THE PLAYWRIGHT AS REBEL

Nicholas Dromgoole
THE PLAYWRIGHT AS REBEL
Essays in Theatre History

OBERON BOOKS
LONDON

First published in this collection
2001 by Oberon Books Ltd.
(incorporating Absolute Classics)
521 Caledonian Road, London N7 9RH
Tel: 020 7607 3637 / Fax: 020 7607 3629

e-mail: oberon.books@btinternet.com

A catalogue record for this book is available from the British Library.

ISBN: 1 84002 147 0

Cover illustration: Andrzej Klimowski

Cover typography: Jeff Willis

Printed in Great Britain by Antony Rowe Ltd, Reading.

For Geoffrey Spain
who shared the trials and tribulations
of boyhood at Dulwich College
and has remained a steadfast
friend ever since

Contents

Introduction

We all fantasise. We all have a secret world where we dream of what it would be like if…where imaginatively we fit into someone else's shoes and project an excitingly different set of circumstances. Those happy moments before sleep, when we snuggle down into the bedclothes and our mind takes us to other places. Perhaps one of the major differences between early childhood and later is that we come to recognise the sharpness of the boundary between the worlds we imagine and the real world we actually inhabit. Yet watch a little girl playing with her dolls and clearly her fantasy world is part of her learning process. She is playing mother, the doll is standing in for her, and she is experiencing what it is like to be an adult. The doll is temporarily landed with the little girl's own identity while the girl has stepped out of herself and is playing what it must be like to be somebody else.

It is sometimes salutary to take a long hard look at our own fantasies. If we fantasise a great deal about sex, it probably means we are getting very little of it in real life. If we fantasise about being someone powerful and important, perhaps in reality we are a remarkably insignificant little wimp. At least part of the process of launching ourselves into a secret, imaginary world, is to allow ourselves to compensate for what we are not getting in actuality.

It is only a small step from private fantasies to enjoying the better organised and more complex imaginings of someone who is possibly better at it than we are, the professional storyteller, the creator of fiction, who tells a tale. As we listen, we identify with characters, imagine what it would be like to be in somebody else's shoes, step into an imaginary world that has been created for us. Bruno Bettelheim in his *The Uses of Enchantment* looks at the fairy tales told for hundreds of years in western culture and shows how they help children both consciously and unconsciously to cope with baffling emotions, feelings of smallness and helplessness, anxieties about strangers, and the mysteries of the adult world including the taboo-ridden territory of sex.

As we grow up, we graduate from fairy tales, yet fiction, narratives created for us as well as our own imaginings, continue throughout our life to be an important, a more or less crucial, part of our mental existence. Long before the invention of writing we may be sure that tales told around the fireside played an important part in the thought processes and cultural life of our early homo sapiens ancestors. The forty thousand years of the Pleistocene, a hunter gatherer society about which we know so little, must surely have nourished as vigorous an oral literary tradition as that of every other society known to social anthropologists.

The teller of the tale around the fireside is edging close to the world of performance. Arab culture did not originally develop the more formal conventions of theatre and performance found elsewhere in the west, but anybody watching the professional storyteller in the souk, the market-place in Marrakesh say, soon realises how close to theatre the storyteller has got. He grimaces, makes appropriate gestures, adopts the different voices of each character in the story. He has already arrived at fiction in performance.

When considering theatre, another whole area of human experience is also involved – music and dance. Both of them seem inextricably entwined and play a vital part in every culture in every society discovered or studied by anthropologists. Music and dance have an important role.

They are inalienably part of being human, it would seem. The philosopher Susanne K Langer, in her *Problems of Art* even speculates that they predate language itself, and possibly helped in its development. The joy of moving to the rhythms and melodies of music is something that most of us still take for granted. We do not have to buy an ecstasy pill before we can wallow in the sheer exhilaration of moving in time to the music. This is something that human beings just do, a simple, shared enjoyment. If we want to speculate about those early Pleistocene, hunter gatherer societies in Europe, can we not be sure that music making of some kind, and dancing to the music as it was made, was a vivid part of communal life?

We have a good deal of evidence that at certain times of year the smaller groups throughout the Pleistocene would all meet up for larger group occasions. We may be sure that music and dance played a part on these occasions. Inevitably some dancers would be better than others, more skilled at physical tricks they had worked on, so that an element of watching and appreciating the display of others, as well as a widespread general participation must have developed. Accustomed as the minds of everybody there already were to enjoying stories, narrative, fiction, it would be quite understandable that the music and dance should start to tell a story. Loaded with religious ritual, it might perhaps enact the story of the hunt that was to take place the following day.

And now we approach the crucial moment in cultural history. The moment when the story became more important than the music and the dance. It is at that moment theatre, as we understand it, was born. The telling of a story, a fiction, by performers to an appreciative audience of spectators. Music and dance still playing an important part no doubt for many cultural ages to come, but the story itself firmly at the heart of the performance and experience. What kind of story? Obviously one that plugged deep into the shared fantasy life of the spectators, closely relating to the imaginative world of creative fiction that every society seems to depend upon and share.

Let me now make big claims for this created fiction. I would suggest that human beings learn who they are, what kind of world they are in, what their relations should be with others, almost as much through fiction and fantasy as through the actual everyday experiences of being born, growing up, dealing with parents, falling in love, producing and bringing up children, growing old and facing death. We learn almost as much about these actual events which most of us experience, through the fictions told about them, as in experiencing them. Our culture, with its prepared stories, prepares us for the actual experience. We interpret what actually happens to us by means of the set of expectations our culture has already provided for us. Thunder and lightning are frightening phenomena, but much less frightening if we already know what is actually happening, that the father of gods and men, the great Jove himself, is angrily hurling his thunderbolts.

And when, all too like another thunder clap from heaven, the overwhelming emotions of falling in love descend upon innocent adolescents for the first time, they too are not altogether unprepared, the adolescent recognises the emotion for what it is. Culture, fiction, fantasy have already explained it. So fiction, the telling of absorbing stories, is not just a matter of idly dreaming the time away. Fiction is one way of coming to terms with life.

The Bellevuehohe in the Wienerwald in Vienna has a plaque which baldly states "Here on July 24th 1895, the secret of dreams revealed itself to Dr Sigmund Freud." The plaque says nothing about the racial hatred of the Austrians for Jews, so that Freud had to end his life in London, forced to flee his countrymen's implacable prejudice. Dreams of the *Herrenvolk*, the Aryan race, were fictions that ended in horrifying events. And did Freud really grasp the secret of dreams? Perhaps that too was his particular fantasy!

What we do know is that whatever cultures evolved during the forty thousand years of the Pleistocene in Europe were swept away almost without trace. We can gaze wonderingly at the cave paintings of Lascaux, and elsewhere at a few strangely effective figurines and the odd artefact, but of the culture we know pathetically little. Why do cultures change? The short and gimmicky answer is technology. The values, attitudes and assumptions that make up an ideology suited to hunter gatherer ways of life must have proved inadequate for a quite different way of life, the coming of agriculture and settled communities. So values, attitudes and assumptions had to alter to meet the new challenge. The old ways and the old beliefs that underpinned them were forgotten, stories changed too, embodying the new values and assumptions.

No media studies specialist has yet examined the *Iliad* or the *Odyssey*, or *Beowulf* in our own Saxon tradition, in terms of the changing values of a newly agrarian society, but no doubt these somewhat dubious pleasures lie in store for us. It is worth remembering that all three of these stirring tales originated as public performances, to a musical accompaniment from a lyre or harp, a tale told to an audience, already almost a piece of public theatre.

Cultural historians like to imagine that what we fondly regard as western culture, western ideology, has its origins with the Ancient Greeks. The high point of their culture, and so an early high point of our own, was Athens five centuries before the birth of Christ. With a few little gaps here and there like the Dark Ages, history can provide written evidence and continuity from then till now, and help us to understand where we came from and how our culture developed. Open any history of European theatre and it almost always starts with the Greeks, so if we are to consider the role of the playwright as rebel, we must clearly start there. This is not the place to give an account of Greek theatre, readers will hopefully find an attempt to cover it in the essay on *Medea* and *Antigone*. It is worth noting that this first emergence of theatre into the written historical record still clearly shows its ancestry in music, dance and religious ritual. In front of the Greek stage was a large circular area known as the orchestra, a word which then meant "the dancing space". Here the chorus sang songs and danced, the songs interspersed between and commenting on the events of the play performed by actors on the stage at the back of the orchestra. The performance was still part of a religious festival, celebrating the god Dionysus. We still have a representative number of complete play texts, written by the outstanding dramatists who emerged: Aeschylus, Sophocles and Euripides for tragedy and Aristophanes for comedy. Here then for the first time, in what is recognisably a theatre, a specialised building created for the performance of plays, we have recognisable dramatists. In what sense can they be considered rebels?

A rebel is someone dissatisfied with, and wishing to change, the accepted order of things. Even the most cursory look at the plays of the most conservative of the Greek playwrights Aeschylus, makes it immediately clear that like his fellow dramatists he is echoing his society's dissatisfaction with aspects of the accepted value system, and pushing his audience in the direction of change. In the *Oresteia* he tackles the traditional blood feud, the duty of a family to avenge the death of one of its number by killing the murderer, and then the subsequent duty of the murderer's family to avenge his death and so on, in a perpetual wearying, wastefully endless cycle of killings. He pushes his audience into a recognition of the need for change.

The shape of the thesis to be argued in this essay should now become clearer. It is suggested that the fictions, all the stories on which a culture nourishes itself, play an important part in telling the culture's members who they are, what sort of a world they are in, what their relations are with other people, and generally help to create a common sense of cultural identity. (The reader need not worry. I do not intend to submerge him or this thesis in any sea of arguments with which modern literary criticism is currently awash; no Lacanian psychoanalysis, no structualist semiotics, no post-structualist theory, no Althusserian Marxism.) At certain key points in history, generally as a result of new technology, new inventions which change the way people live, a new value system has to emerge to match up to the changing way of life. A blood feud may work in a hunter gatherer society, but in the city state it is outmoded. At these moments of change the media of communication play a vital role. Vital, because they present a new set of fictions, stories showing people dealing with and echoing the new value system. At certain times in our history, theatre has become the important media of communication, the important focus, the powerhouse, where the changed stories spread the word, initiating and disseminating changes in the value system. At these key moments of change, the dramatist becomes in Shelley's words "the unacknowledged legislator for mankind". The playwright is then the rebel who changes the world. Athenian theatre in the fifth century BC was such a moment. Athens was changing from a small city state into becoming the centre of a powerful empire stretching across the Aegean. Mathematics, astronomy, physics, philosophy and medicine were making discoveries that started to shift the old explanations. What we call the classical world was being born. A new value system was emerging and the drama was, in a vivid metaphor, "the midwife at the lying in".

It must also be remembered that theatre is very much an art form in its own right. Change, rebellion and revolution are the grist that keep the wheels of every art form turning so busily. There is a sense in which every artist worth his or her salt, is a rebel. At the beginning of the nineteenth century Sir George Beaumont, then president of the Royal Academy, laid it down that every landscape painting should be the colour of an old violin, a rich, deep brown. Then along came John Constable with a range of revolutionary greens, scandalising the traditionalists and helping his viewers to see landscape in a new way. Every art form proceeds through an exciting range of innovations of this kind. Theatre is no exception. It has exactly the same history of stylistic innovations, changes in the way it told its stories, differences in the way it presented them, making each period in theatre history distinct, very much part of its time and different from what had gone before and what was to come. These stylistic variations are not what this essay is concerned with. Moving from an open arena to a closed building, curtains, stages, moveable sets and scenery, lighting, design, stage effects, all play a part in the way theatre has evolved. Each innovation has had its rebels, its revolutions and its diehards. This essay salutes them all, but wishes to look elsewhere.

INTRODUCTION

The theatre which evolved in Europe after the collapse of the classical world and the long night of the Dark Ages, was propaganda theatre, apart from a more exciting mime touring theatre about which we know little. The Church put on theatre free of charge to get its message across. For hundreds of years the majority of people lived in small villages, tied to the land, their value system unchanging, their understanding of the world fixed in a rock-like immobility. This medieval period, the age of faith, produced a theatre that innovated and experimented endlessly in the ways in which it presented its message, but the message itself was a simple and unchanging one. Those who are good go to Heaven, those who are bad go to Hell. The Reformation/Renaissance changed all that. The fifteenth, sixteenth and early seventeenth centuries were a period of increasingly intense religious controversy. Protestants and extreme puritans arrived, and the Church of Rome agonisingly reformed itself to meet their challenge. At the same time the lay ruler gradually became more powerful than the controversy-ridden Church. In the struggle for power between Church and Ruler, Emperor, King, Prince or Duke gradually started to win, and the Church, so pre-eminent throughout the middle ages, started to lose. Power shifted from one to the other. The literature of Ancient Greece and Rome was increasingly studied and increasingly influenced thought and behaviour. The market economy, as opposed to the directed and controlled economy, rose in gradual ascendancy. Technological change from the invention of printing initiated a process that increasingly saw the rise and growth of the city. The world started changing at an accelerating rate. It has not stopped yet. Along with the technological change, there lagged not far behind the striking changes in the value system that had to accompany them.

A world outlook and set of values that suited small village dwellers proved inadequate in the growing city, where religious beliefs were being questioned, the class system changing, the market economy increasingly prevailing, and all the old certainties crumbling. As the Church lost its power, its lands and its monasteries in England, so it ceased to provide the free drama for all which it had developed so carefully. Yet the audience for drama was still there, still wanting more of what it had already acquired a taste for. Is it any wonder that a new commercial theatre should arise to fill the gap and to develop into the most important medium of communication of its time, the arena where the issues of the day, the growing conflict of ideas, the need for a new sense of cultural identity could be argued out? There were books and pamphlets, but literacy was still a skill restricted to the few rather than the many. Few of the typical Globe audience could read. No newspapers, no magazines, no radio, no CDs, no film, no television. Given a choice between a sermon by the parish priest, or a play by Marlowe, Shakespeare, Jonson, Middleton, Tourneur, Webster, Ford, Beaumont or Fletcher, is it any wonder so many thousands of that Elizabethan and Stuart audience did not hesitate? Increasingly they learned in the theatre who they were, what sort of a new world they were in and what its new values were.

One example will have to suffice, but at least it is fashionable and politically correct. The medieval view of woman was perhaps best summed up by the chastity belt. A husband locked his wife up in this contraption and kept the key, knowing that his wife could not be unfaithful until he himself unlocked her. A whole set of assumptions surround that one contraption: that a woman was her husband's property to do with as he wished; that she probably could not be trusted on her own; that she was, by her very existence, a constant temptation to men to sin; that her own wishes, her own individuality were of little account. Women were in a very profound sense, religious as well as social, seen as inferior to men.

Shakespeare in his plays was constantly edging his audience towards a quite different view of women. He showed some women who were more fun than the men around them, more intelligent, more dominating, more impressive. And yet the paradox was that these very roles demonstrating women as a fascinating set of individuals, could only be played on stage by boys, because everybody shared the medieval view that a woman was a temptation to sin, and to put her on stage was to tempt men to fall from grace. The boy that squeaked through the role of Cleopatra was himself an object lesson in how far Shakespeare's audience had to go, merely to catch up with what Shakespeare was already demonstrating.

Can anyone deny that Shakespeare and his contemporary playwrights in England as well as Lope de Vega in Spain, Molière and Racine in France, each in their various ways bestrode the whirlwind of change? They thrashed out for their audience the big questions of the day. They helped to create a new ideology, a new *Weltanschauung.* The reader who looks at the essays in this book on these playwrights will hopefully see them as rebels indeed, not so much changing the conventions and styles of their art form, although they all certainly did that, as helping to change their world, to assist in the birth of a new value system. In many ways, and certainly in England, this was the drama's finest hour.

How sad that at this high point it is necessary to descend from the sublime to the ridiculous. Attitudes to the theatre in England suffered a remarkable sea change in the seventeenth and eighteenth centuries – or perhaps it would be more accurate to say a minority view became a majority view. All through the Elizabethan and early Stuart period the Puritans vigorously attacked and decried the theatre. This is not surprising when we remember that extreme Puritans thought it was a sin even to smile. When they were triumphant in the civil war and executed Charles I, they put a stop to theatre too. From 1642 to 1660 (when Charles II was restored to the throne) stage drama was banned. After 1660, Restoration drama, particularly comedy, flourished, but much more as an aristocratic, minority drama. Increasingly the broad majority of what might have been the theatre-going public became suspicious of drama. They distrusted it. They saw theatre as basically flawed, immoral in ways that bit much deeper than mere sexually licentious shocks and alarms. Drama was generally seen to be bad for everybody.

It was still so considered when Jane Austen published her remarkably trenchant *Mansfield Park* in 1814. Edward Said, in his *Culture and Imperialism*, makes much of the visit of Sir Thomas Bertram to Antigua in this very novel, as an example of the way England's upper class increasingly depended for its wealth on colonial exploitation. One has to look very hard for clues about this in the novel itself. What will strike most modern readers is an astonishing attitude to the theatre. Sir Thomas, a man of considerable moral integrity at home whatever his wealth is based on, visits Antigua. While he is away (and journeys then took many months) the young adults of his family decide to indulge in amateur theatricals and amuse the neighbourhood with the performance of a play. When preparations are well advanced, Sir Thomas unexpectedly returns. Everybody accepts that the play cannot take place, that the idea of its performance was morally unsound, and most of them feel ashamed of themselves. The reader is clearly expected to concur. Modern readers can do nothing of the kind. There is a gap – more than a gap, a chasm – between attitudes in 1814 and ourselves. Jane Austen is clearly convinced, as were the great majority of her readers, of the rightness of her views. Are we then so very different from the *Weltanschauung*, the zeitgeist, the ideology of a mere two centuries ago? And where did this educated consensus of 1814 come from?

Theatre's decline in the eighteenth century was parallelled by the rise of the novel. In 1680 the words poet and playwright were almost interchangeable. Poets and writers of fiction, creators of fantasy, wrote plays. That was what a writer did. But by 1780 all that had long changed. The novel, not the play, had become the dominant art form for fiction. Eighteenth-century French writers credited England with the invention of the novel. It was greatly helped on its way by the introduction in 1737 of censorship in the theatre. Henry Fielding's play *Tom Thumb* (1730) and other successful satires on the government of the day, persuaded the then Prime Minister Robert Walpole, that plays and indeed theatres should be licensed and controlled. London was restricted to two theatres, at Covent Garden and Drury Lane, and plays written after 1737 had to be licensed by the Lord Chamberlain. The effect of this was to drive many good writers out of the theatre. Henry Fielding was himself a sad example. The man who went on to write those much-admired novels *Joseph Andrews*, *Tom Jones*, and *Amelia*, had started as playwright. He ended as one of our distinguished novelists, opting out of a controlled and censored theatre and choosing the adventurous challenge of a new and rapidly developing art form. Yet surely, fiction was fiction, fantasy was fantasy, and imagining invented characters and situations in the novel was not so very different, indeed an extension of what had been done so honourably and for so many centuries in the theatre?

Not so! The moral opprobrium, that descended in stifling folds on the theatre, did not apply to the novel. Jane Austen herself in *Northanger Abbey*, a delicious satire on the new gothic novels of her day, which at one level is an ironic attack on the power of the media to change public attitudes and assumptions, managed to make great claims for the art of the novel. Perhaps she has her fluent tongue lodged a little in her gifted cheek, but there is a serious strand in what she tells her readers. Novels are where "the greatest powers of the mind are displayed, in which the most thorough knowledge of human nature, the happiest delineation of its varieties, the liveliest effusions of wit and humour are conveyed to the world in the best chosen language" – which have only "genius, wit and taste to recommend them". Wow! And this is the self same writer who expects her readers to condemn out of hand the cheerful little enterprise of an amateur performance of *Lovers' Vows*.

Sadly, one of the commonest sins committed by critics is to praise up one art form by decrying and devaluing another. Think of the way opera and ballet have long puffed themselves up by sneering at each other. In eighteenth-century France, still then the arbiter of European taste, there was a tendency to over-praise the novel by knocking the drama. There is a terrible gap between Jean-Jacques Rousseau's views on the novel and on the drama. In 1758, Rousseau attacked Alembert's suggestion that a theatre should be set up in the republic of Geneva. Rousseau regarded the theatre as a snare. Aristotle's theory of catharsis was a mere excuse for indulging in unhealthy feelings – unhealthy because they were false, all pretence and illusion. Actors were liars, pretending to be what they were not. Audiences lost themselves in the false emotions of others, so they fragmented their own identity and imaginatively took on false ones. Sexual morality was also put at risk by the abandoned behaviour of actresses.

Against these recitals of vice, Rousseau set the virtues of the novel. It was an English art form, he thought, because the English were different from the French. They were not constantly trying to win the approval of others, playing a part as Frenchmen did, to get the attention and admiration of the crowd. Rousseau saw the English as more solitary, more confident in themselves, less caring about others' opinions of them. They liked to think things out on their own, and the novel was designed to meet just such a taste. In one of his many striking phrases Rousseau considered the English more concerned with being happy than giving the appearance of being happy. It was the drama which encouraged "silly imitations".

Diderot, a key influence on French eighteenth-century thought, essentially agreed with Rousseau in his *Praise of Richardson* (1760), praise from a leading French critic for an English novelist. Earlier he had already castigated drama for its dependence on ceaseless, feverish action. Theatre was for those who surrendered to immediate pleasure and were essentially facile. The novel was for the calm, self-centered man who left behind the tiresome pleasures of the social round and retired to his own solitary study for quiet reflection.

Madame de Stael's *Literature and Social Institutions* (1800) claimed even more for the novel. Whereas in Classical Greece political decisions were shared out among the citizens of the state, and the epic poem and the drama celebrated the public actions of committed citizens doing their bit for the group, in

1800 it was different. Political liberty depended on keeping a private space around oneself where the too powerful state could not interfere. Freedom meant being free from government intervention. This was a concept no Ancient Greek would have understood. Madame de Stael, recognising this concept as the mainspring for so much English political thought, saw English writers as supreme exponents of the novel, because their fiction celebrated "morality in which minor qualities and fates create a new kind of heroism".

These are only particularly illustrious examples of widely-held views that underpinned Jane Austen's certainty in 1814. The drama was suspect, depending for its effects on what characters did, their actions on stage. The novel looked at the inner processes of thought that preceded action, and could carefully weigh "thoughts that do lie too deep for tears".

Jane Austen's characters attend plays, just as they attend balls in London or in Bath, as part of the round of social activities that make up a morally questionable "season". What matters in the novels is what the characters think and feel rather than what they do, and this, it was felt, was an area where the drama could not compete. As Jane Austen makes clear in her eulogy of the novel in *Northanger Abbey*, the reader has direct access to the mind of the novelist. The poor playwright can only reach his audience through the actions of his invented characters. The novelist can speak directly to readers, sharing innermost thoughts with them as the story proceeds.

It is difficult for us now to realise just how damaging to the theatre these views were. They made the theatre seem an intellectually shoddy place. By the end of the nineteenth century Henry James (himself a failed playwright) could write of the theatre in England "the arts of the stage are not really in the temperament and manners of the people. These people are too highly moral to be histrionic...they have too stern a sense of duty." Morality once again. What he is really saying is that the theatre is immoral, too scandalising for the high moral tone of the English people. It was in this climate that Oscar Wilde wrote *An Ideal Husband*, George Bernard Shaw his theatre criticism, and Archer tried to eulogise Ibsen. They were struggling against a tide of thought that had left theatre increasingly deserted by intellectuals for over two centuries. As Shaw's educated dustman in *Pygmalion* reminds us, "middle-class morality" was undoubtedly the culprit.

The twentieth century saw the tide change. Film, radio and finally television immersed everybody in exactly the kinds of drama that Rousseau, Diderot and de Stael despised. A Schwarzenegger film has just the "ceaseless, feverish action" Diderot would abhor. By the end of the twentieth century almost the whole world was back in the play houses of these new media, wallowing in the illusions and pretences Rousseau was so anxious to save the solid burghers of Geneva from experiencing.

Was he right? Have we changed for the worse? Today's younger generation at Mansfield Park would no longer even understand what Sir Thomas Bertram was talking about. Did he ever have a point?

With hindsight we can realise that the strict distinctions between novels and plays, which the eighteenth century was so anxious to establish, were a little too arbitrary for comfort. The idea that only in the novel can the writer address his audience is obviously unfair. One of the essential roles of the chorus in Classical Greek drama was to comment on the action as it unfolded, to stand back and take the larger view. Would anyone suggest that Shakespeare in his soliloquies, did not take the audience into the mind, the secret thoughts, the motives and the very psychology of his believable characters? And all Rousseau's strictures against unhealthy feelings, pretence and illusion, audiences losing themselves in the false emotions of others, fragmenting their own identity as in imagination they step into the shoes of invented characters and experience their imaginary thoughts in created situations – all these criticisms really apply just as much to the novel as to the play. Any burghers in Geneva weeping over Samuel Richardson's *Clarissa*, *Pamela* or *The History of Sir Charles Grandison* were experiencing very similar emotions to an audience for Euripides' *Medea* or Shakespeare's *Troilus and Cressida*. Accustomed as we now are to the film of the play of the book, we can see that Sir Thomas Bertram got it wrong. And understand why the noble traditions of French theatre from Molière to Racine dwindled into the comfortable after-dinner farce of Feydeau and the melodramas of Dumas. Essays in this volume on Molière, Racine, Feydeau and Dumas pay tribute to them all.

What this widespread distrust of the drama in England and France in the eighteenth and nineteenth centuries makes clear, is why what was happening elsewhere in European drama made so little impact on English theatre. The sentimental excesses of Dumas could sweep to triumph in drama and the novel in England and in France, but the challenging work of Goethe, of Lenz and above all of Schiller in German theatre did little to disturb the stagnant waters of English theatre. The essays on Schiller and Romanticism and on Lenz are still in this sense breaking relatively fresh ground for the average English theatre-goer. How amazing too, as the essay on *Troilus and Cressida* suggests, that only in the twentieth century can we approach this challenging play which middle-class morality quietly suppressed for nearly four centuries.

It is suggested in the essay on Schiller and Romanticism that the Romantic Movement was the last major shift in western culture, and that we are still very much a part of it. In the nineteenth century the growing power and numbers of the newly emerging middle class, produced the first mass consumer demand for the arts, and the purveyors of fiction and fantasy, novelists and playwrights, did their best to rise to the challenge. The industrial city propagated a changing value system, and the stories then duly helped to spread and illustrate the changes. Karl Marx, busily scribbling away in the reading room of the British Museum, as a newly industrialised London expanded all around him, helped give an economic analysis of the process. When power resides with the king, he told his readers, the popular stories are about kings and queens, princes and princesses. When power moves to the aristocracy, they move to the centre of fiction's stage too. And when power moves to the middle class, then all the stories start being about the middle class. Where Marx would seem to have been wrong was in his prophesy that capitalism contained the seeds of its own decay. Looking around him at the ruthless exploitation of the working class, he could hardly have guessed otherwise, but in the twentieth century, the most striking development in the west has surely been the growing prosperity and general betterment of the working class. Whereas in the nineteenth century it was the ill-educated emerging middle class that offered the first mass consumer demand for the arts, in the twentieth century the same process has been repeated for the working class. All the elements of

Romanticism which changed the emphasis of the arts in the nineteenth century to meet the new consumer demand: sentimentality; escapism; alienation; the concept of romantic love, continued to permeate the arts in the twentieth century, as power has started moving from the middle class to the working class, and popular narrative reflects the shifting patterns of power. The popular stories, fictions like *Eastenders* and *Coronation Street* are now about the working class. They have triumphantly moved centre stage in popular dramatic fiction on film, radio and television.

Happily for its future, theatre remains an exception to this process. In spite of all the posturings of culture ministers such as Chris Smith desperately trying to claim otherwise, theatre resolutely remains a middle-class activity. The average member of the working class reads a popular newspaper, goes to football matches, occasionally sees a film, listens to radio in his car and watches dramatic fiction on television more nights than not, but hardly ever goes near a theatre. A pantomime at Christmas, or a musical just possibly. Otherwise never.

Most media analysts have become increasingly concerned at what is popularly known as the "dumbing down" of the media, as they resolutely aim at those lowest common denominators, gossip, wild sensationalism, sexual scandals, immorality and corruption. There is an increasing whiff of these nastinesses about most popular media of communication. The assumptions made by media professionals would seem to be that the average *Sun* reader has a very short attention span, cannot follow any complex reasoning, has a limited vocabulary and needs simple sentences with slogans rather than arguments. The success of *Eastenders* and *Coronation Street* would seem to prove them right.

Worse still, analysts claim there is an insidious side effect from the dependence of the media on advertising revenue. Half a newspaper's revenue comes from advertising, all of commercial television's revenue depends on it. There is a sense therefore in which the media have to try hard to be good media for advertising, and as all the world knows, advertising is most likely to succeed when the consumer has warm comfortable feelings that the world is essentially a good place, and all is for the best in this best possible of worlds. Hence not only dumbing down but a marked preference for a sentimental support of things as they are.

Yet however they have been edged out of the spotlight in the media, the middle class, still paradoxically making up the media professionals, the people who actually run and write the media, remain predominantly the decision-makers in our fragmented society, in politics, in industry, in science and in education, quite apart from their domination of the creative side of the media. Where is the arena providing a fictional world where their problems and views can still be imaginatively rehearsed and thrashed out in a changing society? There is a marked difference between the so-called quality press for the middle class, much smaller in circulation but more influential because it is still aimed at the decision-makers, as opposed to the tabloids with their much larger circulations aimed at the mass market – *The Daily Telegraph*, say, as opposed to *The Sun*. In the same way there is a marked difference between the theatre, still aimed at what might optimistically be called the thinking classes, and the drama of popular film and television soaps.

A theatre audience is almost inevitably well-educated, more demanding and perhaps the most sophisticated that exists in any size for the media. Theatre is still competing against the novel, but the live stage has its own resonances and special qualities that still keep it vigorously competitive. Television provides honourably for its better educated minority audience in features, current affairs and even arts and history programmes for them, but in drama, apart from occasional lavish dramatisations of nineteenth-century novels, and intelligent detectives solving murders, there is a depressing void. Drama for an educated minority seems not to be one of television's priorities.

Interestingly, in the twentieth century the stranglehold of the middle class over the media persisted rather longer than it should have. Censorship, both of theatre and of film, imposed Shaw's "middle-class morality" firmly on these media, particularly during the growing popularity of cinema in the Thirties and Forties. On the radio the BBC monopoly, inspired by Reith's high-minded determination to maintain middle-class standards, tended to treat the working class as a congregation to be carefully sermonised at. Although this country invented television and was the first to provide a public television service pre-war, it was an expensive luxury only the rich could afford. The Russian Bolshevik revolution in 1917 terrified the middle classes everywhere else. The working class was seen as a potential threat. The British Board of Film Censorship firmly suppressed all Russian films and indeed most "art" films made in Europe including German expressionist films like *The Cabinet of Dr Caligari* because they might have a "disturbing" effect. The LCC, then the licensing authority for London, allowed Russian masterpiece films by Eisenstein like *The Battleship Potemkin* to be shown in middle-class film clubs, but specifically banned it from being shown in a trade union film club. It might have been too "unsettling" for the workers. British and American films were severely controlled for the same reasons. The middle class knew best, and the working class had to be protected against themselves.

During World War II, in the rush to rally morale and support the war effort, a wider variety of films were made as, in the stress and strain of war, society and its values started changing at an accelerating rate. After 1945 and the inevitable lull as Britain agonisingly readjusted to a post-war world, television increasingly came to dominate the media arena. The coronation in 1953 sparked off a sudden surge in television ownership, which then continued to expand. Finally the arrival of commercial television, aiming firmly at a working-class popular audience, forced the BBC to rethink its policies and compete in the changed market place. In its first months commercial television took more than seventy per cent of the BBC's viewers. And the middle-class domination of the subject matter of popular culture finally faltered.

Then with John Osborne's *Look Back in Anger* at the Royal Court Theatre in 1956 (later made into a film) the floodgates of change were publicly opened and for a time nothing was ever to seem the same again. In the theatre the "kitchen sink" was in, and "anyone for tennis?" plays were seemingly out. Plays about the working class suddenly became fashionable. A whole generation of actors, accustomed to echoing middle-class characters in middle-class settings, found it much more difficult to get a job in the theatre. Even the playwright Noël Coward began to feel out of touch and out of date. The so-called Swinging Sixties had arrived. This was undoubtedly a moment of cultural change in British society, as television assumed its place as the most powerful of the media of communication, and at last the stories were about the newly powerful working class they were aimed at. The focus of the popular arts changed. Popular stars, public icons tended to emerge from and belong to the working class.

These developments arrived on the back of a revolution in sexual attitudes and in the use of drugs which for a time seemed part and parcel of the same thing. It is worth noting in view of what has been claimed already about technological change, that it was a technological development which triggered a whole revolution in sexual attitudes. The contraceptive pill was an advance in medical technology, yet ideas, assumptions and attitudes changed as a result of it, and these changes were disseminated and underpinned by the stories, the fiction in the media, showing people coping or attempting to cope with the changing attitudes. Benzedrine, marijuana, LSD, cocaine and heroin were all a part of medicine and chemistry before they were dropped into the outside world.

With hindsight, it is now possible to see that much of the thinking behind the change in attitudes in the Sixties was woolly minded and naive, if not downright absurd. The so-called sexual revolution, the blithe assumption that it was now cheerfully possible to pop in and out of bed with a variety of partners in the interests of ever more skilfully-arrived-at orgasms of pleasure, ignored basic aspects of men and women's sexuality. The golden age of sexual adventure never seemed to get any nearer, but its supporters became sadder and wiser as they aged, and many of them, alas, ended up not only with disillusion but with AIDS.

Drugs too were seen to have helped create illusions not reality. Similarly the political revolution that seemed just around the corner in the Sixties receded and then vanished in an ever gloomier-looking future. The high hopes of the

Sixties were followed by the harsh gritty realism of the Thatcher years. What should be noted here, is that this overwhelming social and political revolution began in the theatre. Nowadays, in spite of a recent and challengingly good revival of *Look Back in Anger* at the National Theatre, the play no longer seems the ground-breaking, radically new departure that it seemed in 1956. As Osborne himself admitted later, "it was a formal, rather old-fashioned play". It had the good fortune to seem to say the right things at the right time in the right place. And what was the right place? The theatre. The Angry Young Men, playwrights seeming to be introducing a new kind of "kitchen sink" drama, adventurously examining the problems of the working class, appeared to be spearheading a wide-ranging cultural and social revolution from the platform, the stage of the London theatre. The playwrights were rebels indeed.

In all the wild excitements, the illusions, the widespread self-deceptions and experiments of the Sixties and Seventies, nobody really noticed a depressing paradox. Plays about the working class, sympathetically aimed at the working class, were being watched in the theatre by an almost exclusively middle-class audience, and were all too often written by middle-class writers, rebels against and drop-outs from an Establishment they despised and repudiated, but all too ready to sentimentalise a working class about which they really knew very little. Osborne himself was a striking example. His background was beset with the snobberies of the lower fringes of the middle class. He went to a private boarding school, Belmont College in North Devon, a seedy, run-down establishment aping a public school system and desperately pretending to emulate it. He was expelled for physically assaulting the headmaster. Wesker's *Chips with Everything* really applied to Osborne. The chips on his shoulder were duly served up with every play he wrote.

In the Eighties and Nineties sanity began to predominate in the theatre. Major dramatists like Stoppard aimed their plays firmly at an educated, knowledgeable and sophisticated middle-class audience, challenging them to measure up to the real issues of modern thinking and living. Rodney Ackland's *Absolute Hell*, lucklessly in advance of its time, was revived at the National Theatre, and tribute is paid to him in this volume.

Today the theatre once again has become the power house, the focus for the thrashing out of major problems and issues of our time. With most of the media aimed at the less demanding popular audience, this makes the theatre one of the few arenas where the class which still makes the decisions, can see, think and discuss the problems it must grapple with. Playwrights creating for the theatre are still rebels, still examining controversies, still edging audiences into making value judgments, into making decisions about what is right and wrong, what is worthwhile, what life is about.

Part of the price to be paid for this ferment of ideas, apart from the high price of theatre seats, is that some distinguished theatre creators undoubtably try to haul us down artistic cul-de-sacs. Fascinating and rewarding as a preoccupation with the ideas of Artaud may be in the short term, and Peter Brook for one has the talent to make this French theorist about cruelty, sadism and wordless events re-enacted in the theatre, seem exciting and relevant, this is diverting drama from its mainstream development. Horror films and television programmes can do this just as well. There are areas in modern fiction where theatre has an even more vital role.

In the theatre the audience is still expected to think as well as feel emotion.

Rebels are dissatisfied with things and want to change them. Rousseau would have called this dissatisfaction divine. For modern theatre audiences it illuminates the tragedy and the comedy of being human. We would all be vastly poorer without it. We need the rebels and the debates of modern theatre perhaps as never before. It is one of the last arenas that can attract a sizeable audience and still push them into squaring up to the big issues, just as those Ancient Greek playwrights did so many hundred years ago. Playwrights remain that divine irritant who puncture the complacency the other media spend so much of their time propping up. Long may they thrive to do so.

A final word should be said about the choice of plays and playwrights covered in this book. What is included and what is left out may seem a shade arbitrary. In fact, I had written a number of introductions to plays for Oberon Books, and it is the publisher's suggestion that they should be assembled here in a single volume: so the choice is arbitrary indeed. Yet hopefully they illustrate and expand the theme of this opening essay.

1

Euripides – Medea
Sophocles – Antigone

These days the calmly complacent assumptions of superiority on which so much of European culture is based, are very much under attack. The Ancient Greeks called non-Greeks "barbarians", and later Europeans inherited the same racist attitudes. Arnold Toynbee, at whose feet I literally sat as an Oxford undergraduate, since his lectures were so popular there were not enough seats to meet the enthusiastic demand, announced in his *Study of History*, "When we classify mankind by colour, the only one of the primary races...which has not made a single creative contribution to any of our 21 civilisations, is the black race." Undergraduates, their assumptions of inherent superiority suitably massaged, then went back to their own colleges, doubtless to listen to the jazz music that was then the latest fashion, without ever considering where jazz came from. On their walls were daringly novel prints by Picasso, with motifs and forms of representation deliberately and determinedly adopted into Cubism by Picasso from African art. Toynbee was writing dangerously racist nonsense, voicing notions that were widely accepted as the "given wisdom" of the times.

We are wiser now. Black academics, particularly Martin Bernal's *Black Athena*, have set out vigorously to redress the balance. We now see the Ancient Greeks, not as emerging from nowhere to blaze the trail that led to European wisdom and enlightenment, but as just one of a number of cultures around the Mediterranean, deeply influenced by the Egyptian world so firmly established much earlier and far longer in North Africa. Palaeohistorians tells us that intelligent human life originated in Africa's Rift Valley. In that sense, all our origins are firmly African.

Yet it is still important to remember what was special about the Ancient Greeks, why we still feel that our culture stems from them, and why we feel that Euripides' play *Medea* still has much to say to us, and why we are entitled to claim a special relationship with Ancient Greek drama and regard it fondly and reverently as the founder of our own drama.

Let me first pontificate about that early intelligent human life, even if doing so might make a social anthropologist wince. Since we know so little about early man, my pontificating is as essentially unprovable as anybody else's. Imagine early man in his cave, with thunder and lightning building up a storm outside. These natural phenomena must have been extraordinarily frightening. Yet if they could be explained in terms say, of the anger of the Great God Wuzz, who was angry with us because we had broken his rules, and if early man took his first born to the sacrificial stone at the mouth of the cave and slit his throat to placate the god's anger, what is really happening? The unknowable has become knowable, the uncontrollable has become controllable, and even more importantly, man becomes the centre of the universe since it is all happening because the Great God Wuzz is annoyed with him. It is a truism to point out that much of the force and appeal of early religions depends on this process, making the frightening world explicable, knowable, controllable and reassuring the individual by giving him a false sense of his own importance in the scheme of things. Yet the disadvantages of such religions is that they explain the world in affirmations that demand blind faith and cannot be questioned. If the world is supported, let us say, on the shoulders of a giant, who is standing on a crocodile, supported by a turtle, to question this is blasphemy and such questionings have to be punished.

What was so amazing about the Greeks was that they broke this cultural mould. They seem to have been the first culture known to history prepared to ask awkward questions, and who expected rational answers to such rational questions. In *Medea* Euripides is himself edging his audience towards asking awkward questions about male supremacy. He is appealing to his audience's sense of reason. Belief in the power of reason is a paradox, however, because it is still belief, and there is nothing very rational about belief. Yet Greek and our culture was built on the belief that there are rational answers to rational questions. The whole of European science is based upon it. Partly, this revolutionary set of expectations, once dazzlingly new, although we now take them for granted, stemmed from their religion which was based firmly on human attitudes, assumptions and wishes. Whatever the range of human desires, from wishing to get drunk, to make love, to work hard, or simply to laze around doing nothing, there was a god or a goddess in the Greek pantheon ready to approve. And feminists will have noted approvingly that there were godesses as well as gods, although Zeus himself, who presided uneasily and very humanly over this squabbling set of deities, was all too male.

The Greeks invented democracy too, even if it was based on slavery, and women were excluded. It is their word. Their system of majority vote, by which the minority agreed to accept the will of the majority, although maintaining the right to argue against the majority and try to convince those who disagreed with them, has remained as a tantalising ideal of how to arrange matters between ourselves ever since.

One example will have to suffice. Xenophon was a rich young socialite in fifth-century Athens. The Greeks in his day were considered among the best soldiers around, and when he heard that a mercenary army was being assembled to cross the Aegean and fight for some cause on the far mainland, he asked if he could go along with them for the fun of it. In fact this army of 10,000 men were being bamboozled into marching deeper into the interior of what was for them unknown territory, to support in a pitched battle a pretender to the imperial throne of Persia, the great power at the edge of whose world the Greeks somewhat uneasily existed in independence. They duly fought their battle and did well in it, but the contender for the throne whom they were supposed to be supporting had the bad judgement to get killed in the battle. The Greek forces were then in a distinctly unenviable position, marooned in the depths of unknown and alien territory, facing a victorious Persian emperor they had just been trying to depose. All they wanted to do was get home to Greece and their commanders went to negotiate a truce and safe journey home from the emperor. Seated on his imperial peacock throne of ivory and bejewelled gold, the emperor watched these unpredictable Greek commanders as they marched into his luxuriously tented court. Once they were before him, he had them slaughtered to the last man. His reasoning was clear. Destroy the leaders, and a leaderless army would be easy meat. When they heard this devastating news, the Greeks simply got together and elected a fresh set of leaders – including Xenophon, whose written account of how they successfully fought their way back went on to become the Ancient Greek equivalent of a bestseller, and is still available in paperback. (Not bad going for someone writing over four centuries before the birth of Christ!) Here was an early example of one mindset, one *Weltanschauung*, one ideology, clashing with another. The Persians believed in an autocratic ruler and so believed that removing the leader would lead to collapse of the group. The Greeks had invented a different system. Democracy.

Neither the Ancient Egyptians, nor the Persians (the Greeks' powerful and frightening neighbour), shared that belief in democracy and in that power of reason. Both had autocratic systems and closed theologies. This made the Greeks different and special, so much so that they are correctly regarded as the fount and origin of most of our culture's attitudes and assumptions. J A Smith wrote in his *The Unity of Western Civilisation* earlier this century when assumptions of European supremacy were still unchallenged:

> We are the Greeks, made what we now are by their thoughts and deeds and experiences, our world their world at a later stage of evolution never interrupted, but always one and single.

There is a complacent, Eurocentric air of superiority festooning this statement which we would now more humbly wish to pare away, but for better or for worse, we cannot get rid of our ties with the Greeks. Like a set of in-laws, they are part of the marriage of our European culture and we are never going to get them out of the house.

Greek theatre has dominated European drama in spite of crucial changes in both the actual buildings and in the conventions of making drama. We are becoming increasingly aware that a mime drama, claiming continuity from Ancient Greece, and surviving in fairgrounds and market places, toured Europe until the eighteenth century. It did not use words and so was able to survive the collapse of the Roman Empire and

European disintegration as waves of invasions set up fresh settlements and a bewildering variety of languages. It survived the Dark Ages, flourished in the Middle Ages, and achieved a final flowering in the *commedia dell' arte* of the seventeenth and eighteenth centuries. It cannot be discounted when we are considering Greek influence on our theatre. Scholars have neglected it, largely perhaps because it has no texts for them to argue over.

With classical Greek spoken drama, it has been quite otherwise. This has been an academic battlefield for generations. Partly the trouble has been in the relative paucity of material. Remarkably few plays have survived sufficiently whole for us to make a fair estimate of their quality. It has therefore been relatively easy for academics to become self-appointed experts in Greek drama. They can master the texts, all the available texts, without great effort. Only five Greek dramatists have survived in this way, and one, Menander, belongs to a later century than the rest. The titans were three writers of tragedy, Aeschylus, Sophocles and Euripides, and one writer of comedies, Aristophanes. Of their 44 plays, which have survived, seven are by Aeschylus, seven by Sophocles (496 – 406 BC), and eleven by Aristophanes. The remaining nineteen are by Euripides (484 – 406/7 BC), although one of these is probably by someone else and one is a satyr play written to be performed as an afterpiece to a tragic performance. Even so, we have seventeen plays by Euripides and seven by Sophocles, quite enough to give a fair idea of their powers as dramatists, although sadly that is a small proportion of the plays they wrote. We know for example that Euripedes wrote 91.

What of the theatre they were writing for? Here, although we know a great deal, every detail is a scholastic minefield.

The large open air auditorium in fifth-century Athens, as improved by Pericles, held about seventeen thousand people. It had a raised wooden stage, the *skene,* backed by some sort of scenery and a door for entrances and exits. It was used by actors to play the leading roles. Below it was a large circular space, the *orchestra* or dancing space, used for singing and dancing by the chorus. The *theatron* was the greater part, semicircular rows of stepped seats used by the audience. There were three speaking actors. As they wore masks, they could easily take different parts and did so. *Medea* calls additionally for two children, who appear with their mother on stage. Women's parts were invariably taken by men since women never appeared on the Greek stage. The role of the chorus, (12 to 15 for tragedy, 24 for comedy) was a dramatic convention we no longer share. We think of a chorus as a row of scantily clad and nubile females waving their long legs at the audience. For the Greeks the chorus was an integral part of the drama. At one point they were the centre of attention, dancing and singing lyrics of memorable intensity, which either reinforced or commented on the themes of the play. While the leading actors were on stage, the chorus stood around as respectful spectators of the events on stage, acting as fellow citizens and asking or answering questions, and at a distance, very much part of whatever was going on.

We must remember that drama was still young. Its origins are hidden from us, and can only be a matter of speculation, but we know of no culture that does not possess music, singing and above all dancing, even though some cultures lack what we would call theatre. Singing and dancing can be something everybody takes part in, but gradually can evolve into something done by a specially gifted few, watched and admired by the many. Dance can have an element of narrative, the story of a hunt for example. We can imagine theatre as being born when the story became more important than the dance. In Greek theatre, the song and dance element was still a vital part of the whole, yet already the spoken drama had become differentiated, declaimed by specialist experts from a separate part of the acting area, the stage. The *orchestra*, the dancing space, harked back to an earlier kind of performance.

All Greek spoken drama was part of a six-day religious festival, the Great or City Dionysia, held each March, for which Aeschylus, Sophocles and Euripides wrote in competition, among a host of other dramatists. Three writers of tragedies would each present four plays, making twelve plays in all. During the festival the statue of the god of the theatre, Dionysus, was brought from his temple for all to see in the centre of the dancing space, and all the performance was in his honour. We have very little idea of the dance, yet the language of gesture, *cheironomia*, paramount in the mime drama so popular in the market place and in after dinner performances in private houses, still dominated both chorus and actors, and made a common language that must have underpinned the spoken word for the audience, and must have dominated the choreography too.

What we do have is the text, the words the actors spoke. While it is important to emphasise the dance, the singing and the musical elements, Greek theatre was essentially a theatre of the spoken word. Events, dramatic actions, did not take place in front of the audience. All the action took place offstage, and was reported to the characters on stage by a messenger or an eyewitness. This placed great emphasis on the words themselves. Greek dramatists were above all poets. They survived and made their reputations by their ability to say things well. Whatever else may be said about Euripides and Sophocles, they were those rare beings, true poets.

Theirs was supremely a verbal drama, and it was written by poets. The sheer beauty of the language was its main element, and the poet wrote the songs of the chorus as well as the words spoken on-stage; each seen as reinforcing the other and depending on the other. Gradually this poetry enriched the everyday language of the Greeks. They quoted it, they used it when writing prose, they learned the songs and recited and sang them for their own entertainment outside the theatre. Athenian soldiers made slaves at Syracuse, won their freedom by reciting Euripides' choruses. Greek drama became a part of the mental baggage of the people for whom it was made. (I remember sitting behind an American lady who was attending a performance of *Hamlet* for the first time. At the first interval she turned to her companion and said wonderingly, "I never knew it was so full of quotations." An uninformed Greek lady attending a performance of Sophocles' *Antigone* 400 years after it was written could have said much the same.)

There is another hurdle for the modern reader too. We approach Ancient Greek drama with the babble of more recent controversies in our ears. The Greeks, led by Aristotle, were the first to argue about art, about aesthetics, about what made a good play. They laid down criteria by which art could be approached and judged. They thought they knew why they liked the Parthenon. Its symmetry, its lucidity and seeming lack of anything extraneous to what is essential about it, were the qualities they most admired. A modern viewer sees the Parthenon with different eyes. It uses only the post and lintel form of construction, the most basic and obvious form of building found in every primitive society. The Greeks had no idea of the arch or the dome, clever ways of organising the stresses and strains a large building sets up. Worse still the Parthenon tends to go on doing in stone, which is a quite different material with quite different possibilities, what they had originally done in wood. Its columns are essentially tree trunks with the bark scraped off. There is no real sense of economy about the design either, no sense of pushing the possibilities of the material as far as they can go, no fun in seeing how the problems the material poses have been solved.

It is much the same with Greek drama. A modern audience has a different mindset. The Greeks admired the balance in Sophocles' drama between the songs of the chorus and the dialogue of the actors, the simple effectiveness of the language, the clear and rapid development of the story, the way everything contributed to everything else, the unadorned dramatic purpose. A modern audience misses a drama which approximates more to life, with looser episodes, many-layered plots, the closeness of laughter and tears, the fascination of a wide assortment of characters, the rich splendour of a variegated poetic language, close to poetry at one moment, to prose another. (Are we back at *Hamlet* again?) Then there are the seemingly statuesque characters, no longer balanced by a chorus in a convention which everybody takes for granted. But such is the magic of theatre, that temple of seductive illusion, an audience soon adjusts. After all, if we can adjust to the wildly demanding conventions of opera or ballet, Greek drama should be vastly easier. The strength of Greek drama was the words, and two-and-a-half millennia later, these still creep into our minds, setting up echoes and associations, recreating that Greek world of so long ago.

We can leave behind too all those tiresome historical controversies about what made a good play. Much of Greek and Roman thought was lost sight of in the Dark and Middle

Ages, but the Renaissance was a wonderful rebirth of interest and fascination with the classical world. Greek and Roman literature deeply influenced the Renaissance dramatists who rushed in to fill the vacuum when medieval propagandist theatre passed away. Shakespeare, despite supposedly having "little Latin and less Greek", would have received a thorough grounding in classical language and styles at his Stratford grammar school, and his major influence, Christopher Marlowe, trailed behind him all the glory of a classical education at university. In the seventeenth century, particularly in France, classical models and precepts became something of a straightjacket, teaching the literati to look down on the vigorous Elizabethan drama because it broke too many classical rules. These included the dramatic unities of time, place and action. The ideal play needed to take place within the same 24 hours, in the same place and its plot should proceed without confusing sub-plots. The growing romanticism of the late eighteenth, nineteenth and twentieth centuries has changed all that. We now revere artistic genius, relish breaking the rules and applaud the innovator. Stepping back into the fifth century BC, we can abjure these upsets.

The other eleven plays have not survived from the occasion when *Medea* was first presented during the Great Dionysia, but we know *Medea* was placed last in the popular vote. Throughout his entire career, Euripides won only four "Firsts" for his plays, and that represents a mere four out of ninety one plays. Even with the seventeen plays we have, it is clear that audiences must have found him unsettling, a dramatist who was "caviare to the general". He was questioning, even making fun of what his audience took for granted, and few audiences enjoy too much of that.

Aeschylus, who belonged to the generation before Euripides, established with others the basic concept of Greek tragedy as the grandly endowed hero struggling hopelessly against a fate which relentlessly grinds him down. Sophocles, although of Euripides' generation, shared much the same vision as Aeschylus. Euripides was different. While still enmeshed in the same convention that all plays had to be based on myths, he obstinately refused to deal with mythic characters as anything other than ordinary people in unusual circumstances. Even more unusually he is a master of irony. His characters may be saying one thing, but often we know they mean something else. They may be deceiving themselves but Euripides makes sure they do not deceive us. He teaches us to suspect their motives and discount their claims. And even though the plot is already known, he is full of dramatic surprises.

In the British television series *Till Death Us Do Part*, Warren Mitchell voiced outrageously prejudiced statements about Jews, Blacks, the monarchy and British snobbery, with the clear intention that the audience would respond to all this as satire. Apparently some sections of the television audience reacted in quite the wrong way, lapping up the preposterous prejudices because they shared them, relishing Mitchell's ludicrous views because they coincided with their own. I suspect that sections of Euripides' Greek audience of seventeen thousand must have behaved in much the same way, responding to the excitement of the drama, and the beauty of the language, but missing the irony entirely and positively sharing some of the outrageous views solemnly enunciated by the less attractive characters. Jason's views on women and wives for example. How many Greek males nodded approvingly, blissfully unaware what an insensitive prig Euripides sets out before us. Perhaps by the end of the play they began to feel uncomfortably that they had missed something, and firmly voted against. Every time a man in a Euripides play speaks about women, irony hangs on his words. Every time women speak about other women, automatically accepting the values of a male dominated society, irony mocks.

Earlier this century, feminists claimed Euripides as one of their own. A careful reading of his plays would not seem to support this. He is very concerned with the relationships between men and women. In a male dominated society he is constantly asking audiences to question men's claims about their attitudes to women, to see how men deceive themselves in their attitudes and assumptions about women, and to recognise what is really going on. In fifth-century Athens, as in twenty-first century England, that in itself is probably revolutionary enough.

At one level *Medea* is a play about a woman's revenge on the man who deserts her. She kills his new wife and she kills the two children she herself has borne him in order to hurt him. Revenge was a more acceptable concept in pre-Christian Greece. Since a hero was bound to defend his own concept of his own honour, one of the ways that was publicly done was by revenging affronts and injuries. A Greek audience would understand about revenge. Killing children was something the Greeks took in their stride too. It was usual to do away with sickly infants, or sometimes infant girls were killed simply because they were unwanted. But the crucial decision of life or death was left to the father. Mothers were thought of as being too emotionally attached to their offspring to be rational about it. So even a Greek audience would have been shocked at Medea's decision to destroy her own children.

The myth was well known. Jason and his Argonauts sailed to Aeëtes' kingdom to win the Golden Fleece. Aeëtes imposed impossible conditions, but his daughter, Medea, fell in love with Jason and helped him meet the conditions. When Aeëtes refused to keep his word Medea helped Jason vanquish the dragon who guarded the Golden Fleece and they both fled the country with the fleece, pursued by Aeëtes. To discourage her father, Medea scattered the route with dismembered bits of her own brother. When she and Jason arrived in Colchis, Medea persuaded the daughters of the ruler, Pelias, that she could rejuvenate Pelias provided they first cut him up in pieces and cooked him. She then refused to do anything and left him well and truly cooked. Jason and she withdrew to Corinth, lived happily and had two children. Then Jason fell in love with King Creon's daughter and abandoned Medea. Medea sent a fine new robe as a present to the new bride, and the robe consumed her with fire as soon as she put it on. Medea then cut the throats of her two children fathered by Jason and fled to sanctuary in Athens where she married King Aegeus.

Euripides uses the myth to expose the complacent cruelty of Jason in his treatment of Medea. It has to be accepted that modern audiences are far more likely to be sympathetic to Medea and appalled by Jason's treatment of her than any Greek audience would have been. Greeks took male superiority for granted. So when Euripides shows us Jason as a conceited prig, unable to grasp Medea's suffering, much less respond to it, he has had to apply a little built-in bias against Jason, largely because a Greek audience would otherwise have sympathised all too quickly with the husband.

Medea is far brighter than anyone else on stage. The scenes where she persuades the two older men, Creon and Aegeus, to do what she wants, not what they want, are minor masterpieces of satirical humour. Yet with her husband at first Medea's cleverness fails. She is too wounded, too upset, too emotional. Then she plans her revenge. She wins the acquiescence of the Chorus to the idea of killing the new wife, but then the Chorus find themselves consenting by their silence to the murder of the children. This is a fine dramatic surprise. The audience also, who have been acquiescing all too easily in the murder of the wife, now find themselves facing up to the moral question of the rights and wrongs of killing the children. We can notice in passing how unimportant wives are compared with husbands. Medea wishes to hurt her husband. Nobody sees anything wrong in killing a new wife in order to hurt the husband. The views and fate of the new wife are hardly considered. The theme of the play is clear. How can a mother murder her own children? Is she justified in doing so? The audience observing the appalling insensitivity of the men around Medea, if not condoning her actions, at least understands them and sympathises with her.

Why do men, stripped naked in a modern prison regime, smear their own excrement around the walls? It is a last affirmation of their own individuality, a refusal to accept the humiliations the system is imposing upon them. They use the only weapons available to them. Medea, in determining to show Jason the enormity of his behaviour to her, commits the seemingly inexplicable, but she too is using the only weapons available to her. She has her final triumph and revenge. Yet the final irony is that it has been a hollow revenge. She may have destroyed her husband's happiness, but she has destroyed her own as a mother. Her victory is pyrrhic, long before that battle added a new word to our language. That is the tragedy of any fight between a husband and a wife. Neither triumphs. Both lose. And that implies a dependence between them that few Ancient Greek males would have been willing to admit or accept.

When Aristophanes wrote a comedy *The Frogs*, he took his audience down to Hades where the dead were debating as to who should sit on the chair of poetry, Aeschylus or Euripides. Sophocles, with characteristic modesty even in Hades, had declined to oppose either of his two great contemporaries. Yet by any standards, he could well claim to do so, having written over a hundred plays and winning first prize 18 times, triumphing over Aeschylus with his first attempt and never being ranked third.

In his youth he was praised for the beauty of his voice, his figure and his general appearance. At 16 he took part in a boys' dance as part of the celebrations for the crucial victory of Salamis over the Persians – a battle in which Aeschylus himself fought. Sophocles became very much a public figure, playing a leading part in Athenian life. In 443 BC, as Treasurer of the Greeks, he was one of the ten men administering the Delian League. In the Samian war (441-439 BC) he was elected General along with Pericles and again in 428 BC for the Archidamian war. After the disastrous expedition to Sicily in 413 BC he was one of the ten commissioners appointed to limit the powers of the Athenian council. He lived a life full of honour and public esteem although we learn from Cicero, a very late authority, that when he was 90 Sophocles' sons tried to have him declared unfit to manage his affairs. He proved otherwise by reading the court an ode for his last play *Oedipus at Colonus* which he was then writing, and won his case. He is also known to have been asked in his sixties if he could still enjoy sex with a woman and to have replied, "I am only too thankful to be rid of all that. It is like being chained to a raving madman." (I remember being very impressed with this when I was 19, still shackled to "the lunatic, the lover and the poet", but as I march inexorably towards the sere and yellow, I find myself increasingly out of step with Sophocles. My own father lived to the grand age of 104 and when he was 100 I asked him, purely in a spirit of disinterested enquiry, at what age his sexual urge had deserted him. His eyes twinkled as he told me that he was afraid I would have to put my question to someone older than himself. So hopefully Sophocles did not represent the norm.) Sophocles also shouldered religious responsibilities. He was a priest of Halon and also played a part in spreading the cult of Asclepius from Epidaurus to Athens. Socrates' last words, it will be remembered, were to insist on a sacrifice to Asclepius. It is clear from this long list of public offices in Athens, where Sophocles remained throughout his long life, that he was highly regarded, respected and was ready to play a vigorous part in Greek public life.

Where Aeschylus was positively moralistic, maintaining that out of the conflict of life in his plays, the good emerged, the bad were punished and through suffering men achieved a wry wisdom, Sophocles sought for no explanation or reliance on divine providence. He was much more willing simply to accept and to show in compelling poetry the pleasures of life as it was. Human heroism was a glory in which all could share, beauty and devotion to truth were values in themselves, and although there was brutality, terror and misery, there was also the splendour of life's possibilities. It was left to Euripides, unable to believe or accept, to brood over and to grapple with so many of the issues which still concern us. But in *Antigone* Sophocles came closest to Euripides, and although little is made of the fact that Antigone was a woman, there were no feminist issues struggling to the surface of Sophocles' mind, it was perhaps significant that Sophocles in this play alone edged towards that sympathy for women's plight in a male-dominated society which is so movingly apparent in some of Euripides' work.

We can date *Antigone* with some accuracy since an early source maintains that Sophocles was elected General largely thanks to the success of *Antigone* in winning the first prize, so that *Antigone* must have been written around 440 BC. The play takes place one day after the action of Aeschylus' *Seven Against Thebes*. Eteocles and Polynices, sons of Oedipus, have killed each other and Jocasta's brother, Creon, has therefore succeeded to the throne. He decrees that Polynices' body, because of his treachery, should not be buried but left to lie rotting away above ground. For the Greeks, until the body is properly disposed of with religious rites the soul cannot leave it and enter Hades. It was therefore the duty of a family to ensure this was done. Ismene and Antigone, sisters to Polynices, both think Creon is wrong. Ismene feels she can do nothing about it, but Antigone who is about to marry Haemon, Creon's son, decides to defy the decree and bury her brother. Both Antigone and Haemon appeal to Creon to change his mind but he refuses. The seer Teiresias prophesies doom and disaster for Creon unless he changes his mind but Creon refuses to listen. Antigone, after burying her brother, commits suicide and Haemon kills himself. Eurydice, the wife of Creon, kills herself when she hears of her son's death. Having lost both wife and son, Creon faces death as the play ends.

Since Hegel wrote about it, the play has been seen as a straightforward conflict of interest between the state and the individual, Creon acting in the best interests of the state, while Antigone listens to her conscience and does what she knows to be right. Interestingly, Goethe in discussion with Eckermann disagreed with Hegel's view. He felt that Creon acted not from political expediency, nor from political principle, but simply from his own hatred for Polynices. After all, Polynices was only struggling to regain his rightful inheritance, and this did not justify what was in effect a terrible punishment. Goethe saw the play as weighted heavily against Creon. "Creon upsets the citizens of the chorus, he upsets the people of Thebes, he upsets Teiresias, he upsets his relations and he refuses to listen to anybody until it is much too late."

Goethe's view was probably much closer to how an Athenian audience actually felt. It must be remembered that Athens was a democracy and almost obsessively proud of it. Creon was a despot. There must have been a warm sense of "At any rate, it could not happen here" in the Athenian audience as they watched the play. Look at the behaviour of the guard who is abjectly fearful at having to report to Creon that someone has attempted Polynices' burial, hiding the truth until he gets Creon's word that he will not be punished as the bringer of bad news. This is how ordinary citizens behaved under a despot. It is not how Athenians behaved. Sophocles is manipulating his fellow citizens, massaging their egos without saying a word. He does not have to; the message is implicit rather than explicit. Advertising agencies could profitably study Sophocles, winner of public competitions, triumphant in public elections, popular with the citizens. We do not know which ode he recited to the court when he was 90 to refute the charge that he was too old to manage his own affairs but my guess would be it was those unforgettable lines that tell us just what a marvellous place Athens was.

Antigone and her sister Ismene are in a sense two sides of the same coin. Ismene is afraid of antagonising Creon, or perhaps more simply put, is just straightforwardly afraid of Creon. She loves her sister, but cannot bring herself to support her at first, until finally sisterly love prevails and even then she does her best to reconcile Creon and Antigone. The audience sympathises with her, not a weak-willed person, but one doing her best in an impossible position, forced by a strong-willed sister to face unpalatable choices, instead of retreating behind a smokescreen of well-meaning platitudes and actually doing nothing as so many ordinary people find themselves doing.

Antigone is the rock around whom the play revolves. She knows she is in the right, she is determined to do what is right and it is only the unyielding intransigence of Creon, so like despotic bureaucracy everywhere, that makes her seem an extremist and finally drives her to extremist behaviour. We should perhaps remember the verdict from the trial of war criminals after the Second World War: "There should have come a time when the consciences of the accused prevented their carrying out their orders." This is an easy thing to say in a courtroom. Antigone showed that it is not so easy on the ground (or under the ground in Polynices' case!). It did not exactly trip easily off the tongue of the victors in the Second World War either. It must have sounded a bit hollow in Hiroshima or Nagasaki.

The man who changes, who finally when it is too late realises he's in the wrong, is Creon. Partly he is another victim of Lord Acton's verdict, "All power corrupts. Absolute power corrupts absolutely." A despot has absolute power and Creon at the beginning of the play is revelling in the exercise of power. His personal hatred of Polynices becomes converted into a decree that for him represents the best interests of the state. It would be easy to parallel this with Hitler's hatred of the Jews, McCarthy's hatred of communists, or Milosevic in what was once a stable Yugoslavia. I have deliberately made these modern references because Sophocles' *Antigone*, or Anouilh's 1944 version of it as a veiled reference to a France living under Nazi occupation, both grapple with issues which obstinately refuse to go away. Hegel's interpretation of the play as a straightforward struggle between the rights of the individual and the power of the state was a perfectly valid one and embodied perhaps the relevance of the play for Hegel's generation. Yet Goethe, and the Athenian audience it was written for, were perhaps a shade more politically sophisticated and aware of other issues. There is no exact equivalent in the Ancient Greek language for the English verb "to command", and their only word for "to obey" means literally "to permit oneself to be persuaded". The Athenians were certainly aware of the danger of dictatorships and of giving bureaucrats too much power. There is however one set of modern attitudes the Greeks would never have understood. We have come to see the state as too invasive. Liberty in the twentieth century has come increasingly to mean a private space around each of us, a chance to exist behind our own front door where the state cannot invade and dictate, a chance to do our own thing. Liberty for the Athenians was the chance openly to discuss, to act collectively, to reach majority decisions, to act in concert. The idea of the state as "They" and the rest as "Us" was quite alien to Athenian thinking. It is a cause surely for concern if we have come a little closer to understanding Creon and his behaviour and in the process are in danger of losing some of our sympathy for Antigone, as just another of those awkward extremists, prepared to break the law in defence of what they consider to be right.

2

Lope de Vega – Two Plays:
Fuente Ovejuna and Lost in a Mirror

In spite of all the evidence still available, the clothes, the artefacts, the buildings, the pictures, whole libraries of books and written material, the attitudes and assumptions underpinning seventeenth-century working lives still seem extraordinarily elusive. What did they really think and feel? Even in his most intimate moments, confiding his scabrous thoughts in code to his intensely personal and private diary, Samuel Pepys speaks to us across a distance of centuries, and we are uneasily aware that although we share the same words, all too often they meant quite different things then from now. Even with "table and chair", there are serious stylistic differences and wildly different visual judgements, but what about words like "honour", "hero", "reputation"?

If we can find ourselves bogged down in incomprehension even in our own English history, across such a relatively short time span, then it is doubly difficult for the English reader to come to terms with Spanish literature. It is not so much that we see a play by Lope de Vega in a quite different kind of theatre from his, nor that it comes to us filtered through a translation which, however painstaking, sensitive and well written, interposes yet another barrier between the playwright and ourselves. It is more that the play was written for a particular kind of audience, sharing sets of commonly agreed values, a cultural view of the world, a *Weltanschauung*, different even then in crucial areas from an English audience's, but one which now seems foreign to us in every sense. We are not the kind of audience for which these plays were written. If the plays still succeed in the theatre, and they do, it is often in spite of, rather than because of the author's intentions; often just because they happen to chime in with our preoccupations, however different from the author's, so that we decode these signals from a distant era, all too often in terms of what is significant for us, sometimes blithely oblivious of what they originally conveyed.

A modern audience responds to Shakespeare's *Romeo and Juliet* in terms of romantic love, part and parcel of the Romantic Movement, and now almost a cliché of popular films, novels, serials in women's magazines and a staple of television fiction. (If you think I should be writing about Lope de Vega and not Shakespeare, bear with me. They were contemporaries, and it is sometimes easier to move from the known to the unknown.) Shakespeare's audience knew nothing of our romantic attitudes, but doubtless remembered with secret and acute embarrassment the fools that they made of themselves in early adolescence, when they first fell in love. Shakespeare was reminding them, not of the clumsy, cringe-making ways they actually behaved, but of how their calf-love had seemed at the time, as devastating as a thunderclap from heaven, a vision of poetry and finer feeling in a mundane world. In their society of arranged marriages, where women were so strictly controlled they could not even act on stage the equality between the sexes that Shakespeare was radically championing, where Juliet herself had to be played by a boy, the Elizabethan response, the understanding they brought to the performance, must have been wildy different from our own.

Yet the play still works, and surely this is what matters, even if the negotiation between text and audience, between signifier and signified, is now profoundly different. Living theatre is about here and now; that mysterious moment when the curtain rises and conversation stills into a hush of expectancy from an audience that has paid for the privilege of being entertained, in that peculiarly vivid magic which only live actors in direct communication with a responsive audience can create.

When the drama historian raises a shrill voice, gnashing his aged and ill-fitting teeth, and brandishing his categories like an unwanted Polonius, to tell us we have got it all wrong, who really cares?

Perhaps, at heart, we all do. Once the play has succeeded in our terms, in our imaginative world, it has established its fascination for us, and we are naturally curious about it. When we gossip about our friends, it is not just love of gossip as such, but love of our friends too, that motivates us. They fascinate us and we want to know as much as possible about them. It is the same with plays and playwrights. We have that nagging desire to know. Are we missing something? So that the more we know about the context of the play, the social milieu for which it was written, the kind of theatre in which it appeared, what clues there are to the author's original intentions, what he thought he was saying, and how his original audience might have reacted, the more we can add to the impact of the play on ourselves as twentieth-century playgoers. Because part of the burden of coming at the end of a long and remarkably rich theatre tradition, is that we simply have to be knowledgeable about that tradition if we are fully to benefit from it.

It was probably always thus. Five centuries before the birth of Christ, Athenians at the theatre must have prided themselves on being at the end of a long and noble theatre tradition. Elizabethan audiences probably lamented the demise of the mystery plays, so carefully and opulently organised by the Church only a generation earlier, and intellectuals probably sounded all too recognisably superior as they drew parallels and recognised influences. But it has only been with the arrival of the Romantic Movement, that Europeans grew so obsessed with the past, wallowed in nostalgia, became historically conscious, and systematically and sympathetically studied previous centuries. Only in the nineteenth century, as part of that romanticism, were plays consciously presented in sets and costumes which attempted to be historically accurate. Shakespeare's and Lope de Vega's plays were presented in modern dress.

So perhaps we should look first at the kind of theatre Lope de Vega was writing for. It was a popular theatre. Historians of English drama tend to see the rise of English Renaissance theatre, a commercial popular theatre, as being forced on us by the weakness and impoverishment of the Church after Henry VIII, so that where Church and Guilds between them had organised theatre, as their influence waned, commercialism and free enterprise touring companies stepped in to fill the vacuum and take advantage of the nationwide enthusiasm for drama already created. Events in Spain should teach us to approach this simplification with caution. While helpful enough as generalisation, it ignores too many factors in a complex situation. The Church continued throughout Spain's golden age of theatre from 1492 to 1700, to organise and present drama as it had done in the Middle Ages. Yet independent touring companies and theatres built specially to house them grew up alongside the Church theatre. In fact throughout Europe, and including England, a sub-culture of touring theatre companies had existed from the days of the

Roman Empire, and seems to have survived throughout the Dark Ages and certainly flourished throughout the Middle Ages. Because of language and dialect problems, this theatre, the theatre of fairs and feast days, was a highly accomplished mime theatre, a theatre of gesture rather than words. In the absence of scripts, written evidence about it is scanty, but quite enough to put its continued existence beyond doubt. With the emergence of common national languages in the sixteenth and seventeenth centuries, a new kind of verbal theatre developed alongside and gradually superseded the mime theatre. It is worth remembering that the play within the play in *Hamlet* starts, as plays usually did, with an account in mime of the plot. Even in Shakespeare's day audience's "read" mime gestures much more easily than understanding the words. When a modern audience "reads" the programme note in order to understand a ballet at Covent Garden they are doing the exact opposite. Nothing could better illustrate just how far removed we are from those audiences of Lope de Vega and Shakespeare. (One reason why the actors seem not to have required directors was that they and the audience shared a common visual language of gesture, a centuries old European tradition that everyone so took for granted it was hardly ever mentioned.)

The difference in these developments between England and Spain was in the setting up of specialist commercial theatres. This happened earlier in Spain and between 1565 and 1635, the year Lope de Vega died, a network of such theatres (*corrales*) was established across nearly all Spanish cities and towns. They represented a happy combination of municipal planning and private enterprise. Municipalities granted the right to build and administer theatres to charities, and the charities in their turn acted as impresarios to the repertory companies, ploughing back the profits made from administering the theatres into their hospitals and almshouses. This gave the theatre in Spain a respectability which enabled it to shrug off attacks from the moralists of the day, a phenomenon as old as theatre itself. The Puritan Revolution closed down drama in England. In Spain all too many charities simply could not do without it.

Corrales were the yards enclosed by a block of houses, so this was not a street theatre but a yard theatre. The form dictated by building practise, was rectangular. A stage, with an apron projecting into the pit, would be built at one end of the rectangle. It tended to have its own roof, although the greater part of the spectators remained open to the sky, except for some roofing over seats at the side and the back, which were generally tiered. The windows of the houses giving on to the yard could, where appropriate, form boxes (*aposentos*) with rooms looking onto the stage, available for annual hire at a suitably extortionate price. The main bulk of the poorest spectators stood for the performance in the patio, where our word pit had its origin. At the back of the rectangle, the ground floor of the building giving on to the yard became converted into theatre entrances, separate ones for men and women, and a refreshment bar. The wealthy in the boxes did as they liked, but the rest of a Spanish audience was strictly segregated, seating for men only and seating for women only. As in Elizabethan theatres, one fee was charged for entrance and then an additional fee gave access to the more privileged parts of the audience accommodation. From 1574, right through into the eighteenth century, Madrid had two such theatres and the practise quickly spread throughout Spain. The stage was even more flexible than Shakespeare's. The projecting apron, the mid-stage, and the back stage, which could be curtained off, were similar enough, but the back of the stage was a house with windows and balconies waiting to be used. For large-scale battles, part of the pit could be roped off with ramps leading onto the stage, or an actor could jump from his real horse in the pit directly on to the stage before climbing up to a balcony at the back. "The furthest heaven of invention" could be the top balcony at the back of the stage, ready with its cloud machine for angels or the odd *deus ex-machina* to descend from the celestial sphere, while traps on the main stage could belch out the fumes of hell, spew up ghosts, or cover sudden disappearances in fire and thunder.

Performances were given in the afternoon, and if they ran late they risked a heavy fine. As in Elizabethan and Jacobean drama, a dance or mime to music opened the performance. In between the acts or *jornados* brief dance and mime plays were performed as in England, and the performance ended with more music and dance.

Once a performance started, there were no gaps to allow an audience to grow restive. Theatre audiences were uninhibited, and there was always an uneasy possibility of violence, probably not helped by the segregation of the sexes. It was exceptional for a play to run for more than a week. Two or three days was the norm, and with two theatres open all the year round in Madrid, only closing for Lent, the demand for new plays, if it did not create a new literary form, at least ensured that writers with talent arrived, as writers will, to make the most of the new opportunities and to jostle for a share of the funds newly available. Among them was a major talent, who was to extend and refashion the possibilities of the literary form and dominate the theatre during his lifetime. So much so that "*es de Lope*" entered the language as a common expression meaning "it's of real quality!" In El

Greco's masterpiece, *The Burial of the Conde de Orgaz,* at Santo Tome, Toledo, where St Stephen and St Augustine have miraculously appeared at the funeral to lower the Count into his tomb, among the distinguished contemporaries watching the scene are three from the arts, Cervantes, Lope de Vega and El Greco himself. Philip II, although alive when it was painted is, of course, among the angels. Jan Morris wrote of this picture "it epitomises the alliance between God and the Spanish ruling classes… (who) expect miracles as a matter of policy and are watching the saints at work rather as they might watch any foreign expert sent to do a job." It is indicative of the importance of theatre, that Lope stands prominently amongst those very ruling classes. He may have been on the fringes of gentility by birth, but through his plays he could almost claim to rule the minds of whole generations of Spaniards.

As in England, theatres became associated with resident companies, only opening their doors to other touring groups when they themselves were summoned to perform at Court or for the local grandee. Touring companies, perceived as being of lesser quality than the resident companies, continued the rounds of great houses, inn yards and fairgrounds that had been the staple of touring companies throughout the Middle Ages. Resident companies, whose actors' lives were a source of wonder and gossip, maintained in their picaresque private lives that engaging mixture of sexual promiscuity and emotional insecurity which has tended to make backstage theatre life the human equivalent of a libidinous rabbit warren with weasels on the prowl. Each company was directed by a manager (*autor de comedias*), buying his plays from playwrights (*poetas* or *ingenios*). The company would have about eight actors and six actresses. Stars would be the *prima galan* and the *primera dama*, and two clowns (*graciosos*) and two of the other men would expect to play older character parts.

As in England, drama was a poetic drama. Playwrights were *poetas*. In the hands of Lope de Vega, however, the verse language heightened the drama in a complexity of structure more sophisticated than elsewhere. As he developed it during a richly productive life as a writer of plays from the early 1580s to 1630, his polymetric versification used separate metres and strophes for groups and categories of scenes, events or feelings. Unselfconsciously echoing Ancient Greek drama, perhaps more by chance than by design, this produced much the same variety and complexity in dramatic language, contrapuntal effects in the verse akin to changes of tone in an orchestra, which it is quite impossible to reproduce in translation. Although the process began before Lope de Vega, and the polymetric system was refined even further after him, his work established a convention, adventurously explored its dramatic possibilities and accustomed audiences and other playwrights to the stimulating demands of such a complex literary form. He established other conventions too. The three act form became accepted in his time largely because he opted for it. He also developed the use of a sub-plot to complement the main plot, and built up the character of the *gracioso*, the clown, who played an important part both in plot and sub-plot, and served both to bring comic relief, and to comment as an outsider on the action of the main plot so as to sharpen the audience's understanding and appreciation of the basic theme of the play.

He was amazingly productive. His protégé Juan Perez de Montalban in his *Fama Postuma* claimed that Lope had written over 1,800 plays for the *corrales* and over 400 *autos sacramentales*, plays for religious festival performances. Even if these claims are far-fetched, and modern scholarship contests them, careful academic researches by Morley and Bruerton and others tend to agree that we have 315 plays for the *corrales* that are unquestionably Lope's and of an additional 187 attributions, 27 are probably his, 87 probably not, while 73 are uncertain. Morley and Bruerton have done invaluable work in collating stylistic differences and developments, both to date the plays that are undoubtedly his and also to exclude for stylistic reasons plays incorrectly attributed. These, of course, are the plays that for one reason or another, have survived. Accepting a round number of something over 400 plays, this is in itself a staggering total. Imagine the daunting prospect for scholars if Shakespeare had written over 400 plays! Allowing a mere three weeks to study, analyse and make careful notes on each play, it would take a student six years of uninterrupted work simply to familiarise himself with the plays themselves. It is not surprising that academic experts on Lope de Vega are hardly elbowing for room on the campus.

Lope also wrote not only novels but, in his *Arte Nuevo de Hacer Comedias en Este Tiempo*, published in 1609, a 389 line poem on the problems and skills involved in writing for the wide cross-section of society that a typical *corrales* audience represented. It was not until the 1670s that English dramatic poets began to take criticism seriously and write treatises about writing plays as well as actually writing plays. Spain and France began earlier – Lope's poem shares much with Boileau's *Art Poetique* and both are indebted to Italy which began even earlier and was, in turn, dependent on the Ancient Greeks. Lope is therefore very much a conscious part of the classical tradition. Indeed the first two decades of the seventeenth century endured a series of written attacks on Spanish drama for ignoring some of the classical rules and making up some of its own, and in a sense Lope's treatise is both a justification and an answer to classical purists. He was in the same difficult position that Dryden later found himself in. A large body of successful plays had established a dramatic form and a set of expectations in the audience which clearly broke some of the classical rules. To accept the classical rules was to condemn what common sense could not condemn. It was not until the later part of the seventeenth century that writers began to entertain the possibility that they might not only be as good as the ancients, but were possibly even better. Nobody had played with heretical notions like that since the Dark Ages engulfed Europe and the glory that was Greece and Rome, if shattered in fact, became all powerful as a mythology of past greatness. Lope sensibly sidestepped the question of the dramatic unities. While emphasising the unity of action, he completely ignored unity of place, and of time he recommended as short a time span as possible, except for history plays which by their nature spread themselves over years. Where possible he felt the action of each act should take place within the limit of a day. These are the confident tones of a seasoned practitioner in mid-career, writing from experience of what works in the theatre as he knows it, aware of the classical tradition, feeling very much a part of it, but adapting and selecting, rather than slavishly obeying. It is like Wren's boldly inventive use of the classical architectural vocabulary for his own purposes, and very far from Burlington's stitching himself up in a straightjacket of classical rules.

Then there is the question of tragi-comedy. Plays for the *corrales* were known as *comedias*. Literary historians until recently found it difficult to fit Spanish dramatists into the category called "tragedy", and so tended to find them unable to write it. Readers of *Fuente Ovejuna* and *Lost in a Mirror* will know otherwise. Lope could write a powerful, serious tragedy as effectively as any other outstanding master of the theatre, but, like Shakespeare, he also introduced humorous scenes and events into a serious play, whenever it seemed appropriate, and he argued persuasively in favour of doing so, whatever the classical rules laid down. He was aware of the fierce controversy in Italy over Guarini's *Il Pastor Fido* written in the early 1580s, mixing tragedy and comedy and then vigorously defended by Guarini. Lope not only used some of Guarini's arguments, but the very success in Spain of *Il Pastor Fido* may well have influenced Lope's practice, particularly in the development of the *gracioso* and comic sub-plot to comment on the serious main narrative. The poem is full of shrewd, practical observations and advice for would-be playwrights. They should forget classical rules about not putting monarchs into comedies. After all Plautus had written a comedy *Amphitryon* and thought nothing of including Jupiter himself as a character. It was what was appropriate to the subject matter, once chosen, that mattered.

And who was this confident spokesman for Spanish drama, still with twenty-six years of prolific writing ahead of him? First and foremost he was a poet, a spinner of magical words, but during his long writing career, from the early 1580s to 1635, he taught himself by trial and error the craft of writing plays. In his early days he clearly wrote with a fatal facility, and must have thrown off a play from a brimming creative imagination, seemingly without much thought and effort. Some of his early plays can seem almost naïve in their inability to organise the talent always on display. But he learned quickly. What impresses always is the sheer power of his writing, a passionate appetite for life, a revelling in exuberance, in the joy and fun of living. He has tended to be categorised as the sensualist with a zest for life where his successor Calderon is seen as a thinker who relished the play of the intellect. This, however flattering to Calderon, is monstrously unfair to Lope, who was one of the most impressive and creative minds of his generation, who seems to have led as full and active a life in reality as in the imaginative world he created for the stage, who after more than his fair share of the fleshpots of physical pleasure became a priest, spanning in his own lifestyles the contradictions inherent in the Renaissance between the older, if newly discovered, classical freedoms of the senses and the Christian emphasis on the mind and the soul.

The range of his plays in subject matter and style is sufficient tribute in itself to his zest for life, the breadth of his understanding, and his all encompassing imagination. While obviously the aim of seventeenth-century Spanish drama was to entertain and give pleasure, there was also an evident belief that the drama taught its audiences lessons about life, gave them a better understanding of themselves, of the world around them, and of their relations with others. Since this was the *raison d'être* of the religious drama, the *autos sacramentales* co-existing with the popular theatre of the *corrales*, and since the whole purpose of medieval art had been to instruct, this attitude was not surprising. Both audience and playwright expected a moral to he drawn. This made characterisation and action in seventeenth-century drama subordinate to the main theme of the play.

The careful touches with which Shakespeare creates believable characters in realistic situations, and the subsequent bias towards naturalism in English theatre, towards making theatre as life-like as possible in the eighteenth and nineteenth centuries were alien to what Spanish seventeenth-century drama was attempting to do. A Spanish audience expected to see a theme running through a play, and indeed to see the play as the working out of that theme, so that it is the theme, rather than the action, which brings cohesion and unity to the play. What happens in the play is designed to emphasise the force of the main theme, and should be understood in those terms. This makes Spanish drama essentially a theatre of ideas, where what actually happens in the play, and the characters around whom the play appears to he constructed, are all designed to illustrate a set of ideas. Audiences came away from a Spanish play tending to think not along the lines of "if only Hamlet had been able to make up his mind" but pondering a general lesson, such as "how foolishly snobbery makes us behave". This is so even in Lope de Vega's most light-hearted and frothy plays, amorous intrigues with a lineage stretching back to Plautus and Terence. It certainly applies to the two of his most serious and best known plays discussed here. They are both tragedies and it may be useful to emphasise that Renaissance playwrights, particularly in Spain, tended to regard historical or biblical plays as serious plays. Events that had actually happened fitted more appropriately into the mould of tragedy, whereas an invented plot allowed free play for fantasy and imagination and was therefore more appropriate as comedy. However odd these assumptions may seem nowadays thcy were an accepted seventeenth-century convention in Spain. Dramatists certainly approached history with this apparent seriousness and respect, but it did not prevent them from altering the facts and reshaping the characters to make the theme more effective.

Both *Fuente Ovejuna* and *Lost in a Mirror* are taken from life and concerned with the difficult subject of honour, where attitudes taken for granted in the seventeenth century require more explanation in the twenty-first. It hardly needs emphasising that there are two very different, almost mutually contradictory strands in our culture, which have persisted to the present. In my own schooling the two extremes of this cultural contradiction were made very clear. I attended a Christian boarding school with a school chaplain who took his duties very seriously and, looking back, I seem to have spent an inordinate time in a variety of religious services whose main aim seems to have been to set me down as part of an imprisoned congregation, while the chaplain thundered at us that this life was a vale of tears, a preparation for the life to come, and that if we were to win salvation in the after life, we must make strenuous efforts at all times to resist the Devil's blandishments in this one. If we had any pretensions to learning we were put, as previous generations of pupils had been for centuries, to study Latin and Greek. After we had reached a certain level of proficiency, we were exposed at the callow and impressionable ages of fifteen and sixteen to classical authors in the original. These authors had a very different message for us. Life might be short, but while it lasted it could be unbearably sweet. Physical passion, the pleasure of the senses, the company of women, feasting and wine, music and conversation and, above all, the fascinating interplay of human relationships in love and friendship, these were what life had to offer. Intoxicated by such heady promises during the day in the classroom, we were then herded back into the stalls in chapel to be to told all over again to resist temptation, put the Devil behind us, and concentrate firmly on confessing our sins of thought and deed, (alas largely in thought alone for most of us) to prepare for salvation in the after life. The system, particularly for the intelligent, the imaginative, and the sensitive, was schizophrenic beyond belief. And yet it faithfully represented what had been Christian culture since the Renaissance.

When the doctrines of Christianity conquered the minds and hearts of the classical world, most cultural historians would agree that the major shift in European sensibility which resulted was a change for the better. If we assume for the sake of argument that you, gentle reader, are a monster of sexual perversion, just for the sake of argument you understand, had you lived in classical Greece or Rome you could have wandered down into the market place, and provided you could produce the necessary cash, bought some attractive youngster of either sex on whom to practise your hideous perversions, and nobody would have dreamed of denying you such a right. The classical world was a slave society, a brutal and callous world, where a whole class of fellow human beings had almost no rights at all. Christianity with its concepts of equality before the Lord, of an individual soul to be respected, of mercy and forgiveness, of love and charity, civilised whole areas of human intercourse.

Unfortunately, the whole civilisation which Christianity arrived to civilise was destroyed in waves of barbaric invasions. Europe disappeared, as far as history is concerned, into the Dark Ages, into general chaos, and the primitive society which emerged from the collapse, knew little or nothing of the grandeur or achievements of Greece or Rome, apart from the broken monuments still littering the landscape around them. Christianity survived and gradually converted the barbarians all over again. Medieval society was very much a third-world society, primitive, technologically backward, superstitious, with an all-powerful Church which not only imposed a powerful ideological grip on the minds of everyone, but siphoned off what little surplus wealth there was for its own aggrandisement.

We tend to think of our culture as representing first the achievements of the Greeks and Romans, and then the triumph of the shift towards civilising values which Christianity brought. Actually it was not like that at all. Upon a primitive backward, superstitious, closed world "steeped in error", upon that medieval society, growing acquaintance with Greek and Roman texts opened up the kind of fissures still apparent in my schooling. The Renaissance was exactly what the French word means, a rebirth of interest and enlightenment in things classical. Yet in many ways, classical ideas were diametrically opposed to medieval Christianity. Both had to try and adapt, and certainly by the seventeenth century, and some would maintain even by the twentieth century, there were still areas where one set of assumptions opposed another.

The concept of honour is one such battleground. The classical Greeks had a highly developed sense of male personal honour. Schoolboys in Athens followed a curriculum that seems wonderfully simple in a later technological era. They learned to read and write, they did a little maths, some music, but otherwise their academic, as opposed to athletic studies, were restricted entirely to a study of Homer. The Greeks felt that Homer was in himself a complete education for life. This Bronze Age poet was, in our terms, a powerful medium for communicating his society's dominant ideology. If we look at Homer's assumptions about honour, we are looking at a value system that was shared across all the Greek city states, a common set of attitudes and beliefs which bound them together, and kept them haughtily conscious of their superiority to the barbarians who made up the rest of the world.

On the Trojan expedition, about which Homer wrote in the *Iliad*, Achilles, the Greek hero, the personification of the concept of honour, saw himself as insulted by Agamemnon, the overall commander. The Greeks had captured cities and acquired booty *en route* to Troy, and in the share-out of the plunder, a pretty slave girl Briseis, had originally been allocated to Achilles. Agamemnon decided to re-allocate the spoils, and in the redivision, he awarded Briseis to himself. Achilles therefore decided to sulk. When they arrived at Troy, Achilles and his troops took no part in the battles because Achilles felt himself to have been wronged, his honour insulted.

We, embedded in a twentieth-century viewpoint, might think that he was "not pulling his weight", "not being a good member of the team", "thinking of himself before others", "selfishly putting himself first", but that was not how Homer and his audience saw it. A Greek hero jealously guarded his "reputation", what others thought of him, and his honour depended on that public respect. Slighted by Agamemnon, Achilles was suffering what a very similar Japanese code would call "a loss of face", and his first duty, in caring for his public reputation, was to make it clear that he would not countenance such an insult. (Notice the similarity in our own language between the Japanese "loss of face", and our refusal to "countenance" an injury.) The Greeks saw the heroic individual as being, first and foremost, careful to guard his public reputation, "jealous of his own honour", his status in his own society, seen as dependent on his readiness to defend and, if necessary, fight for the respect of others.

Of course the hero had other attributes. In the *Iliad* the reader comes to admire the Trojan hero, Hector, and at the end of the *Iliad* the two heroes fight each other in individual combat. Indeed, most of the Greek-Trojan conflict is described by Homer in terms of individual combat. Finally, Hector, after a noble fight, is vanquished and lies defenceless on the ground, while above him Achilles stands, spear poised. Hector, understandably in the circumstances, pleads to be spared. We might think that Achilles should show generosity, magnanimity for such a brave and doughty opponent. Nothing of the sort. Achilles says the Homeric Greek equivalent of "no way" and in goes the spear, and Homer tells us in loving detail what it does on the way in, and what parts of Hector's anatomy are dragged with it on the way out. So much for Hector. Concepts of generosity, magnanimity, forgiveness, would be considered as weaknesses in classical Greek times. A hero is ruthless, competitive, prepared to step on others in order to get what he wants, judged by success "it's the results that count", and judged also by his readiness to jump to the defence of his public reputation, his status in the eyes of others, his own honour.

Christianity saw the hero in quite different terms. The Christian was, above all, attempting to imitate Christ. Concepts of forgiveness, generosity, charity, love of one's neighbour, turning the other cheek, were all at variance with what classical Greeks admired. The Christian was concerned with following Christ's teachings and attempting to do what was right in their terms. He wrestled with his own conscience, "a man has to do what a man has to do", irrespective of what others thought of him. He had to justify his behaviour to God, and to his own conscience, and the rest of society, his public reputation, came a very poor third in such a judgement. "Conscience doth make cowards of us all" is not a statement an Ancient Greek could feel at home with – no Ancient Greek saw himself as a coward.

The Christian view dominated Europe throughout the Middle Ages. It was built on the conversion of barbaric hordes who had their own concept of honour. The English jury system emerged from a whole set of Saxon concepts about an individual being worth the number of other men around him prepared to stand by him, concepts closer to classical Greece than to Christianity. But Christianity triumphed, and as the Dark Ages receded, and Europe prospered, the Middle Ages represented a triumph of Christian ideology. Charging interest on a loan was seen, throughout the Middle Ages, as being un-Christian and a crime. Only non-Christians like the Jews were allowed to get away with it. Charging more for something in a shop than it was worth was seen as un-Christian and a crime. Trying to pay a workman less than a fair wage was seen as un-Christian and a crime. However backward, primitive and superstitious medieval society was, some of its commonly held values seem remarkably attractive to us in retrospect. Economic historians would remind us, however, that throughout the Middle Ages, another battle was going on. The lay ruler, the monarch, the prince, the duke, was struggling for supremacy of power with the Church. By and large, the Church won this struggle for most of the Middle Ages. Spectacularly when, for example, Henry II was scourged by the monks at the shrine of Thomas á Beckett after walking barefoot in penance in 1174.

By the Renaissance, the Church was losing, partly because of its own corruption and venality. "All power corrupts" and the Church in the later Middle Ages became a vivid example of just how far power's corrupting influence can go. At the same time alien ideas had been spreading through Europe since as far back as 1085 when the fall of Toledo unleashed libraries of Greek texts, carefully preserved in Arabic by Arab civilisation. Arab culture in Spain reached a high point, superior to backward Christian Europe in technology (there was public lighting in the streets of Cordoba), in toleration (different races and creeds lived freely together), and in scholarship (a careful preservation and adaptation of Greek writings), science and medicine. It was not until 1492, about the same time as the discovery of America that the last Arab state in Spain was defeated and Arab influence no longer officially ruled anywhere in Spain. After the fall of Toledo the influence of Arab culture and the Greek culture it had made its own, permeated European universities and centres of thought, such as the courts of enlightened monarchs, and gradually built into that ferment of new ideas values and assumptions we call the Renaissance. In the nineteenth century history was rewritten to imply that only when Constantinople fell to the Turks did fleeing scholars bring the precious texts of our European Greek and Roman heritage back to us. This conveniently eliminated the Arabs, who were not Europeans at all, and therefore seen as not being entitled to membership of the club. Indeed it did more, managing to indict the Turks for destroying Constantinople, one of the great cities of European civilisation. Actually Constantinople was sacked and its influence effectively destroyed by a Venetian-led European army, ostensibly on a Christian crusade, but actually out for whatever booty it could get in 1204. This sort of awkward fact never appeared in Victorian school history books.

Along with all the other bewildering rich echoes and assumptions from a forgotten classical world, Greek ideas about honour arrived at a remarkably convenient time to underpin the struggle for supremacy between Church and State in late medieval Europe. If the ruler and the state were to wrest control of economic power from the Church, as Henry VIII did in the dissolution of the monasteries, for example, they needed an alternative ideology, a set of values and assumptions which, while grudgingly allowing the Church to maintain its control over the so-called "spiritual" aspects of life, effectively divorced it from much of the everyday business on which the growing prosperity of Europe depended. Classical Greek concepts of honour, alongside a clutch of other concepts, effectively established the difference between the aristocrat, the gentleman, the new representative of the power of the state, as opposed to the priest, the old representative of the power of the Church. The more different the new representative values and assumptions were seen to be, the more readily could it become clear that the priest, the old representative, was irrelevant in whole areas of such a changing world.

In England the extremes of this position were clear for all to see. Sir Thomas More was beheaded for not being able to adjust to the new order, for attempting to maintain the Church's old hegemony in a world where the Church was not only losing power with its actual territorial estates being confiscated, but where its influence was being increasingly confined within so-called "spiritual" boundaries. It was no accident that the drama became secularised in Shakespeare's time. This was a small part of a much larger social and cultural revolution.

In Spain, as in the rest of Catholic Europe, the revolution was subtler, arrived more slowly, and was never quite as effective as in Protestant Europe, but it was a revolution nevertheless. Once again it was no accident that the drama of the *corrales* became secularised, but the fact that some of the profits from this commercial, secular theatre were siphoned off into religious charities emphasises how much gentler, how much more imperceptibly the changes were introduced in Catholic Spain. In England the jagged results of abrasive change could be harder to bear. "Hark hark, the dogs do bark, the beggars are coming to town" refers to the gangs of uprooted labourers and former monks who terrorised defenceless villages in late Tudor times. Spain suffered much less from this kind of social upheaval, but the alternative ideology of the aristocrat and gentleman arrived just as inexorably in the Spanish Renaissance, as it did elsewhere in Europe.

From the early Renaissance, handbooks on being a gentleman spread the new concepts with all the authority that a host of classical references and quotations could give them. Since Italy was the spearhead of the Renaissance, setting the tone for later developments in Spain as much as in England and Northern Europe, these textbooks on how to be an aristocrat were largely Italian. It was no surprise that one of the earliest and most influential, Castiglione's *The Book of the Courtier*, given over forty editions in the sixteenth century after its first printing in Venice in 1528, was banned by the Spanish Inquisition in 1576. As usual the Inquisition knew what it was doing. These books were to dominate an important area of European thought. Indeed they took root in Spain faster and more radically than anywhere else. Spain was entering upon its Golden Age. If England's great period of commercial prosperity and territorial aggrandisement centred around the eighteenth and nineteenth centuries, Spain's was the sixteenth and seventeenth. The discovery of America and the granting by the Pope of much of its wealth and territory as a monopoly to Spain, meant that Spain became the siphon through which the wealth of the New World reached Europe.

It brought problems too. Syphilis, endemic in America, spread to Europe. Inflation arrived with the vast consignments of silver bullion, itself accelerating the erosion of the old order, and underpinning the establishment of a new, monied class.

The new ideology was ready and waiting to fit this new class as neatly as their newly ostentatious suits of bejewelled clothes. The classical ideas of a gentleman, carrying the responsibility for protecting his own honour, and that of his family, were carefully elaborated. Honour, or the public respect due to the virtuous man, was seen in theory at least as being as important as life itself. Without it, a man was socially lost, consigned to a social grave if not an actual one. Lost honour could be won back, sometimes by legal means, but generally by the spilling of blood. In the last analysis a man not prepared to die to defend his honour was seen as being without honour. A slight to a man's honour, or that of his family, however small in itself, therefore became immediately and grimly important. A slap on the face, a push in a crowd, a chance remark could all become – if seen as public loss of honour – grounds for mortal combat. Hence the rise of duelling, still remarkably slap-happy and unscientific in the seventeenth century, but by the eighteenth a nastily specialised set of skills which no would-be gentleman could do without. The code of honour became even more ritualised. Calling a man a liar was seen as being no more and no less grave than invading the sanctity of his own body space by pulling his beard. Neither of these were really any more or less a cause for demanding satisfaction than the seduction of a wife. Don Juan, in another context, remarked cheerfully that, given the choice between pulling a man's beard and seducing his wife to give him grounds for a challenge, after careful and prolonged reflection, he was inclined to pursue the latter course. Certainly in Spain it was legal to avenge dishonour to oneself or one's family. Courts accepted the killing of both the seduced wife and the seducer, even where adultery was only suspected, provided such suspicions were public knowledge. The emphasis was always on a public reputation. As the Duke says in *Lost in a Mirror*:

> But how can I find out
> What has gone on
> Without witnesses knowing
> My honour has gone?

The code of honour excluded not only the Church, but Christian teaching. Where his honour was concerned, a gentleman brushed the Church aside. The priest's role was to bring the comforts of the last rites to the dying victim after satisfaction had been exacted. No set of rituals could more cleverly or more effectively have established the divisions between Church and State or reasserted more convincingly the values of classical Greece and Rome. These assumptions about the need to protect individual honour have persisted with amazing resilience. Even in the last century English politicians called each other out to fight private duels, as did Americans. The insistence in so many Hollywood films on the need for the hero to "prove himself", to establish his personal reputation and honour as a member of the group, makes it clear that, however garbled, Renaissance teachings about the role of the gentleman bit deep. It might surprise Clint Eastwood fans to know that his spaghetti westerns were faithfully reproducing fifteenth-century Italian ideas of what a virtuous man should do to protect his own standing in the eyes of those around him.

Both *Fuente Ovejuna* and *Lost in a Mirror* are concerned with the concept of honour, and Lope de Vega wrote a number of other plays attempting to come to terms with what, in his own time, was a remarkably powerful and radical concept, at odds with many of the assumptions inherent in earlier Christian doctrine. In *Fuente Ovejuna* he tackles the subject head on. One of the most important aspects of the code of honour is that it is class-related. By accepting the obligations of the code, an aristocrat and a gentleman, just as much as an Ancient Greek hero, is distinguishing himself from the common herd. What is all right for ordinary people is not all right for him. He has to be jealous of his honour, ready at any time to put his very life at hazard in its defence. We can remember that Aristotle felt it was this willingness to hazard the most precious commodity we possess, life itself, which made being a soldier a more honourable profession than any other. By participating in and belonging to the gentlemanly code from the Renaissance onwards a gentleman cloaked himself in the same mystique that surrounded the medieval knight of chivalry, or Aristotle's soldier. In *Fuente Ovejuna* Lope de Vega asked the unanswerable question: why is the peasant villager not allowed his share of honour, his share of reputation, his share of public respect? Fernand Gomez sneers "your honour" at the peasants who seem to be getting ideas above their station and this is the voice of aristocratic privilege taunting those beyond the pale. Lope is asking his audience to think about the true nature of honour. That is the main theme of *Fuente Ovejuna*. It has other themes too, which we shall look at, but in asking his audience to reflect on honour, Lope is echoing the advanced thought of his day. Gomez, the Comendador, is a despicable tyrant, and the villagers agree not only to his killing but, by their mutual collective silence afterwards, they prevent the authorities from discovering his murderer. The audience is in no doubt that Gomez deserved to die. They admire the villagers' determination to stand together after it. These are honourable men, committed to an honourable course of action.

Lope is edging his audience towards thinking that true honour depends not on class, not on noble birth, but on virtuous action. The accident of birth at best implies an obligation to behave virtuously, but virtue is won by actions and the man or woman deserving honour is the one whose deeds have earned respect, irrespective of social class. It is not the result or the success that matters, so much as the intention, the determination and fortitude shown in attempting to realise them. This is a sophisticated view of honour. It still accepts many classical assumptions which are basically pre-Christian. It is right to kill the Comendador, and honour consists not only in killing him but in standing by each other afterwards. In accepting this, the audience still see the shedding of blood as conferring honour. But at least Lope is attacking the idea of class, the idea that honour is an aristocratic preserve. The play's assumptions are that every man or woman, whatever their status in society, can win honour and reputation and self-respect. Indeed, it is a woman, rather than a man, who finally shames the villagers into action, shame being bound up with honour, the woman personifying the reputation they will have to live with, as her husband will have to live with her, for the rest of their lives. Virtue in the play is shared equally between the king and the villagers. The wrongdoer is the Comendador. Virtue and vice, honour and dishonour are seen to have little or nothing to do with barriers of class, birth and social position. In the claustrophobic and semi-feudal snobberies of the seventeenth-century Spanish class system, the play must have seemed radical indeed.

The peasants are, of course, idealised. The grim actualities of their hard lives do not form part of the dramatist's intentions. They belong to the bucolic pastoral, a strand in European literature tracing its wayward path back to Horace's *Beatus Ille*, which has persistently refused to be anything but sentimental about shepherds and agricultural workers. There are recognisable echoes and allusions in Lope's poetry making these antecedents clear, and even more irritatingly reaching some of the high points of his verse. But it is no good interposing a twentieth-century desire for realism for facing the hard facts of how tough actual village life must have been. In seventeenth-century drama characters and actions are subordinated to the theme. This is a theatre of ideas and of poetry, and if real life does not fit, it is left outside like the muddy boots the farmer discards at the door.

There are other ideas in *Fuente Ovejuna*. The discussion in Act I between Barrildo and Mengo about love crystalises the secondary theme which underpins the play's main analysis of honour. As the villagers stand by each other, they learn, as does the audience, the importance of being able to trust each other, that love and confidence which the play reassuringly asserts as a vital bond to link disparate elements of society together. Here Lope and his audience are harking back to an earlier Christian medieval view of society, welded together in love and trust from the highest to the lowest, each doing his best in the station fate has allotted. "The rich man in his castle, the poor man at his gate". In the twentieth century, it seems even more idealised than the bucolic pastoral element, a charmingly naïve view of a society that will never change, where the king rules through divine right, where the nobility by the accident of birth have higher responsibility thrust upon them, which it is their duty to live up to, and where the cheerful yokel, doffing his cap to his betters, earns wide respect through hard work and pleasing humility. It seems incredible in the seventeenth century, when social change was proceeding at a faster rate than for hundreds of years previously, audiences went for this self-deluding nonsense. Yet they undoubtedly did. Just as the Church reassured them about the fundamental righteousness of their society, so this medieval view of the nature of the state, suitably backed by Church teaching, helped to shield them from the realities of social change until long after the changes had actually taken place. In learning collective trust and love, putting their community before their own self-interest, the villagers are learning in the play about the love of God, whose representatives the king and queen are, and whose pardon has as much force in changing the outcome of the play, as the priestly pardon brings to the individual in the confessional. It brings the play to its second high point.

We know from his *Arte Nuevo* that Lope accepted the classical view of the development of the plot from protasis (exposition) to epitasis (complication) and catastrophe (unravelling), and his three-act form generally fits this mould neatly enough. But in *Fuente Ovejuna* the thrilling high point of the Comendador's death is followed by the cerebral high point of the play's resolution, and whatever we may think of the values which underpin it, it rounds off the drama with an exhilarating and satisfying sense of completeness. The theme has worked itself out in a logical and coherent way, appealing in its development to both the hearts and the minds of the audience.

The poetic metaphors of the play use a range of animal imagery, which probably had an immediacy in the seventeenth century which an urban industrialised twentieth century has lost. Gomez names Frondoso "dog", and as a metaphor for faithfulness that is acceptable enough, but it is Gomez who is seen as a running dog, to be killed like a dog. Simile and metaphor are the stock in trade of a poet, but Lope builds his dramatic effects with a verbal language whose subtlety adds layers of richly textured meanings and ironies. Add to these the skilful varieties and carefully chosen range of his polymetric system to emphasise and isolate out different aspects of situation and emotion and we can only admire the level of sophistication in a tragic drama which can grapple with such intellectually demanding subject matter and find the theatrical meanings and the language to measure up to the challenge of its theme.

Lost in a Mirror is a late play written in 1631. It took its plot from a novella by Bandello which was itself based on a real life incident. It made, therefore, a fit subject for tragedy, its authenticity giving it a gravitas for seventeenth-century Spain which mere fantasy, created by an author's imagination, could never acquire. Whatever we may think of this artificial distinction it predisposed audiences to take the subject matter seriously if they knew the events echoed historical reality, just as modern cinema audiences are sometimes assured at the beginning of a film that the events depicted are a "true story". Even today Hollywood could hardly introduce a comedy in this way, and it is this distinction which Spanish audiences and playwrights clearly felt was crucial.

There are three central characters and Lope makes no attempt to idealise any of them. They are presented as fully rounded, believable individuals, each striving to lead a satisfactory life, but each flawed by weakness which ultimately destroys. The Duke of Ferrara's weakness is plain for all to see. He has a bastard son, and his cheerful womanising is spelled out early in the play. Once again the metaphors are those of the countryside:

> The Duke looks,
> Just like a fox.

And when he can appear in public as somebody else, then the sensualist can forget his public reputation and honour:

> When you're in disguise,
> Nothing's forbidden, anything goes.

So the Duke can:

> Dance to love's tune
> On the tiles of the Moon

The fact that the Duke is married does not prevent his happy whoring. Nor is there any suggestion in this play that his wife's honour is besmirched by his infidelity, that she requires satisfaction, that only the death of husband and mistress can satisfy the wrong done to her. This double standard, which had existed throughout the Middle Ages, was still largely unquestioned in the seventeenth century. What was acceptable behaviour in a man, was certainly not acceptable, was indeed unheard of, in a woman. A man's honour was bound up in his wife's chastity, but the reverse was not even feasible. Nothing could more clearly indicate the subordinate status of women in European society, a general view of them as male chattel, than their humble role in the relative hierarchies of the codes of honour. While the Duke is away on a Papal war, something perceived as an honourable Christian activity, his bastard son begins an affair with the Duke's wife, According to the codes of the time, this was incest. Their act of love represents the weakness of the other two central characters, the bastard and the Duchess. The son is betraying his father's trust, as is the wife. Enmeshed in the code of honour, as was the rest of Spanish society, the Duke's first aim on discovering the wrong done him when he returns from the war, is to keep the matter secret:

> This is what the laws of honour say!
> That there must never be public knowledge of my
> injury for that would double my dishonour.

One of the many ironies in the situation is that the Duke is betrayed, not by a legal son, but by his own bastard, by the very evidence of the Duke's own fall from grace. In that fall he created the instrument to punish himself for doing so. It is a neat twist that a Catholic, Spanish audience would relish to the full. "The evil that men do lives after them" with a vengeance. The Duke has returned from the war a changed man, ready to live honourably and cherish his wife. The blow, when he discovers how she has cheated him, is akin to the discovery of AIDS in the twentieth century. The knowledge leads inexorably to death. It is not a question of whether, but where and how and when. Acting in his capacity as a ruler and judge, he decrees a punishment that he and his audience see as inevitable and just. The son is persuaded to kill the wife in error, and then himself punished for the murder. The Duke's public reputation remains untouched and he has managed to preserve his own private sense of honour as well. The Duke's punishment is clear enough. He has killed his own son. He has lost the virtuous wife he thought he possessed. That the public sense of his honour and reputation remained intact, must have seemed a hollow sham even for seventeenth-century Spain:

> Honour my fierce enemy!
> Who invented your cruel maze?

Lope was here asking questions that were unanswerable in seventeenth-century terms. Just as in Greek tragedy we watch the hubris of the proud man slowly ground to dust by the force of circumstances over which he has no control, squirm and struggle as he may, so the options open to the Duke leave him equally little choice. He is left at the end of the play facing a bleak future, and yet his audience might well have pondered as they left the theatre, how could it have been otherwise? The code of honour required him to act as he did. Had he been a virtuous man, there would have been no bastard in the first place, so he lives betrayed by his own weakness. The moral is clear. That the son should have betrayed his father so monstrously is spelled out as weakness. The son's willingness to desert the Duchess for another marriage on his father's return shows him in the same mould as his father, ready to use women, surrendering to the pleasures of an affair, and then move on. The audience could share his pleasure in the affair and find his actions all too believable, but ultimately they had to condemn him as shallow in his love which could not weigh in the balance against the betrayal of his father. He was seen to deserve his fate. For us, Casandra, the wife, is perhaps the most sympathetic of the three protagonists:

> Because of the wrongs done by the Duke
> My soul leans towewards wickedness.
> I'm like a mad woman trying to take
> Revenge and pleasure at the same time.

She here justifies her behaviour because of the wrongs done to her by her husband, and for a modern audience this seems justification enough. It has to be stressed that this would have seemed mere sophistry for Lope's Spanish audience. It could never have aroused the sympathy it undoubtedly arouses today. Fidelity and purity were so bound up in being a wife and mother, that her fall would have been complete in Spanish eyes. A Spanish audience, watching her become a wicked woman, would consider her fate as deserved as it was inevitable.

It is Lope's skill as a playwright that this ancient package of outmoded conventions and assumptions still works in the theatre. The issues are presented so straightforwardly and the characters, even if they exist for us only in a strange time warp, are so believable that they persuade us to share, for the brief excitement of the drama, their alien view of the world and its twisted obligations. It is a strange reversal of time that just as Lope could respond to the force of classical drama from an entirely different standpoint – that of a seventeenth-century Spaniard with pretensions to gentility – so we in the twentieth century can respond to the force of Lope and to the influence of classical drama upon him, while sharing even less of his views than he had in common with the pagan world.

For Lope's audience *Lost in a Mirror* was most decidedly not a tragedy about a doomed couple. The tragedy was the Duke's, and the tangled web through which the weakness of each of the three main characters helped to destroy the other two. As in most seventeenth-century drama, character and action served to illustrate the theme, and it remains a theatre of ideas, challenging us to puzzle out the ideas inherent in the drama, inviting us to ponder the moral in the play, which remains paramount. Once an honourable man stoops to dishonour, he may retain a mask of public reputation, but his life becomes a hollow sham, and he is really no better than anybody else who surrenders to temptation. It is a bleak message. Although Lope ended his life as a priest, there is no hint in this play of redemption or forgiveness. The code of honour co-existed alongside Church teaching, and made few connections with it. In a period still dominated by the Church, the theatre of the *corrales* was ostensibly "real life". Yet with the hindsight the twentieth century brings, we can see that Lope and his audience had a warped view of "real life", a world where a man's honour justified his killing wife and lover, and where legal courts accepted such actions as just and worthy, while in the next street, churchgoers sat raptly listening to sermons about turning the other cheek, loving one's enemies, and forgiving them, while making mental reservations that, of course, this did not apply where a man's honour was concerned, might seem at first glance rather far removed from our own. Yet the incompatibility between the pagan and the Christian world still persists, if weakened, in our own time. Its echoes are all around us. They are still strong enough for us to sympathise with Lope's characters, even while we tell ourselves that, of course, things are altogether different now. It is like responding to tunes and songs from armies in half forgotten wars. The music still works, even though we have forgotten, or never knew, the words. Lope is above all a poet and his siren voices still enchant.

3

Shakespeare – Troilus and Cressida

U nlike so many of Shakespeare's plays, where we are dazzled by individual characters, share an insight into what makes them tick, and where we may see the inmost part of them, *Troilus and Cressida* is not so much about people as about ideas.

Astonishingly there is some doubt whether it was performed at all in Shakespeare's lifetime. In the last century Peter Walker put forward the theory that it may have been put on as a private performance for "the witty young masters o' the Inns o' Court", but there is no direct evidence. Dryden rewrote much of the play, and his version, very different from what Shakespeare intended, held the stage from 1698 to 1734. Shakespearean scholars, editors and critics wrote about it in varying degrees of bafflement, shock and incomprehension, but Shakespeare's own play seems not to have been performed from 1602, when it was probably written, until a William Poel, London production in 1912.

So the first sobering reflection engendered by the play has to be that it has taken the England for which it was written approximately another four hundred years of experience and development, before we feel able to come to terms with so much of its content. Four hundred? Only a little over three hundred before the 1912 production surely? Poel was a pacifist, and apparently used the play as a director's sermon against war. Only as we creep gingerly into the twenty-first century, can we begin to feel a grasp of what this exciting play is about. Indeed, in an astonishing *volte-face*, for many play-goers this has become their favourite Shakespeare play, peculiarly modern in the way it tackles problems that a post-Marx, post-Darwin and post-Freud audience feels better able to analyse.

Only a third of the play is about Troilus, Cressida and Pandarus, the ardent lover, unfaithful heroine and scandalous go-between – a tale loosely based on Chaucer's poem. The other two thirds are about Homer's heroes of the Trojan war. As the prologue tells us:

> our play
> Leaps oe'r the vaunt and firstlings of these broils
> Beginning in the middle, starting thence away
> To what may be digested in a play.

We may feel wiser than that Elizabethan audience, but in some respects we are a good deal less educated. Ben Jonson might well say slightingly that Shakespeare had "little Latin and less Greek", but that was from the standpoint of someone who prided himself a little too vociferously, on his classical scholarship. Shakespeare had the typical grammar school boy's education of his day, and by our standards would have emerged with an enviable grounding in Latin authors and history. It is clear from the many allusions and references throughout the plays, that Ovid must have been among Shakespeare's favourite poets. The love of grand sounding, slightly over decorated language, must have been part of the same heritage. It is not so much that Shakespeare himself was moulded by these influences, as that he shared the same background of learning and knowledge with a good deal of his audience. Some of the arguments in *Troilus and Cressida* are based on Aristotle's *Nichomachean Ethics*, explicitly referred to in the play by Hector, an engaging anachronism since Homer and his war are located firmly in the Bronze Age whereas Aristotle flourished only five centuries before the birth of Christ. Of course, the arguments are still effective for those who know nothing of Aristotle, but Shakespeare seems to have expected his audience to pick up these references. How many in a twenty-first-century audience can do that? In the same way Shakespeare obviously expects his audience to know both Homer's epic and Chaucer's too. But those of my readers who have had the benefit of a modern public school education should take heart. Shakespeare probably knew his Homer in translation too.

And now let us leap over the vaunt and firstlings of the play and ask what makes it special and challenging for a modern audience? Remember it was written in 1602. Most scholars agree that the final version of *Hamlet* was produced in 1601. The wonders of *Lear*, *Macbeth*, *Othello* and *Antony and Cleopatra* lay well ahead. But after the light-hearted *Twelfth Night*, so obviously a relaxation from the "ferocious ironies" of *Hamlet*, Shakespeare turned again to what Harold Bloom calls the "bitterness", the "rancidity", the "dangerous" ideas of *Troilus and Cressida.*

The voice of Hamlet is there in the play too. Think of Troilus, watching Cressida betray what he thought of as their love, and give herself to Diomed. Like Hamlet, Troilus is attempting to deal with a terrible shock to his system, and his sense of the rightful order of things.

> TROILUS: This she? – No, this is Diomed's Cressida
> If beauty has a soul, this is not she;
> If souls guide vows, if vows be sanctimonies,
> If sanctimony be the gods' delight,
> If there be rule in unity itself,
> This is not she. O madness of discourse,

> That cause sets up with and against itself
> Bifold authority; where reason can revolt
> Without perdition, and loss assume all reason
> Without revolt. This is and is not Cressida.

We cannot date the *Sonnets* – but they seem to have been written over the twenty years from 1589. Is it a rash speculation that hears some of the same passionate dismay in some of the sonnets, that may well have been written at much the same time?

But we have not got there yet. Jonathan Bate in his brilliant *The Genius of Shakespeare* thinks that *Troilus and Cressida* is "cynical" and "deeply ironic" about "traditional codes and values".

Indeed it is, and of course there are many layers and complexities in this richly challenging play, which Bate only refers to as an illustration in the particular thesis he is arguing. Almost in passing he suggests it is this very cynicism that kept the play unperformed throughout the eighteenth and nineteenth centuries. Yet in the excellent Arden edition of the play, Kenneth Palmer, while generally agreeing about the cynicism, also finds similarities between Alexander Pope's mock-heroic style, much admired in the eighteenth century and the mock-heroic style of *Troilus and Cressida*. Cynicism and irony are well-established weapons, along with parody and satire in the use of humour. Perhaps Troilus himself sums up the mood of the play best when he says:

> I have, as when the sun doth light a storm,
> Buried the sigh in wrinkle of a smile,
> But sorrow that is couch'd in seeming gladness
> Is like the mirth fate turns to sudden sadness.

It is that sadness which seems to pervade the play. But Shakespeare in *Troilus and Cressida* is standing back, looking at the larger picture. It is not so much individual situations that interest him here, nor what makes the individual tick. It is what makes society tick. He seems to be taking a hard look at the basic myths that underpin our culture and help to give us our view of ourselves.

I am always suspicious when scholars (and I suppose grudgingly I must even allow A L Rowse that title) when scholars tells us a writer "must have" felt this or that. A L Rowse was particularly prone to make these intuitive leaps, especially when claiming, without any evidence, to have discovered the identity of the Dark Lady of the *Sonnets*. But surely Shakespeare "must have" been aware of what he had done to Richard III? The Tudor Henry VII, Queen Elizabeth's grandfather, seized the throne by force from Richard in 1485 at the Battle of Bosworth Field. The more of a villain Richard III was, the more the seizure was legitimised. The Tudors immediately married into the royal line to legitimise themselves, but popular mythology required that Henry VII be a hero and Richard III a villain. Shakespeare duly obliged. When he had finished with Richard III, the "murderer" of the little princes in the Tower (probably in fact organised by Henry VII!), the public had a villain in spades. It is difficult to believe that Shakespeare was unaware of this convenient manipulation of historical facts. Richard III seems actually to have been quite estimable as monarchs go. Shakespeare converted him into a monster, and a monster he remains on stage to this day.

The Renaissance, a French word meaning re-birth, was given its title by historians because it was indeed a re-birth, a renewed interest in and careful study of classical literature.

Shakespeare's careful grounding in the classics at his Stratford grammar school was a late example of the way the Renaissance changed the cultural world. That classical world was steeped in Homer. As we have seen earlier, five centuries before the birth of Christ, Greek school boys learning their three R's would, as the young Shakespeare had, learn to read and write and do some maths. They also did a good deal of music and athletics but they were otherwise rather charmingly considered educated if they had studied Homer, a Bronze Age poet whose origins were even then lost in the mists of time. Homer therefore was a basic creator in establishing the value system and attitudes of Greek culture. Every Greek had been brought up on him. Homeric values were what underpinned concepts of honour and incidentally much of Aristotle's *Nichomachean Ethics*. In the Renaissance, Homer's epic poems, and the way they pervaded the classical world's assumptions, once again became a dominant force in Western culture.

Shakespeare in effect sends Homer up, makes fun of him, satires him. It is as though Shakespeare were saying to us: "This is what Homer tells us happened in the Trojan War. Now let us see what really happened!" And the events are tellingly different. Achilles – unlike the real hero Hector – gets his Myrmidons brutally to slaughter a defenceless Hector, and then claims he defeated him in single combat in a fair fight.

In the 1914–18 war, the British troops in the trenches at the Front, read the same daily newspapers that were being delivered that same day to most homes in Britain. They read of non-existent victories, that said nothing of the appalling losses suffered by our own troops. From that time dates the widespread feeling that newspapers lie. That "you cannot believe what you read in the press". Is it any wonder that post-World War I audiences, knowing how the truth had been rearranged, re-edited for propaganda purposes, felt in tune with what Shakespeare was saying in this play. But how on earth was Shakespeare so prescient? Because he knew all about it. As a leading creator in the main medium of communication in his day, the theatre, he had already re-edited the facts for propaganda purposes. His whole cycle of history plays consciously told his audience who they were, what sort of a world they were in and how privileged they were to be English.

In World War II Anouilh re-wrote Sophocles' *Antigone* knowing that his audience, suffering under the censorship of the Nazi occupation, would make the parallel between Sophocles and France in the 1940s. Shakespeare's audience could make no such parallels. *Troilus and Cressida* might have persuaded them to start doing so. Is there any wonder it seems not to have been performed? Shakespeare in effect is looking at the power of popular mythology, at the way the media of communication create popular mythology, often transforming fact into fiction in the process.

Dare I take a bold leap in the dark? Suppose he had decided to satirise, not the mythology of the classical world of Homer, but the mythology of Christianity? Suppose he had written a play saying: "This is what the *Bible* tells us happened. Now let us see what really happened!" (And remember that Homer was an almost equally powerful story for the Ancient Greeks.) Just think of the uproar such a play might have caused. Apparently even sending up Homer was enough to get the play effectively suppressed on any stage for over 300 years.

Not of course that I am suggesting Shakespeare would have wanted to satirise Christianity. We have no evidence any such thought ever crossed his mind. I merely wanted an extreme example of what he was actually doing at the time he wrote this play.

A surprising number of the characters in *Troilus and Cressida* are in love, not with themselves but with their image, with what posterity will make of them. It is not just Shakespeare who is standing back, and taking the longer view, but so many of his characters as well.

The famous scene where the lovers join hands and plight their troth, is pervaded with a sense of what future ages will say about them. They are consciously making, not so much history, as an image of themselves to project onto posterity. And the fun is that the audience knows it is all going to end in tears and sick, that Cressida will become a byword for infidelity, Pandarus give a word to the language and what of Troilus? He is not so much in love with Cressida as in love with love itself. They are all posturing in front of a mirror, all hoping the press photos as it were, will be carefully retouched, when in fact, events and the tabloids are going to dish the dirt on the lot of them.

Not only are characters constantly watching themselves and refurbishing their image when required, but others are watching them too. Shakespeare manipulates with enviable authority, not just the characters, but the very conventions of theatre. We watch and listen to people who are watching and listening to other people who are watching and listening to other people. Shakespeare is playing with us, the audience, almost as much as with his characters, who are also making up an audience, and yet Shakespeare does this so effectively we hardly notice how sophisticated it all is. If the play was performed for those discriminating lawyers at the Inns of Court (and I like to think it was. Surely no such finished masterpiece could have been left without the excitement that only a live performance can bring to a script – and this play cries out to be performed) that close friend of Shakespeare, Ben Jonson, steeped in classical scholarship must have (oops! – "must have" again) must have been in the audience, consumed with the envy of a fellow creator even as he could not help enjoying the sheer brilliance with which all his classical knowledge was being turned upside down.

Harold Bloom, always a pleasure to read on Shakespeare, wonders that he can never remember it is actually Troilus who says such memorable things such as:

> This is the monstruosity in love, lady, that the will is infinite and the execution confined, that the desire is boundless, and the act a slave to limit.

We all remember the words. Shakespeare has a gift for saying things that once heard, continue to echo and resonate in the mind, becoming part of our mental baggage, because quite simply he puts things so much better than anybody else, but it is appropriate in this case that we hardly remember the individual speaker. *Troilus and Cressida* is a different kind of play from so much that Shakespeare wrote. Of course Shakespeare being Shakespeare his characters come alive as individuals but that is not his primary intention. In this play he is dealing with types rather than individuals, parodying the styles and conventions of the drama itself, giving his audience the perceptions that come from that flash of recognition, as we realise how effective styles and conventions are in creating the illusion that is theatre. It is the mock-heroic that illuminates for us the style and the limitations of the heroic.

In *Troilus and Cressida* Shakespeare is giving us not just a battle of Trojans against Greeks, but the battles of dramatic styles too. He is more than ironic about both, his wrinkle of a smile turns to a sudden sadness at the ease with which audiences can be taken in.

Look at Ulysses' superb speech in defence of order and degree, still plangent with meaning for Michael Portillo quoting them to his fellow Conservatives in 1994 as Jonathan Bate points out. It is a beautiful defence of a hierarchical society. Yet having made it Ulysses' goes on to suggest they dishonourably gerrymander an election. In context, this makes nonsense of the style and the sentiments of the previous speech. It is exactly in that distinction between what the characters grandly say and what they actually do that the mock-heroic lies.

How is a director to deal with these stylistic variations? It is generally accepted that Shakespeare directed his own plays, although we have no clear idea of what that entailed. After 1604 he seems to have given up acting altogether and stuck to writing and producing. This means that if it was performed Shakespeare played one of the characters in the play. We would dearly love to know which. He would have been 38 years old. My guess would be the unimpressive Agamemnon, so unlike a true commander that Aeneas quite fails to recognise him – although judging by what Shakespeare was confiding to the sonnets, if indeed these are to be believed as personal confessions – then perhaps the cuckolded Menelaus would have been more appropriate. My guess would also be that Shakespeare as director would have begged his actors simply to play it straight, as Hamlet also asked his visiting players to do. The play can then speak for itself, each stylistic switch requiring no exaggerated alterations in diction and style. Yet there must be a continual temptation for actors and directors to exaggerate slightly. That is how parody works, imitating but exaggerating slightly with an intention to amuse. That is what much of the play with its wide variety of styles undoubtedly sets out to do. Is Troilus to use artificial language like: "What makes this pretty abruption? What too curious dreg espies my sweet lady in the fountain of our love?" entirely with a straight face? The language is parody, and most actors and directors will want to add a little something of their own to that. The director's choice is whether to aid and abet Shakespeare's intentions or leave this master dramatist confidently to his own devices.

Parody turns to satire when those who are imitated and exaggerated slightly in order to amuse, are themselves authority figures, and there are plenty of authority figures in *Troilus and Cressida*. Two thirds of the play in effect dishes the dirt on the leaders of both armies. The structure of the play turns on the two set-piece debates, one among the Greek leaders and one among the Trojan leaders. These two debates make sense of the suggested audience as lawyers at the Inns of Court. They would appreciate, not just the use and even citation of Aristotle, but the almost courtroom style as the argument ebbs and flows.

In the debate among the Greeks, Shakespeare first makes explicit a main theme of the play, even though it seems to have been not explicit enough for many critics and commentators. Agamemnon first attempts to raise the morale of what is beginning to look increasingly like the losing side. (Although with hindsight of history the audience knows the Greeks actually won). Nestor in effect agrees with Agamemnon. Ulysses then, after fulsome praise of a leader who clearly has little to praise about him, offers to comment

103

on the causes of the Greek failure of morale. He then praises hierarchy, degree and order, and considers the Greeks are in danger of losing this sense of themselves. Nestor agrees and Agamemnon asks: "What is the remedy?" At this point Ulysses mentions Achilles. We would expect him to say that while Achilles and his myrmidons sulk in their tents and take no part in the fighting, the Greek forces are dangerously weakened and the invasion loses its impact. Ulysses says nothing of the kind. Instead he describes in speech and no doubt, mime, how Patroclus and Achilles captivate the crowd by making fun of, and satirising, Agamemnon and Nestor:

> ULYSSES: and in this fashion
>   All our abilities, gifts, natures, shapes,
>   Several and generals of grace exact,
>   Achievements, plots, orders, preventions,
>   Excitements to the field, or speech for truce,
>   Success or loss, what is or is not, serves
>   As stuff for these two to make paradoxes.

> NESTOR: And in the imitation of these twain,
>   Who, as Ulysses says, opinion crowns
>   With an imperial voice, many are infected.

Harold MacMillian might have said just the same sort of thing about the satirical television programme *That Was the Week that Was*, which so effectively satirised and lampooned him and his government in the 1960s that he was almost turned into a public buffoon. As Nestor says "In the imitation of these twain…many are infected."

So what is Ulysses really saying? He is commenting on the power of the debunker, of ridicule, of parody and satire to bring down a government – or in this case destroy the morale of the Greek army. And he is talking about "performance". It is Patroclus in performance, imitating and making fun of Agamemnon and Nestor, that can so powerfully destroy their authority. The play *Triolus and Cressida* is itself doing much the same thing to Homer. Shakespeare too is making paradoxes. There can be no doubt that he is doing so consciously and with a wrinkle of a smile. He is commenting on the power of the media. They can make or break reputations, just as he himself broke Richard III and puffed up Henry V. He is quite explicit about it. Yet his message was neither understood nor heeded for 400 years, and only in a modern age when the power of the media is everywhere apparent, can we both appreciate the message and wonder at his prescience. Ulysses is a spin-doctor like Mandelson and his remedies for problems are equally short term and *ad hoc*.

The Trojan debate is much more of a set-piece. The Greeks felt they had right and natural justice on their side, and so had no doubt over their motives. The Trojans on the other hand ask themselves how they can justify holding onto Helen. It should be perhaps be noted that in Shakespeare's time this seems to have been a common subject for a set debate, exactly the kind of "moot" the lawyers themselves may have taken part in, so that Shakespeare, leaning heavily on Aristotle, was very much on his mettle in getting the Trojan leaders to rehearse the various arguments. Troilus argues passionately and well, but not altogether rationally in favour of keeping Helen. Hector, light years away from the detestable hubris of Achilles, argues convincingly that natural justice, very much an Aristotelian concept, requires the return of Helen to the Greeks. He convinces any theatre audience, so that his sudden *volte-face* is all the more surprising. He moves from absolute to relative values. Aristotle placed honour well below the demands of absolute good and natural justice, but Hector opts for it all the same. A hero must defend his own concept of his own honour, and so he opts to keep Helen, much as Fortinbras fights over territory that is of no value to anybody. Honour requires it.

In a sense, Hector is the opposite of a Ulysses who will use whatever general argument happens to be at hand to achieve an immediate, desirable end. Hector has in this sense, been taken in by his own propaganda. On the battlefield he expects Achilles to abide by the code of honour they both subscribe to. Achilles, like Ulysses, is more interested in results. Hector is unarmed and defenceless. This is a good opportunity to kill him. Hector assumes a code of honour will protect him. ("Gentlemen of the British Guard please accept the honour of being able to fire first!" Were we supposed to say: "No, no, gentlemen of the French Guard, after you we insist." Or did we just grab the opportunity with every flintlock we had?)

Shakespeare provides two additional characters who themselves stand outside the action and comment on it much as a Greek chorus did. They also from time to time become embroiled in the action and interact with other characters in the play. But Pandarus and Thersites are definitely not the cool, calm, authoritative voice-over, even if they do strenuously try to tell us what to think about the events as they unfold. Pandarus is of the earth, earthy, and somehow reduces everything he is involved in to the basic level of human lust. He seems less of a commentator and more an essential role in the play as the pander, the go-between relishing the lustful aspects of bringing the two young lovers together. Only occasionally as in his last astonishingly bitter admonition to the audience does he seem to stand outside the action itself.

It is Thersites who is more than ready to provide a running commentary on what is happening. His comments have all the elements of a modern tabloid. He over simplifies, he sensationalises, he gives the scandal rumour and strikingly sexual shock with which the tabloids try to spice the events of the day. Shakespeare could not have foretold the development of Fleet Street, with its striking division into a quality press and tabloids deliberately trying to "dumb down" the news they provide. *The Sun* readership was outside his ken. Or was it? If we see Thersites as some awesome MacKenzie of *The Sun*, interpreting the subtle and complex personalities and events of the day in simple sensationalism, sexually shocking scandal and arresting headlines, "Gotcha" or "Up yours, Delors" we come closer to understanding what is going on in *Troilus and Cressida*.

Shakespeare knew that a significant element in his Globe audience responded more to melodrama than to drama, and could only be reached by "dumbing down". It is the wonder of his popular plays that they succeed at so many levels – there is something in them for everybody, enough to keep all levels of his audience happy. In *Troilus and Cressida* we are not expected to agree, to nod our heads wisely as we listen to Thersites. He is too reductionist for that. We are slightly shocked, slightly tantalised as we are with *The Sun* banner headline, and of course we accept this is one way of interpreting events, one way of seeing how the world wags, but it not the only way – there is more to it then that. *The Sun*, and Thersites oversimplify, sometimes with a shatteringly effective: "All the argument is a whore and a cuckold" but these headlines do not give the whole story. It is the play itself which does that.

We warm to Hector most of all the characters in the play, but he is still essentially a type, the Sir Philip Sidney of his day. It is the ideas he represents that still tantalise. And this is perhaps the best key to both these debates at the heart of the structure of the play. Shakespeare might well be reminding us not only that his characters are besieged by conflicting ideas but so is his play itself. Shakespeare passes judgement on the media long before the word was given its modern meaning. *Troilus and Cressida* is about the gap between what people say and what people do; and about how they say it too, and about the gap between what they profess and how self-seeking impels them actually to behave. Yet it is about much more than that. It is about the myth makers, the storytellers, the imaginative creators, the media professionals' spin systems that deceive us, about how easy it is to sway the mob, as Marc Antony did in his praise of Caesar. It is also about the conventions and styles that drama uses to create its illusions.

Max Beerbohn created a character, Savonarola Brown, who wrote a play that is in itself a gorgeous send-up of the Elizabethan style. Had Beerbohn read or seen *Troilus and Cressida*? He stopped being a drama critic in 1910 so he just missed Poel's first production in 1912. Otherwise he would have realised that Shakespeare had already been there and done that long before Savonarola Brown.

4

Molière

Jean Baptiste Poquelin de Molière (1622-1680) was stage-struck most of his life. He was born into a comfortable middle-class merchant's family. In 1631 his father bought the office of upholsterer-in-ordinary to the King, giving him an entrée to the court, and a hereditary post for his eldest son. Molière was well educated, first at the Collège de Clermont, a Jesuit school for the sons of the nobility, gentry and prosperous merchants, then taking a degree in law at Orléans University. At the age of twenty-one he abandoned the upholstery business and his richly upholstered prospects, to start a theatre company in Paris, taking the stage-name of Molière. He and his company were a disaster. He stuttered, but fancied himself as a tragedian, a fancy not shared by his audience. Within two years he was in prison for debt, his company having gone bankrupt. His father paid his debts, but far from being repentant, Molière embarked with the members of the Béjart family with whom he had originally started his Illustre Théâtre, on a thirteen-year tour of the provinces, directing his own company for most of the time. It was in these thirteen years, about which we know little, that he learned his trade as an actor, a playwright, a director, a theatre manager, a publicist and a manipulator of men.

In 1658 he gave a command performance before the young King Louis XIV, opening with a tragedy which was not well received, but achieving instant success with a farce written by himself in which he took the leading role. From then on he was installed in Paris at the King's command, originally sharing the Salle du Petit Bourbon with an Italian *commedia dell'arte* company, directed by the famous Tiberio Fiorillo (Scaramouche). Hostile critics long maintained that many of Molière's best ideas were cribbed from the Italian *commedia.*

Long before the concept of the Romantic artist, Molière single-mindedly devoted himself to the theatre. He sacrificed family, position, and comfort to belong to it. He lived for it and through it. His amorous affairs seem to have been almost exclusively with fellow thespians, and in the end the theatre killed him. He wrote a leading part for himself in *Le Malade Imaginaire* to accommodate his terrible cough, but at the fourth performance was overcome on stage with a convulsive fit of coughing and died a few hours afterwards.

Molière was undoubtedly one of the great comic actors of his generation – even if he never succeeded, as he longed to do, in a leading tragic role. Yet his real achievements were elsewhere. He transformed the writing of comedy, in the process changing the expectations of his audience. Like most great artists, he was not satisfied with repeating himself. He wanted to innovate and experiment. As a result, he was well ahead of the accepted opinions of his day, almost perpetually involved in controversy, squabbles and sometimes a critical hostility that verged on open warfare. Some of his plays were banned and he aroused the anger and hatred of the medical profession, the clergy and a range of other social groups whom he pilloried and satirised. By the end of his career he had achieved for comedy what another seventeenth-century writer, Racine, achieved for tragedy.

Yet to say this is to use the superior voice of literary hindsight. We can look back and see the seventeenth century as a whole. When Molière achieved his first triumph in Paris in 1658, attitudes and assumptions were quite otherwise. It was no accident that Molière opened his crucial performance before the King with a tragedy. Tragedy was supreme. He ended and triumphed with a comedy, a comedy close to farce and the clowning of the *commedia*, and the young King could not stop laughing so of course the rest of the court hooted and applauded too. But none of them would have dreamed of giving that kind of comedy the same status and importance as tragedy. By 1680, when Molière died, his full-length plays, a new kind of comedy, were holding the stage in their own right and were beginning to command a new kind of status. That was Molière's real achievement.

It is sadly necessary at this point to say something about literary criticism in the seventeenth century. By modern standards it hardly existed at all. There were plenty of people writing animatedly and well about plays, novels and poetry in the seventeenth century. Yet by our standards they were too blinkered to be thought of as critics. Blinkered because they accepted basic assumptions, and grounded their views firmly upon them, which we can no longer accept.

Firstly, they believed that the purpose of art was to do good, to leave ordinary humans morally better after experiencing it than they were before. Art's job was seen therefore as somehow managing to sweeten the moral pill. And Aristotle had laid down a set of guidelines by which this could be achieved, and to ignore them was to court disaster and failure. Critics therefore asked first what moral improvement resulted from experiencing a particular work, and to what extent it had achieved its ends by following the guidelines laid down in classical antiquity. Since we no longer ask these questions, the answers seventeenth-century critics so copiously produced seem to us curiously dated and irrelevant. But they mattered a great deal at the time. They hampered and made almost impossible any worthwhile discussion of what artists were trying to do. Indeed by modern standards the seventeenth century is remarkable for the range and splendour of a whole series of artistic creations which it never seemed capable of understanding or appreciating at the time. The tastes of the audience acted as a heavy break on creativity too. Listen to the great Pierre Corneille on how Sophocles could not possibly be a model for a seventeenth-century *Oedipus*:

> I realised that what a previous era had thought miraculous, would be too upsetting for our own. That unlikely and well-spoken part where he pushes the bronze pins into his own eyes and blinds himself, taking up most of Act V, would not suit the tender feelings of the ladies in my audience, and their hostility would spread to others. And as a final remark, there being no love affair, the play is missing what the audience most want. So I have avoided what is offensive, and brought in an affair of the heart between Theseus and Dirce.

One can almost hear a Hollywood producer saying "This business of putting out his own eyes, I mean that's too gruesome for this kind of classy film, and where's the love interest? You've gotta have love interest. What about this Theseus guy? Couldn't he and Dirce maybe…?"

So one of the great tragedies of Ancient Greek theatre had to be sentimentalised almost out of existence to please the ladies. Yet Corneille's *Oedipe* was one of the theatre successes of 1659. Another was *Les Précieuses Ridicules* by Molière. Corneille played with high-sounding rhetoric on themes well within his audience's expectations. Molière was doing something different. He was bringing real-life characters, speaking a straightforward, down-to-earth language into the theatre, and making fun of the kind of grand-sounding diction and elaborately worded sentences his audience was so vigorously applauding in their tragedies.

He was doing more than this. Surrounded by busy theatrical activity and all too readily voiced opinions on all sides, he was feeling his way towards a new kind of writing. He needed, of course to take his audience with him. He and his company had royal favour, but they also needed a paying public. Their standard of living depended on their share of the box office takings, and these in Paris could be as precarious as in the provinces.

Royal favour was equally important. Louis XIV was an enlightened despot, an administrative genius who ruled France probably better than it has ever been governed before or since. Like most rulers since the Renaissance, he consciously used the arts to assert his own importance and grandeur. Molière needed the King, not only for royal commissions for court performances, but as a protection against the growing number of social groups Molière's plays infuriated and antagonised. Wisely Molière never made fun of the monarchy. On occasions the King broke all court protocols and had a simple lunch alone with Molière. He enjoyed his company. What would we not give to listen in to such an occasion. The young King, doffing his immense powers, to enjoy the company of his brilliant playwright and actor– *Le Roi s'amuse.* At several crises in his career the staunch support of the King made all the difference to a beleaguered Molière. Despotism is seldom enlightened, but that was what made Louis XIV special. Under the Sun King the arts were warmed and flourished.

It is not only absolute monarchy that separates us off from the 1650s. The mind-set of that French society can now seem bewilderingly alien. What were they doing, all those aristocrats and gentry in their elaborate costumes? The simple answer is – nothing. The whole of French society were labouring long hours to keep them in rich idleness. And this was the last moment in history when nobody questioned the fairness of the system. Because God had ordained the system, and to question the system was to question God, something which, as that awful affair at Loudun was to show, could still provoke punishments medieval in their horrifying severity.

The gap between the aristocrats and the rest had never been greater. They were not only waited on hand and foot, wore different clothes, ate better, lived in fine buildings, kept warm, had time for cultural pursuits – the arts, very much a minority affair. They had dancing masters, who taught them not only to dance, but how to carry themselves in almost every social situation; how to bow, how to enter through a door, how to sit at table, how to sit in a chair and so on. Life was elaborately choreographed. They even walked differently. For riding, and only the rich had horses for their leisure pursuits, they wore long thigh-boots in soft leather. When alighting they rolled the tops of their boots down to their knees. This made walking difficult. They had to turn out their feet, so that the toes of each pointed away from the other foot, and they waddled rather like a duck. In time this became formalised, so that even when not wearing the boots, gentlemen walked as if they were still wearing them to show they were gentlemen and could afford horses, boots and the rest. As a result, aristocrats waddled around pointing the feet outwards. Nobody else did. (This, incidentally, became the basis for what is called 'the turn-out' of the feet in classical ballet which was being codified as an art form by the Royal Academy of Dance set up by Louis XIV.)

All this meant that style, *esprit*, became as important to a gentleman as any of his other attributes. He rode, he hawked, he hunted, he learned to fight with a sword, but he also learned to display himself elegantly, to reveal a well-filled mind, to discuss intelligently, to say witty things. It was as important to look good in a lady's salon as on a horse, or attempting to skewer your opponent with a sword. For the first time, mere words could destroy almost as effectively as duelling pistols. Hence the existence of men of breeding and culture in Molière's plays, who say things well, who intend to be witty and are enjoyed as such. That was very much part of his aristocratic court world.

But there was another world. A world he also knew well. The world of his own father. Merchants who worked hard to get on, who spoke a forceful, colloquial language, who had little time for so-called culture and floundered a bit when discussing anything but business. A contemporary called Molière "a constant threat. He takes his eyes and ears everywhere with him!" And what he saw and heard around him Molière introduced into his plays.

Then there was the *commedia dell'arte*. Drama historians like to banish these lively performers to a footnote or a final paragraph. There are so few surviving texts or indeed written references to them, and drama historians are only really happy arguing about texts. People started writing about *commedia dell'arte* in the seventeenth century, but it has a long history which hardly figures at all in textbooks about drama. Alongside the Ancient Greek drama festivals, with plenty of texts left for scholars to fasten on, there was another kind of theatre altogether. A mime theatre – a drama which almost dispensed with words. As Athens and then, in turn, the Roman Empire became steadily more cosmopolitan, its audiences an ever wider ethnic mix with a bewildering array of different languages, mime theatre could speak to them all. This mime theatre began in market places, flourished as entertainment at dinner parties, but by the grand days of the Roman Empire was recognised as a powerful art form. In the reign of Augustus mobs clashed in the streets, fighting over the respective merits of the two great mime artists of the day, Bathyllus and Pylades, much as mobs clash in Glasgow over football teams. The plays of Terence and Plautus (Molière is said to have known all the plays of Terence in Latin by heart) owed much to the comic situations of this mime drama.

When the Roman Empire collapsed and Europe was plunged into the anarchy of the Dark Ages, mime drama did not perish. Far from it. In view of the diversity of languages from district to district, it was the only form of theatre that could survive for small, struggling theatrical troupes. We have enough references to know that it was alive and kicking. Attila the Hun, that scourge of Europe, was, so we read, entertained after dinner with a mime play. When the Dark Ages receded and Europe became steadily more stable and prosperous in the Middle Ages, the Church was very concerned about mime drama. Indeed, most of our knowledge that it existed at all comes from the records of the Church's frequent attempts to suppress it. Where there were markets, fairs, pageants, feast days, celebrations of any public kind, there would be a small temporary set-up, charging its audience and offering the clowning and buffoonery of a mime drama. With dialects so dissimilar from place to place, only mime could tour, and small companies had to tour to make a living. Gradually the Church established its own drama festivals in the Middle Ages (from which the *Oberammergau Passion Play* and the *York Mystery* plays, for example, have happily survived), but there was always an alternative drama "base, common and popular" that everybody knew and felt a bit guilty about enjoying because the Church disapproved.

This mime drama kept sufficient characteristics of the Roman mime to make it clear that the continuity was unbroken. They wore masks, they used the same stock characters and their farmyard humour, to use a word that seventeenth-century *précieuses* added to the language, verged on the obscene. Just as Latin remained the common language of the educated right across Europe in the Middle Ages and the early Renaissance, so this mime theatre, going everywhere and seen by so many, established another common language throughout Europe, a language of gesture. We have lost this language, just as surely as we have lost Latin, and we only know about it because specialist art historians have to study it to understand what gestures in paintings from these periods mean. But there was a time when everybody not only recognised it, but doubtless used it. Actors on Shakespeare's stage would step effortlessly into mime routines as they spoke, because the audience understood the mime rather better than the words. Indeed the plays began with an outline of the plot in mime.

The *commedia dell'arte* in Paris in the seventeenth century came close to being a final sophisticated flourish of this long European mime tradition. It was to survive in French boulevard theatre well into the nineteenth century. Italian players could keep French audiences happy without much of a language barrier. The words were not what mattered. Molière appears to have adored the *commedia* from his early youth. It must indeed have seemed a marvellous dramatic outlet for someone with a stutter. He took lessons from Tiberio Fiorillo, the famous Scaramouche, in his early days as a would-be actor. When at the King's command Molière's company shared the Salle du Petit Bourbon with the Italian *commedia*, they were led by Molière's former teacher. He had taught Molière well, so well that Molière brought with him into his new approach for French comedy detailed, specialised and at the same time a wide-ranging knowledge of most of the tricks of the mime trade. He was part of a tradition that led back in unbroken continuity to at least five centuries before the birth of Christ. During that time theatre had learned a thing or two as clown, buffoon and artist succeeded each other. Molière learned what they had learned. He never forgot it and put it to good use.

It is a contribution largely ignored by his friends and only made much of by his enemies. Yet it is essential to a full understanding of his plays. Who pays attention to the fact that his early plays were performed in masks, for example? Or that the sometimes summary seeming endings of his plots as in *L'Ecole des Femmes* (*The School for Wives*) would have been masked by a final dance? Dance was an integral part of *commedia dell'arte*. It played a much greater part in Molière's plays than modern productions allow.

For drama historians, 1662 is important because it was the year Molière's *The School for Wives* was first produced; the first play in which Molière is thought to have found his authentic voice as a playwright; his first play to be assailed by great waves of controversy, misunderstanding and hostility. Yet at the time the court was much more star-struck about a ballet that year – *Les Amours d'Hercule* by Bensarade and Lully, in which both the King and Queen took leading roles. Louis XIV prided himself on his dance ability. Such was the divinity that hedged about a king, we shall never know just how good or bad he really was. But drama historians tend to dismiss the considerable part dance and ballet played in so many Molière productions as being there simply to please the rather strange preoccupations of the young King. This is nonsense. Dance, social dance, was central to the business of being an aristocrat, one of the ways in which men demonstrated their virility, strange as this may seem to a twentieth century which views a male ballet dancer with some suspicion. Theatre dance, or ballet as it was becoming known, was in Molière's time an extension of a language of movement that was an integral part of people's expectations about the theatre. Molière took for granted and used dance as a matter of course, just as he used the movement routines of the clown and the buffoon. It was part of his theatrical language.

There were little more than four years between that farce, *Le Docteur Amoureux*, which so captivated the King on Molière's first appearance before him, and the full *The School for Wives*. Corneille and many others had written comedies. There was nothing new about comedies. But *Le Docteur* was not a genteel comedy, it was low-brow, it was buffoonery, it was farce. *Les Précieuses Ridicules* which followed it in 1659 was more adventurous. It made fun of so-called women of culture, suggesting they were blocking off real life and escaping into a pretty pretty fantasy world, and did so by exposing them to some quite brutal, low-life forms of farce. This was dealing with ideas, and very contemporary ideas, through the kind of knockabout farce with which Aristophanes had made fun of Socrates. It is not surprising that Molière was George Bernard Shaw's favourite playwright. Both were fascinated by ideas, both had an innate response to the subtleties of language, and both had a wild, almost anarchic sense of fun. *Sganarelle, ou le Cocu Imaginaire* in 1660 was an even more significant success. It was a one-act comedy, but was poetic drama. To say that it was in verse merely implies that it followed stock poetic forms. It did more. Its language, in places as demanding and densely packed as in any tragedy by Racine, was the best part of it, even though its subject matter, close to the stock situations of *commedia* was exhilarating fun.

The new language was trotted out again in 1661 for the five-act *Don Garcie de Navarre,* but the poetry, the straightforward language, the over-complicated plot were too ambitious and the piece was an artistic failure. The next two three-act plays, *L'Ecole des Maris* and *Les Fâcheux* were uncomplicated, closer to the *commedia* and avoiding the flightier excesses of poetic diction. They were both successes. In 1662 with *The School for Wives*, Molière found his true dramatic voice; a combination of vivid ideas, straightforward but poetic language, using the tricks and routines of broader farce to underpin a believable drama about recognisable people. It was an enormous success, and like all such successes aroused a swarm of denigrations, and conventionally-minded people unwilling to accept anything new. But new it was.

Molière took an idea from Scarron of a Spaniard who so educated a simple young girl that she would lack any of the attractions that might appeal to other lovers, and so he would have her to himself. Molière combined this with a *commedia* situation where a young gallant confided his growing success with a girl to an older man, quite unaware that it was this same older man he was making into a cuckold. It was an effective combination, but even so, it was merely a scaffold on which Molière built a believable portrait of a narrow-minded merchant for whom the scandal of being known to be a cuckold was much worse than any unhappiness he might cause his future wife. This was to be the first of the major character creations which Molière's plays laid before a startled and delighted public, played it goes without saying, by himself. Startled because in a theatre they found themselves confronted with people they could not only believe in but people whose ridiculous traits they recognised only too well. Jourdain the spendthrift, Harpagon's greed, the various snobberies of Alceste, Dandin and Philaminte, Argon's hypochondria, Orgon's exaggerated piety, obviously evoked an immediate response from the Parisian audience.

In a sense each of these outrageous roles share the same characteristic. They are all variations on a theme. They are all afraid. Afraid of not being in control. They want to be in control of their own households, and in the theatre that is a dramatic way of making the point that they desperately need to be in control of themselves. And as the play unfolds, the comedy, and their tragedy, is that they lose control. Their very fears help to bring about exactly what they are most afraid of. Even as the audience laughs, it experiences that shock of recognition which is theatre's special gift, as the audience recognises its own dilemmas, its own destiny, in the plight of characters on stage it has come imaginatively to accept as real people. In *The School for Wives*, Arnolphe is obsessed with the public disgrace of being made a cuckold. All his elaborate precautions against this fate fail. What he is most afraid of actually comes about largely as a result of everything he has planned to keep disaster at bay.

Fortunately the practitioners, the poets and playwrights of the seventeenth century had a better idea of what they were doing than their literary critics. We know what Molière thought about comedy, partly from his *L'Impromptu de Versailles,* a one-act play which shows actors in rehearsal and characters arguing about what they are doing and why. In this Molière played a Marquis who hated Molière, while another actor, Brecourt, puts Molière's own defence. Not only was Molière shown arguing against himself, but at the rehearsal he demonstrated to Brecourt how to act Brecourt's own part. Molière was thus playing the role of Brecourt playing the part of an aristocrat who is putting Molière's case. This is extraordinarily sophisticated drama in its own right, quite apart from the ideas about comedy which fill their conversation. Yet in performance this one-act play is perfectly clear, even simple and straightforward as far as its audience is concerned. Nothing could better demonstrate Molière's skill and this little play doubtless inspired the Duke of Buckingham's *The Rehearsal*, which in turn produced Sheridan's *The Critic*, to say nothing of Anouilh.

We also know about Molière's views on comedy from another play, *La Critique de l'Ecole des Femmes*, in effect rebutting the main hostile arguments the controversy over *The School for Wives* had aroused. Even more importantly the second part of the *Lettre sur l'Imposteur* seems undoubtedly to have been inspired, or even dictated by Molière himself.

Comedy for Molière lay in anything that was contrary to rationality or commonsense. This is a very wide definition. As W G Moore has pointed out, nobody laughs at Hitler talking of peace when he was preparing for war. Millions of people were to die as a result. Yet the idea of talking about peace while planning for war is contrary to reason. It is comic. It is also very much Molière's kind of comedy, shot through with hints of tragedy so that even if we laugh, we laugh in despair at the human condition.

Molière offers us no remedies. There is no known remedy for being human. In Molière's plays those who claim to bring remedies, like the medical profession, are all confidence tricksters. They are part of the problem, not its solution. A strong element in humour is the selecting of a scapegoat to laugh at. We reassure ourselves as we laugh, that we belong to the solid majority, and as social animals we need to belong, even as we laugh at Molière's unfortunate outcasts and scapegoats. Deep down in our insecurities we know as we watch these outrageous characters struggling in vain, that there, but for a kind destiny, we too might be equally defenceless against a fate we cannot control. Our laughter is a glorious release from fear.

Why did *The School for Wives* arouse such fierce controversy when it first appeared? Like so many innovations in art, it was misunderstood. In particular it seems to have aroused the ire of the *précieuses.* Preciosity was a movement, admittedly limited to a small leisure class, but a movement nevertheless towards feminism, a set of principles argued by women of culture and intelligence in the face of oppressive social features of their lives: inferior education, married off for convenience almost as business transaction, and the insistence in marriage of a wife's complete submission to her husband. What had started as a development of polite society around fashionable salons, bringing together men and women of social standing with artists and men of letters, cultivating the art of conversation and social graces generally, developed into something else. It became not just the civilising influence of women in society, but a cult, perhaps the first, of feminism *per se*, an intellectual society ruled by women spending much of the time discussing affairs of the heart, and developing a new jargon, a special kind of language to elaborate these discussions. As a reaction against the inferior position of a wife in marriage, the *précieuses* set up an ideal of love, not so dissimilar from the ideal of courtly love in the Middle Ages, insisting that the male lover deferred in all things to his mistress, proving his submission by long years of unrewarded worship, while some *précieuses* insisted on a wholly platonic form of love.

It is clear from *La Critique* that the *précieuses* were very much upset by *The School for Wives*. Arnolphe's strictures against women and his view of an obedient wife were certainly the very things they were fighting against. Clearly Arnolphe's views reflected those of narrow-minded traditionalists in the audience. But is Molière endorsing these views? He is surely making fun of them. He is doing more. He is positively suggesting that a marriage based on Arnolphe's principles must almost inevitably drive an oppressed wife to look elsewhere for the sympathy, appreciation and respect she needs. He was, in effect, making common cause with the *précieuses.*

Perhaps seeing Molière playing Arnolphe so brilliantly and effectively on stage made it difficult to separate Molière the author from the views expressed on stage so trenchantly by Molière the actor. We should remember too that *The School for Wives* when it first appeared was very much a new kind of drama, bewilderingly different and not easy to absorb in its novelty.

Most of the battles fought by the *précieuses* have long since been won. Their views have largely prevailed. It says much for Molière that in a much-changed twentieth century, where political correctness prevails in all the media, his *The School for Wives* can still be presented with impunity. We can now see that Molière's heart was in the right place. He is still showing us people as they undoubtedly are and allowing us to laugh at our discomfiture when confronted with such manifest faults.

The Misanthrope is set in an aristocratic world and shows us these aristocrats in action. Words could be used as weapons, almost as effectively as sabres. This is the world of *The Misanthrope*. Talking well, writing an ode, winning admiration, mattered immensely in the idle social whirl of court life.

Social dance incorporated into court performances became the basis for the new kind of theatrical dance that was turning into classical ballet. Opera was developing in popularity at the same time. It was the aristocratic courts of Renaissance Italy and France, attempting to revive Ancient classical drama, who almost by accident invented these two art forms. They knew classical drama had singing and dancing, but of course they had no idea what kind of music, nor what kind of dance. So they invented what was necessary in attempting to bring back an ancient art form. Both singing and dancing soon specialised and gradually the specialist performer ousted the aristocratic amateur. In Molière's time this process was only just beginning. Molière incorporated song and dance into his drama because they were seen as part and parcel of any dramatic repertoire. Singing, dancing and acting were what actors did, just as they were something aristocrats did. We are the poorer in the twenty-first century because theatre in our time has become even more specialised.

Although the mists of time have obscured so many seventeenth-century attitudes, *The Misanthrope* has gradually emerged for later generations as one of Molière's finest plays. It edges closer and more obviously into the dramatic territory of tragedy, reminding us that in the theatre we laugh or cry at much the same subject matter, the human condition, the fate we laughably or tearfully delude ourselves we can control.

It was first presented in 1666, four years after the first major play in which Molière found his true dramatic voice, *The School for Wives.*

Molière wrote *The Misanthrope* at what must have seemed a moment of real crisis in his professional career. Perhaps this statement would have more force if Molière's professional career had not in effect staggered successfully from crisis to crisis, resembling the highs and lows of a fevered patient's temperature chart. *The School for Wives* had by its very novelty aroused opposition particularly from the *précieuses.* It was accused of vulgarity, immorality and generally failing to meet the literary standards of the day. Even its resounding success at the box office was sneered at. Molière's next play *Tartuffe,* in a trenchant version we no longer have, was forbidden public production. The Church managed to get it banned outright. Worse still, *Don Juan* which Molière wrote as a replacement for this terrible gap in his theatre company's repertory was also banned after fifteen performances and never again appeared in Molière's lifetime. It was not a good year. As well as having his last two plays censored out of existence, his health began to give him serious trouble with the first signs of the tuberculosis that was to kill him, and his emotional private life began to go seriously wrong. Only a true man of the theatre and an artist whose integrity we can only marvel at, could then produce a third play that was both vastly different from the previous two and yet in its own way just as radically new.

The Misanthrope went some way towards standing criticisms and critics, on their pompous heads. Ostensibly it obeyed the rules of the day, the dramatic unities of place, theme and time. It concerned itself with aristocrats, the class for whom the rest of society laboured and was organised. It avoided any suggestion of improper or outrageous behaviour, ignoring the much loved stock characters, dramatic situations and farm-yard elements of *commedia dell'arte*. It was in acceptable alexandrines, and in five acts. It was everything the critics said a play should be. And yet in its way it was just as unsettling as *Tartuffe* or *Don Juan*. It was essentially about hypocrisy, about the way people seldom say what they mean, about the differences between what people maintain and what their motives really are. These were obvious truths which a long line of writers and preachers from Seneca down through the impassioned sermons of medieval friars had already castigated. What was new was creating believable characters in recognisable situations which embodied these very faults, and inviting the audience to laugh at them.

A criticism of Molière is that his characters do not develop. While they come vividly to life as recognisable individuals, they do not grow, change or mature before our eyes. In other words they do not learn from experience and alter as they do so. They are what they are and they stay like that all through the play. Macbeth is a very different man, as is Lear or Hamlet, at the end of the play from what they were at its beginning. Molière's characters are not like that. In that sense they are closer to Ben Jonson's classical *humours* than to Shakespeare's individuals. Yet it is hardly a helpful criticism. There is not much point in belabouring Molière for not writing the kind of play a particular critic prefers. Molière's plays are about ideas. His gift was to embody these ideas in gloriously funny and believable people and to create ludicrous situations which allowed these characters and the ideas they represent, to come into conflict with those around them. Alceste in *The Misanthrope* represents an idea we can all share. If only people would say what they really think, we would all know where we are with each other. But we deceive each other, sometimes with good intentions, more often for selfish motives, nursing our little vendettas and private agendas. Alceste carries this idea to the point of obsession, of absurdity. The comedy lies in the absurdity and in the vivid way the characters bring it to life.

Alceste is certainly believable, his stream of words rising at times to a positive torrent of denunciation. He is in himself almost an object lesson in the difficulty of remaining sincere in polite society, struggling hard, half the time at odds with the constraints good manners and etiquette imposed. He takes time because of this to reach the heights of rhetorical denunciation with those he dislikes, good manners initially holding him back, as with Oronte but he can be much more immediately forthright with his friend Philinte. We like him because he *is* sincere, however much he oversteps the mark. We believe in his love for Célimène, we recognise that he truly cares little for material possessions, that he does fight to avoid lies, deceit and hypocrisy. We believe that, unlike those around him, he has kept in touch with his feelings, and absurd and obsessed as he appears, we keep a soft spot for his passion for truth.

It is these very contrasts in his character that create the drama. He is against society's ills, but believes totally in his own judgement, never even imagining that he could be at fault, that he himself might be so doctrinaire as to be considered ill. His attitudes attract us but this total belief in his own rightness repels us. Can he be right and everybody else wrong all the time? This is as absurd as the wrongs he castigates, and the absurdity is the essence of the comedy.

The very truths which he enunciates so well, become almost untruths when carried to these absurd extremes, against human nature and the way society is. His obsession that society is not as it ought to be, ends up making him behave as he ought not to behave. That is not tragedy, it is comedy carried to an extreme of folly. It is funny, it is believable and it is ultimately ludicrous.

Célimène has a special place among all the women Molière created. She does not reflect one or two character traits to help the rest of the drama along, she comes alive as a many-faceted fascinating personality, a woman who is both lovable and admirable to set on a pedestal to worship, until Alceste finally discovers the feet of clay. As the adorable coquette, the amusing woman of the world becomes unmasked as essentially without love, having so little to give once all the masks she wears have been removed, we see with growing horror the real cause which turns Alceste into a misanthrope. We realise that neither Alceste nor Célimène ever really saw each other for what they actually were, but cherished fond, spurious illusions about each other. Each was in love with what they wanted the other to be. Neither saw the reality behind the mesmerising mask. Is this, Molière wanted us to ask, the reality of the human condition? Do we fool ourselves as we fool others? And this remember, is the seventeenth century, a time of certainty, stability and religious conviction. It is not surprising that *The Misanthrope* was almost too powerful for its day.

The very changes in social attitudes and beliefs, *Weltan-schauung*, the ideologies of the twentieth century, have altered some of the ways we interpret and respond to some of the lessons the play is signalling. Eighteenth and nineteenth-century Romanticism has changed many of our basic assumptions.

In the seventeenth century, unrequited love was almost automatically seen as something comic. We take the concept of romantic love much more seriously, and it does not seem so necessarily funny to us. Romanticism brought with it the idea of alienation, of the individual not wanting to belong to a corrupt and debased society which is quite foreign to the seventeenth century. A misanthrope for the seventeenth century is closer to a romantic hero for the twentieth century, ready to denounce and disassociate himself from a world where society is corrupt and the law is weak. We should not forget too that Rousseau in Steiner's memorable phrase "closed the doors of hell". If men are basically good, then when they do wrong, it is not really their fault, it is because of what their parents or a vicious society has done to them that is to blame. Redemption, saying sorry and being forgiven, the sentimental happy ending always lurks just around the corner. The Ancient Mariner has only to pray and the albatross falls from his neck. We can confidently expect the hero and heroine to walk hand in hand into a Technicolor sunset where they will be happy ever after. These sentimental preconceptions may leave us dissatisfied with the ending of *The Misanthrope*. The knot remains untied, the dénouement does not leave everybody happy, the situation is unresolved. Molière is perhaps more realistic about the actual reality of the human condition. We can laugh or cry, but there is no known remedy for being human. The mercy is that with Molière we laugh.

George Dandin, first presented at Versailles in 1668 and later in Paris, was an immediate success. Molière presented three new plays that year whilst still recovering from the first onset of what seems to have been tuberculosis. Of the other two, *Amphitryon* and *L'Avare*, only *L'Avare* failed immediately to please the public. It is easy to see why *George Dandin* succeeded. It seems essentially designed for a bourgeois Paris audience since it pokes delicious fun at the foibles of the aristocracy, although the court apparently enjoyed seeing themselves sent up too. Dandin is a prosperous bourgeois who has married into an aristocratic family and is constantly being snubbed by his father-in-law as he invariably goes wrong in the niceties of social etiquette. His wife intends to have an extra-marital affair and Dandin, desperate to expose her intentions, finds himself cleverly outwitted by her and made to look a fool. There is a crucial moment before she turns the tables when he appears at last to have her in his power and to be able to expose her to her confident and unbelieving father. She begs for understanding and none is forthcoming. It is a key point. He fails her as a man, fails her as a husband, intent only on proving himself in the right and the audience in consequence inclines to her side. The husband as cuckold is a familiar figure from *commedia dell'arte* and Molière imparts fresh dramatic energy by making him such a believable figure for a bourgeois audience.

Scapin was first performed in Paris at the Palais Royal, the home of Molière's company, in 1671. The plot, which to modern eyes seems fearfully contrived, had a long and illustrious history. It is based on the *Phormio* of Terence, along with other more recent *commedia dell'arte* versions. Scapin, the son of Brighella, was a familiar figure in the *commedia dell'arte* canon. Molière, able to recite the plays of Terence by heart in the original Latin, only took from his admired predecessor just what he wanted. The contrivance of the final dénouement, Argante's "Good Heavens! Not *that* bracelet! Why, this is my long-lost daughter, who disappeared when she was four years old!" does creak a bit. It reminds us of the moment when Sheridan satirises this sort of thing in *The Critic* (ironically inspired itself by Molière):

> I am thy father; here's thy mother;
> There thy uncle – those thy first cousins and those
> Are all your near relations!

As Puff declares "There, you see relationships, like murder will out."

Maurice Sand writes "Molière upon being reproached with the follies of *Scapin* replied 'I saw the public quit *Le Misanthrope* for Scaramouche: I entrusted *Scapin* with the task of bringing them back again.'"

Of course *Scapin* is an engaging piece of nonsense when compared with some of Molière's major creations, but the public flocked to see it and it has maintained a place in the Molière repertory perhaps because its virtues as an engaging piece of nonsense seem ever more apparent as the years go by. Fathers wishing to arrange a marriage while their offspring have other ideas, were a staple of mime comedy long before Plautus and Terence gave them words to speak on stage. The cunning, untrustworthy servant making rings round his master, has an equally long heritage reaching back well into the days of classical slavery. Molière makes a good deal of fresh fun out of this rather worn material and, such is the irony of history, his comedy routines have now outlived the *commedia dell'arte* and survived because Molière liked them and incorporated them in his own plays. The servant belabouring his master in a sack, as he pretends to be someone else, must have been the fantasy of many a hard-beaten slave. It still comes alive in Molière's practised hands, and in the original production of the play, Molière himself played Scapin, the clever servant showing off all his *commedia* expertise no doubt, as he did so. Molière has survived the *commedia dell'arte* because his comedies still show us people as they undoubtedly are, allowing us to laugh at our discomfiture when confronted with such manifest faults that we undoubtedly share.

Alongside ten one-act plays, a couple of Molière's plays have two acts, nine have three acts, and twelve have five acts. He was nothing if not versatile, and each play fitted its subject like a glove. There was no padding. W B Yeats spoke of "a theatre…joyful, fantastic, extravagant, whimsical, beautiful, resonant and altogether reckless." In his development of the comedy ballet, of which perhaps *Le Bourgeois Gentilhomme* and *Le Malade Imaginaire* (*The Hypochondriac*) represent his finest achievements, Molière did all that Yeats wanted. He was in fact creating a total theatre long before Wagner or Brecht attempted it. For him, song, music and dance were an integral part of a theatre performance, and it is perhaps no accident that his last play, *The Hypochondriac*, made splendid use of them all. By then he had lost favour at court to Lully, who had intrigued against him, and had not only obtained all the rights to any words for which he wrote the music, but also engineered in 1672 a Royal Ordinance reducing the numbers of musicians Molière could use in a production to six singers and twelve instrumentalists, later to be reduced again to two singers and six instrumentalists. It is not surprising that Molière did not ask Lully to compose the music for *The Hypochondriac*, nor was it presented at court at all until well after Molière's death. Charpentier wrote the music, and these song and dance routines must be seen as an integral part of the play that Molière created. The musical interludes both comment on and reinforce the action of the rest of the play, and in this sense Molière was designing a seventeenth-century equivalent for the Ancient Greek chorus which in its song and dance routines played much the same role. Perhaps it gave Molière a wry satisfaction to be able to use some of the mechanisms of Greek tragedy as he raised the status of comedy in his own time.

The Hypochondriac is rooted in actual experience. Molière was a sick man when he wrote it, and the play about the head of a household preoccupied to the point of obsession with his own health, allowed Molière to make dramatic use when playing the leading role, of his own real and painful cough. At the fourth performance he was taken ill on stage, and although able to finish the evening, he died a few hours later. The central character, Argan, shares some characteristics with other major character creations which Molière's plays laid before a startled and delighted public, played, it goes without saying, by himself.

In *The Hypochondriac* Argan is obsessed with his own state of health, and attempts to regulate his family affairs around his illness. The play is not so much about hypochondria, as about capitulation to the bizarre demands of the medical profession, the worship of doctors by insecure patients, the medical profession's delusions of grandeur and the social effects on Argan's family as his obsession begins to create havoc in their lives. It may seem, to a man obsessed with his own state of health, reasonable to marry off his daughter into the medical profession on which he so desperately relies. To his daughter it does not seem reasonable at all. His calculating second wife, with the dubious lawyer at her side, intends to use her husband's obsession to persuade him to change his will in her favour. She can only do so because his obsession blinds him to reality. Yet his control slips away from him as a result of that same obsession. The very thing he most fears, losing control, is in danger of being caused by his own obsession.

In the end, Molière did have a remedy for the human condition. George Saintsbury has called him "the master of the laugh". And that glorious, if temporary release from fear as we laugh has been his generous legacy to posterity as well as to his own time. He can still make us laugh. It remains a rare gift.

5

Racine – Britannicus

That particular form of theatre called tragedy has long been regarded as a high point of French culture in the seventeenth century; and Racine has equally been regarded as the pinnacle, the unassailable, incomparable peak of French tragedy. It is true, this is very much a French assessment. Racine, like some of the best French wine, does not travel well. It is not so much that he is difficult to translate, although most poetry loses an intangible something in translation. Racine is after all a favourite author in A-level French for British students. His language is simple, and he uses a relatively small vocabulary. American academics have established, with beaver-like industry and that insatiable American demand for numbers and facts, that Shakespeare uses a dramatic vocabulary of 21,000 words, the King James Bible uses 6,500 words while Racine manages brilliantly with what must seem in comparison a poverty stricken, mere 600 words. Not being American, I have not worked out how many words Robert David MacDonald, for example, uses to translate Racine into English, but my guess is that he uses more than Racine. He is faithful to his author, but English makes more words available, with all the subtleties, echoes and associations that they create. MacDonald also keeps Racine's Alexandrine hexameter, but can be cavalier about the French rule of the mid-line caesura; justly so, since this depends on the equal stress of French syllables, where English verse and ordinary speech has less certainty and a much more inexplicable variety.

Therefore, although MacDonald's sure judgement satifies even the harshest critic, there still tends to be a great gulf fixed between French culture and the rest of the world over Racine. The French quote him frequently, his plays still hold the French stage, he remains very much a part of their mental baggage. Elsewhere his influence remains slight. Compare and contrast, an examination question might say, the influence of Shakespeare on Russian or German literature with the influence of Racine. There is no contest. Compare and contrast the influence of Shakespeare on French literature with the influence of Racine on English literature. Again there is no contest. Yet for the French, Racine is one of the undoubted glories of their literary heritage. He is part of what makes the French special and different. The closer we get to Racine, the closer perhaps we shall get to what it actually feels like to be French.

That would sound better if Racine had been a nicer man, as well as a giant of French theatre. Sadly literature is studded with examples of great writers who were less admirable in their private live than in their works. Racine survives because of what he wrote, not as a result of what he did or did not do in private life. His play *Britannicus* is about life at court, the court of a despot with absolute power; and a nagging doubt intrudes. Did he have entirely to imagine what that kind of life would be like, or did he have some practical experience? In his play the despot is the young Nero – on his way to becoming one the most despicable tyrants of history. Racine lived in the age of Louis XIV, the most able and effective monarch France ever had, an administrative genius, but with all the ruthless *Realpolitik* of Machiavelli's Prince too. With due respect to Taine's "the race, the social context, the particular moment in time", *Britannicus* and its author need to be seen as the product of a key moment in history and perhaps Racine should be seen as an individual, a person in his own right before any approach to the play.

He was a bourgeois in the seventeenth century. That meant a great deal. This was an age when nobody in France (in England they were busily beheading Charles I) questioned the divine right of kings. God, after all, had ordained things the way they were. To question the system was to question God, and as the affair at Loudon was to show, hideous medieval punishments still awaited anyone blasphemous enough, foolish enough to question God. Just as the king ruled by virtue of birth and primogeniture, so did the nobility, the aristocrats who felt themselves equally as God-given as the king. Power and money in the seventeenth century were slowly but increasingly passing to a growing class, the bourgeoisie, the middle class, and as well as a *noblesse de sang*, a nobility by right of birth, there also grew up a *noblesse de robe*, a nobility dependant on office at court. Molière's father had just such an office – upholsterer to the king – and intended to pass it on to his son, but Molière was obsessed with the theatre and could not have cared less about an office at court. He threw all such chances away and devoted his life to forming and running a theatre company, acting leading roles and writing plays for himself and his company to perform.

From an early age Racine had no father nor mother. Born in 1639 he was orphaned while still an infant, and was brought up on the charity of others. His relatives were Jansenists, an extreme sect of the Catholic church, and he was educated at Port Royal, the abbey which was the spiritual centre of the sect, and given a wide-ranging and altogether excellent education, including a thorough knowledge of Ancient Greek that was unusual for the period. A further two years at the Jansenist college at Beauvais gave Racine a network of contacts within aristocratic circles. The Duc de Luynes had as his chief steward a cousin of Racine's, and the Duke encouraged Racine who was already showing his gifts as a poet. To read the list of aristocrats to whom he dedicated his ten successful plays is to realise how assiduously Racine took advantage of the network of contacts opening before him. The King frowned on Jansenism, so the Duc de Luynes did too and Jean Racine followed their lead. Already by 1660 he was working on a play of which we know nothing. In Paris he became a friend of the free-thinking hedonist La Fontaine (of the Fables) and of Molière, who put on Racine's first surviving play *The Thebaïd* (1664) which was a success. He wrote another play entitled *Alexander the Great* in 1665 which Molière also staged, and by then Racine was in more than Molière's theatre as a playwright, he was in the bed of one of Molière's leading ladies, Mlle du Parc, as her lover. He then showed a more calculating aspect of his nature. He owed Molière much. Molière had encouraged him, shared his expertise and a wide knowledge of the theatre, put on his first and second play, been tolerant of the affair with du Parc. But the rival theatre of the Bourgogne was anxious to score off Molière wherever possible, and was certainly considered better at tragedy than Molière's players. As soon as it was successful Racine took *Alexander the Great* away from Molière and gave it to the Bourgogne company. Worse still, Mlle du Parc went with it. Molière was mortified, never forgave Racine, and cordially loathed him from then onwards. Ill fortune awaited Mlle du Parc.

Firstly, how could Racine do it? Perhaps it is important to remember his network of aristocratic acquaintances. Actors and actresses were then considered the lowest of the low. The Church condemned all theatre, excommunicated all actors and would only bury them in sacred ground if they had repented of their sins on their deathbed and received absolution. Otherwise, even in a cemetery, the self-respecting souls of the corpses around them would be insulted and outraged by their very presence. In writing plays, Racine clearly had to be involved in the theatre, but equally clearly he never felt *of* the theatre. He despised the very creatures on whom he depended for his successes. No doubt he found the theatre an exciting place (how could he write so well for it otherwise?), and no doubt equally exciting were the beds he shared with some of its actresses. But he never dreamed of marrying one of them as Molière did. They were just actresses. The theatre was just the theatre. Men of quality visited both but only for brief pleasure, brief affairs. Real life was a much more serious matter.

Secondly, there was the infamous, almost unbelievable, scandal of La Voisin. The worst of this was kept secret from Racine's contemporaries, but even the little they knew outraged the whole of French society. La Voisin was a horrifying fraud. She was a midwife, the wife of a jeweller, who practised fortune-telling. She sold love potions. She dabbled in black magic and sorcery generally. For those clients who needed it, she sold poisons. For those who were desperate, she would, with an unfrocked priest Guibourg, hold a black mass which included the killing and sacrifice of a newborn child. Here her profession as a midwife gave her access to a suitable supply of the infants required. Worse still she was not alone, but one of a ring of similar fortune tellers and accomplices in the black arts. Learning about her is like lifting the lid off this pompous, self-important, outwardly religious and responsible aristocratic world, and seeing what actually went on in terms of greed, lust and the selfish self-obsession of the rich.

La Reynie, *lieutenant de police*, had been alerted to the prevalence of poisoning by the recent but earlier scandal of the Marquise de Brinvilliers, who had poisoned her father because he sent her lover to the Bastille. She was in the habit of making charitable visits to a hospital, and she made sure the poison worked by testing it first on patients there who duly died as did her father. She then poisoned her two brothers to get all of her father's estate. Evidence against her emerged on the death of her lover, and she was arrested, tried and executed in 1676. Two years later La Reynie started investigating La Voisin and soon discovered an alarmingly widespread ring of accomplices. A carefully chosen court was set up to speed the legal system and more and more came to light. Thirty-six were found guilty and executed, five sent to the galleys, twenty-three banished, but as the investigation proceeded increasing numbers of high-ranking aristocrats were seen to be involved and the whole legal apparatus faltered. The King's mistress from 1668-1680, Madame de Montespan, who had born the King no less than seven children, had been a client of La Voisin since 1666, had administered various potions to the King himself, and had taken part in no less than three black masses with the consequent sacrifice of three infants. When her attractions faded, hell having no fury like a woman scorned, she had planned to poison both the new mistress and the King, and was only prevented from doing so by the investigation. This was too much. The King destroyed the police report (although the notes for it have survived) and the court was closed with its findings kept secret, although very much alive in rumour and gossip. Amidst these frightening events in high places, one fact went almost unnoticed. La Voisin remembered that she had provided the poison that Racine used in 1668 to murder his mistress Mlle du Parc. A warrant for his arrest was drawn up, but the court was dissolved before it could be put into effect.

Remarkably little is known about Racine's private life from 1664 to 1667. His sons, to protect their father's reputation, destroyed anything that showed him in a less than satisfactory light. The fact they seem to have destroyed all his correspondence would imply there was a good deal to hide. There is a hint in a contemporary verse, that his current mistress left him for another before he wrote his last play for the professional theatre, *Phèdre,* whose heroine has long angst-ridden speeches luxuriating in the pangs of rejection. What is known is that after writing ten successful plays from 1664 to 1667, he stopped writing for the professional theatre. He became reconciled with the deeply religious Jansenist circle that had originally nurtured him. He married for money, a marriage where, in his son Louis' words "Love was absent." Abruptly, the style and circumstances of his life changed. Cynics might notice that the La Voisin affair had an equally traumatic effect on Louis XIV and the court. The King, shocked at the revelations both of what had and might have happened, became more pious, and his court became more outwardly respectable. He still had a mistress, Madame de Maintenon, but she was herself both pious and a positive pillar of respectability. With the support of Madame de Maintenon's sister (how adept Racine was at knowing the right people at the right time) Racine was appointed jointly with Boileau to the enviable post of Historiographer to the King, moving up from his bourgeois origins to a desirable position among the *noblesse de robe.* It became his duty to be in personal attendance on the King and record the history the King was of course busily making.

There has been much speculation as to why Racine suddenly stopped writing for the theatre in mid-career when he was surrounded by success, admired by the public, admired by the learned and the intelligentsia, and admired by the King. Much of the speculation seems to miss the main point. As a courtier in regular attendance on the King himself, he could hardly be seen to be associating with the riff-raff of the theatre. More importantly, he did not stop writing. The creative problems of recording instant history, surrounded by the exciting events occurring at the centre of the most powerful and influential nation in Europe, must have proved a challenge indeed. Sadly, what he wrote as historiographer has not survived, and it remains a particular irony that the work of possibly one of its best historians was obliterated by history itself.

After twelve years, he was summoned back to drama at the request of Madame de Maintenon, to write a play, *Esther* (1689) for the girl pupils of a boarding school. Although only performed in private for the court, this was such a *succès d'estime* that he wrote another for them, *Athaliah,* in 1691. Both plays rank among his best achievements, but the Jansenists and other bigots did not approve of drama, even in private performance by a respectable girls' school, and such was their outcry, he wrote no more plays. He died in 1699, able to look back on sixty years of steady advancement, including twelve plays already accepted in his lifetime as masterpieces, a court post that was the envy of many true aristocrats, a prosperous marriage blessed with children, many mistresses much admired in their day, successful early forays into the corrupt world of sensuality and eroticism, the odd murder that went unpunished and the undying resentment of one of the nicest true men of the theatre. After Racine's death the adulation of French posterity has continued to grow steadily.

Before looking in detail at his fifth successful play *Britannicus*, armed and forewarned by this knowledge of Racine the man, it becomes possible to consider what qualities made Racine's plays so pre-eminent. Like all artists, he belongs to Taine's "the race, the social context, the particular moment in time", but what keeps his work alive is his ability to transcend Taine's categories with a much more universal appeal. Great tragedy in drama is a rare phenomenon. Five centuries before the birth of Christ, the Athenian Greeks achieved it, and it is no accident that Racine, exceptionally among his contemporaries, had a thorough grounding in ancient Greek, including the tragedies of Aeschylus, Sophocles, and Euripides. For the Ancient Greeks, vividly aware of the glory, the excitement, the pleasure of life, tragedy lay in the all too evident fact that life, with all its joys, must inevitably give way to annihilation and death and that even as the proud man enjoyed all the gifts and potentialities of life, an inexorable fate he could not hope to control could grind him down to nothingness and dust.

With the very dubious exception of Seneca in Roman theatre, tragedy did not achieve very much in European theatre until the Elizabethans in England and Lope de Vega in Spain. Medieval drama, propaganda for Christianity, showed the bad being punished and the good being rewarded, with absolution and the forgiveness of sins always lurking, like some *deus ex machina,* to descend from the clouds and offer the prospect of a happier ending. The Renaissance, among other developments a rebirth of interest in the Ancient Greeks and Romans, set up new tensions in European drama, contrasting the classical world's emphasis on the possibilities of life here and now, with a still fervently accepted Christian belief that this life was a mere vale of tears, a preparation for the afterlife to come. It is this tension which makes Marlowe's *Faust* so effective as tragedy. His audience was dazzled by the possibilities of making the most of the here and now, bringing back Helen of Troy from the dead ("Was this the face that launched a thousand ships?") – and yet believed just as implicitly in the devils that emerged from the pit of hell to drag a screaming Faust down to everlasting fire. Great individuals brought low by misfortunes they cannot avoid and cannot control were still the stuff of tragedy, but there was an added turn of the screw in Renaissance tragedy: its heroes made a choice, a very medieval kind of choice, grabbing at what they want in the heat of the moment and what their conscience tells them is right, and then their very choices set in train the circumstances that bring them down.

Racine's audience was essentially no different from Shakespeare's or Lope de Vega's. They were deeply Christian. And yet they were aware, none of them more so than Racine himself, steeped as he was in Greek literature, aware of all the excitement, the sheer fun and the temptations of life in the here and now.

Racine's Jansenist background gave him an even bleaker view of life than most of his contemporaries. For Jansenists, man was not only born in sin, but was basically corrupt. Without God's grace to bolster the rather pathetic human longing for virtue and to stiffen the weak and wavering human will, the corruption of the flesh and the temptations of the world would triumph. Song and dance and theatre were all part of the world's insidious corruption. They trampled virtue and overcame the weak will. Racine returned to his Jansenist beliefs. In writing tragedies, he was in a sense like a man taking a beautiful woman to bed, wallowing in the pleasure of erotic, but secretly despising himself and her for succumbing to temptation at all, for doing what he felt to be wrong, besmearing virtue and surrendering the will.

(Incidentally, does this get any closer to understanding how it was possible for him to poison Mlle du Parc? Was she despised for leading him astray in the first place, for being so clearly corrupt and in the wrong, an actress on stage, a pretty one at that, a constant temptation to men to fall from grace? Was he merely putting an end to a squalid life gone terribly wrong? Was he God's chosen instrument? There is the making of another Racine tragedy in these very circumstances.)

It is this Jansenist background, with its bleak view of mankind as being essentially corrupt, which probably gave an edge to Racine's tragedies. When he wrote for the professional theatre, he had rejected the religious beliefs in which he was raised. The very fact of writing plays for the theatre at all makes that clear. He brings no panaceas. No *deus ex machina* descends from the clouds to save his characters, there is no last minute resolution of the problems in his plays. They regard corrupt, weak-willed, self-seeking human beings with an all-seeing, but not a forgiving eye. And they leave their audience profoundly troubled at what that all-seeing eye reveals.

What makes his plays special, is his ability to show what is going on in the mind of his characters. The audience has a clear idea what each character is thinking and feeling. The audience knows more than the characters on stage, they know what the other characters are thinking and feeling. Yet as each character speaks and reveals their motivation, sometimes the very mainspring of their existence, the audience can both share in that particular viewpoint and at the same time perceive where each individual is making a wrong choice, making a faulty judgement. The audience can do this because they know more, much more than the character on stage. As a result the audience often comes close to playing God in a Racine play, seeing all, understanding all and judging all. Perhaps this is the essence of Racine's tragedy, because the audience is a God who may be all-knowing, but a God who cannot intervene, and can only be appalled at the inevitability of the tragedy, as the characters intermesh and inter-relate with each other.

Characters in his plays are not petty. They are grandly mythological or historical personages. They are also intelligent. They speak in a language that is simple and direct, great poetry, a major ornament of French literature, but easily understandable and always remarkably apt for each speaker and each situation. Above all, the plays are marvellously theatrical. They move with pace and vigour, even if remarkably little actually happens on stage. It is not the action, so much as the reaction of the characters to the action and to each other, that fascinates his audience.

He accepted, seemingly with ease, the restrictions that current critical writings demanded from seventeenth-century playwrights. The dramatic unities: everything happening in one place; everything happening within twenty-four hours; and every action having some relevance to every other action, all part of the same story. An audience watching a Racine play does not feel that this obedience to the unities is a restriction at all, it seems simply how this play happens to be.

Some of his attitudes and assumptions have dated. The insistence on rank and aristocratic privilege now look snobbish. Phèdre can contemplate lust with her son-in-law –

but it would, as has been pointed out, be quite beneath her dignity to make similar advances to a mere stable boy.

The way each protagonist in the drama sets about a rational analysis of their own motives and psyche generally, added to an equally rational attempt to analyse the motives of everybody around them, has come to seem very French. Characters in French fiction and drama have been doing much the same ever since. Yet to say that Racine is quintessentially French is to say more than just this. His characters clothe themselves and the world around them in a poetic language that is almost alienatingly rhetorical. This is not just fine-sounding language where a spade is never a spade but is always "an instrument of toil" or something equally wrapped up, almost smothered in a grandly ornate language that seems far from everyday speech. It is rather that the characters are always "putting on a show", making a theatrical event out of every exchange, never just leaving the room, always making a grand exit. Even when they are on their own, they seem to be a shade too self-regarding, always adjusting the impression they are making in some mirror seemingly permanently perched in front of them. They are always "on view". No doubt Britannicus urinates and defecates like the rest of mankind, but it is almost impossible to imagine his doing it. That would be hidden away in a closet, offstage and well out of sight. Racine's characters could never even break wind in public. They are much too grand for that.

This too is what we mean by being French, partly why Racine so permeates French thinking and is so greatly revered by his countrymen. Is there any other European nation quite so fond of striking public attitudes, dressing everything up in rhetoric, and finding it difficult to say in plain words exactly what they really think and mean? Perhaps because he so poetically represents the best of this element in the French character, Racine fails to travel well to other languages and other nations. It is not so much T S Eliot's "I gotta use words when I talk to you", because after all Racine does not deploy a large vocabulary. Nor does he deliberately hide his meanings from his audience. It is just that his characters seem to be constantly admiring themselves in different mirrors at the same time. The Hall of Mirrors in Versailles is aptly named. In Versailles Racine the courtier often sat with other courtiers, admiring performances of Racine the dramatist. There is something in French culture that sometimes makes it difficult to tell the difference between them.

Occasionally a modern audience longs for someone in a Racine play actually to do something, to be less dignified, less always on their best behaviour, if only a scratch in an intimate place, a spitting, a farting. There is nothing lavatorial in Racine's plays. But these are impious thoughts. Racine's world must be accepted on its own terms if we are to relive the frightening excitements he offers us.

Courtiers spend much of their time currying favour. Enough has been said of Racine's character to make it clear that he was essentially a courtier, good at making friends and influencing people, well practised at currying favour. In Paris, the theatre, like so much else, revolved in Racine's time around the tastes, the preferences, the attitudes of Louis XIV. He was the fount of most honours, posts and privileges. Only with the King's support could Molière survive the open hostility of the Church over *Tartuffe*. One of the keys to understanding Racine's plays is to grasp that they were written, not just to massage Louis' ego, that would have been too obvious; rather they set out views and ideas with which the assiduous courtier, Racine, must desperately have hoped the

King would find himself agreeing. We know that *Britannicus* had at least one direct effect on the King. Before this play, Louis had been accustomed to take a leading role in court performances. He enjoyed and prided himself on his dancing skills. Such is the sycophancy that surrounds a monarch, we shall never really know for sure just how good he actually was. After *Britannicus*, with its explicit references to Nero appearing in performances before his court, Louis never appeared on stage again. It is reasonable to assume from this that the King took the play seriously. Racine in his second preface to *Britannicus* refers to the hostility that greeted its first performance, "but the critics gradually disappeared. The play remained." What silenced this very vocal hostility? Partly no doubt the sheer intellectual quality of the play. But the approval of the King must have been just as important. Racine the courtier appears to have struck the right note. To ask what it was that the King found so much to his liking in *Britannicus,* is to go to the very heart of the play.

Yet it would be wrong to undervalue the sheer impact of *Britannicus* as exciting drama. Thomas Gray, that admirable intellect, poet and literary dilettante, creator of the famous *Elegy in a Country Churchyard,* saw a performance of *Britannicus* in Paris in the 1760s and was so carried away that he set about writing a play on the same lines in English. He gave up after two hundred lines, a fascinating fragment and vivid testimony to the power of the drama decades after Racine's death.

The play is essentially about politics – not the politics of a democratic system, but the politics seething within the court of an all-powerful ruler, circumstances in their way just as applicable to Louis XIV as to the subject matter Racine chose, the young Emperor Nero in ancient Rome. This could have been very dangerous territory indeed for Racine. Like all ambitious courtiers, he had to take risks to achieve his ends. His previous play *The Litigants* had been a comedy. (Racine? A comedy?) Surprise, surprise, it proved to be exactly along the line of the very reforms the King was introducing into the legal system, and won the positive support of the monarch. As we have seen, so did *Britannicus*. So what was it that won such royal favour?

On the surface there could be no comparison. The play shows us the young Nero in the early years of his reign, not the despicable tyrant he later became. But everyone in Racine's educated audience, well-versed in Tacitus and the Latin classics, knew all about Nero. Racine did not have to labour the point. Clearly he had chosen a ruler, an absolute ruler, who was in no sense like Louis. Parallels were therefore prohibited from the start. And yet, and yet… The play is as much about Agrippina as anybody. Britannicus is the son of the Emperor Claudius and Messalina. Claudius then married Agrippina who already had a son, Nero, by her previous marriage. By a series of wily crimes she ensured that Britannicus, the rightful heir, did not succeed as emperor on the death of Claudius, but her son Nero did instead. Limited by the convention of the dramatic unities to a period of twenty-four hours for his play, Racine shows us a crisis reaching breaking point. Agrippina has been in effect all-powerful and running the empire for the first two years of Nero's reign. She has not done well, and the people are discontented. Nero is about to take control into his own hands. As the play opens Agrippina is seeking an audience with her son, but the door to his apartments remains firmly closed. She is falling from power. As the play proceeds it becomes clear that although she has formerly been a brilliant tactician she is losing her grip. The audience can understand why. All her plots and strategies have been designed to put Nero on the throne. Now her protégé, her own son, is turning against her, everything she has worked so hard for suddenly becomes unreal. She is fighting from the deck of a sinking ship. Yet the long list of crimes she has committed already ensures she does not get much sympathy from Racine's audience. That sympathy goes to Britannicus, the rightful heir to the throne, who is virtuous, admirable, a true hero. Nero falls for Junia, whom Britannicus loves, and forces her to lie to Britannicus and tell him she no longer loves him while Nero secretly listens and enjoys the situation. Nero decides to poison Britannicus, his rival to the throne as well as his rival in love, and is at first dissuaded from doing so by Burrus, an advisor who represents conventional wisdom, and then persuaded by Narcissus, a much more realistic advisor. Britannicus is duly poisoned. Junia seeks refuge as a vestal virgin (the nearest Roman equivalent for a seventeenth-century convent) and Narcissus is torn to pieces by a resentful mob. Agrippina, in an impassioned prophetic speech, foresees the long catalogue of crimes awaiting Nero that will end in his final suicide. The stage is set for Nero to become the tyrant of history and for the final curtain.

At one level, although the love of Britannicus is doomed and Britannicus dies, the audience is comfortably aware that justice is done. Agrippina has been swept aside into impotence. Narcissus has been torn to pieces. In the fullness of time Nero will commit suicide. Evil has engineered its just deserts. And what has all this to do with Louis XIV? As the King watched the play, what chords were struck? What was Racine the courtier saying? Britannicus may be virtuous and a hero, but he has also been outmanoeuvred. His heroic virtues chimed in with the feudal, chivalric attitudes of the aristocrats whose passionate convictions had so bedevilled France in the civil wars of the Fronde. Both Louis and Racine had read their Machiavelli and knew that a ruler must be decisive and unscrupulous if necessary, that reasons of state could overrule private morality. Even in the nineteenth century Cavour could say "If we did for ourselves what we do for our country, what villains we should be!" In disposing of Britannicus, Nero is being a realistic ruler, snuffing out a potential rival, safeguarding his throne. In dealing with Agrippina, are there not parallels in the way Louis had to deal with his powerful but corrupt minister of finance, Fouquet. Having lied and cheated Louis, Fouquet spent the rest of his life in impotent imprisonment in the Bastille. Far from simply being a straightforward contest between good and evil, *Britannicus* is more about the necessary evils a ruler has to commit to grasp and hold on to power. Did Louis possibly feel as he watched the play, that here at last was a playwright who glimpsed what the art of ruling, *Realpolitik,* was all about?

Louis XIV has long since turned to dust in a distant grave. Over three hundred years separate us from Racine's seventeenth century. Yet can anybody maintain that the subtext of this play, the tensions between public and private morality, the difficult choices that face any government, have lost their relevance? The Nazi persecution of the Jews, the death camps, the Jewish persecution of the Palestinians, ethnic cleansing, the behaviour of the Serbs, Islamic fundamentalism, the IRA, are there not still discernible gaps between public attitudes and private agendas, official morality and reasons of state? Louis probably sat fascinated as these characters from another age analysed their own and their opponents' motives, estimated their own chances, summed up the opposition, desperate to perceive where advantage lay. Despite itself, a modern audience is still caught up in the same excitement and enjoys the privilege that every Racine audience always enjoyed, that of knowing more than the characters on stage, taking the larger view.

In Racine's ultimately bleak world everybody is a victim and everybody is doomed. In the end he seems to have returned to his Jansenist beliefs in the grace of a God that could dissolve the sins of the world. That saving grace is hard to discern in *Britannicus*. There is no happy ending, only a tragic acceptance of what being human means.

6

Schiller and Romanticism

Average theatregoers in this country, almost by definition middle-class and reasonably well-educated, know surprisingly little about Friedrich Schiller. The chances of their having seen a single play by Schiller are slim indeed. They may have a vague impression that Schiller was a German romantic poet, but can our theatregoers actually name a poem? Unlikely.

It is difficult to believe we are talking about a major figure, not only in European drama, but in European art. Perhaps a musical illustration would make this clear. Beethoven set Schiller's verse to music in his Ninth Symphony and Brahms, d'Indy, Lalo, Liszt, Mendelssohn, Schubert (fifty settings), Schumann, Richard Strauss and Tchaikovsky have all used Schiller's writings as the inspiration for their music. Schiller remains in the regular repertory of most German state theatres.

Born in 1759 and dying after 45 crowded years in 1805, Schiller can already claim, at that sadly early age to die, to have had a powerful effect on German letters and German theatre.

His death was duly reported in *The Gentleman's Magazine*, a useful guide to what the cultivated Briton ought to know and feel, on May 9th 1805:

> At Weimar of a nervous fever, the celebrated German Poet, Friedrich Schiller, born in Ludwigsburg (actually Marbach) in the Duchy of Wittenberg, November 10th 1759.

After its readership had duly digested this information, the same magazine told them a month later what to think about it:

> Schiller had not attained his 45th (actually 46th) year; but his genius was in full force. What the literary world regrets most is his *History of the Low Countries*, of which he has given but the first volume. All Europe, at an early period of its publication, placed this work among the writings which have done most honour to the age. His *Don Carlos*, his *Mary Stuart* and his *Wallenstein*, with their irregularities and even whimsicalities, must live eternally; but his tragedies are only to be read in German. This language, in its nature so energetic, has become sometimes untranslatable from the pen of Schiller.

Don Carlos and *Mary Stuart* even with their so-called "irregularities" and "whimsicalities", and even in this trivial and remarkably flawed appraisal, were selected out to "live eternally". There was little excuse in 1805 for ignorance. Most of Schiller's major works had by then been translated into English. It is true they were seldom well received, much less with any perceptive understanding. Coleridge's 1800 translation of *Wallenstein*, soon after its German debut, was so savagely attacked it put him off his original intention to translate Goethe's *Faust*. There were political undertones too. Coleridge and Schiller were perceived as "Jacobins" with dangerous revolutionary tendencies. On the strength of his first play, *The Robbers*, Schiller had been, April 26th 1792, proclaimed as Honorary Citizen of the French Republic by a French revolutionary Assembly, which actually had rather more pressing practical problems of revolutionary government it should have been attempting to manage.

Attitudes in England have remained depressingly constant since *The Gentleman's Magazine.* In 1813 Madame de Stael's *De l'Allemagne* was published not only in France but in English in London, giving the first systematic account of the intellectual ferment in Germany that was to make it such a potent centre of European intellectual life throughout the nineteenth century. Thomas Carlyle was so impressed by de Stael that he set about learning German (he became fluent in nine months) and not only translated Goethe's *Wilhelm Meisters Lehrjahre* but published a biography of Schiller in 1825. Yet Carlyle could write as late as 1831 in an article on Schiller "we are troubled with no controversies on romanticism and classicism."

It took the British a long time to absorb, much less contribute to, what elsewhere in Europe was a vital intellectual debate. Even when they did, Schiller remained very much at the margin. Whereas, for example, the European George Steiner's *The Death of Tragedy* is full of references to Schiller, that distinguished English writer Raymond Williams' *Modern Tragedy* does not mention him once. Even as late as 1960 Kenneth Tynan, one of the leading drama critics of his day, could dismissively complain of "four hours of Schiller's *Don Carlos.* A Spanish tragedy composed of themes borrowed from *Hamlet* and *Phèdre",* as if Schiller had nothing much else to offer himself. He would not have dreamed of dismissing Shakespeare so cavalierly, just because Shakespeare too borrowed themes for some of his plays from elsewhere. Not that Tynan's sneer is acceptable anyway. There is precious little of either *Hamlet* or *Phèdre* in *Don Carlos.* Neither Racine nor Shakespeare would have understood what Schiller meant by "freedom of thought". And that romantic theme is at the heart of any understanding of *Don Carlos.*

Although a later arrival and younger than most, Schiller was a leading spirit in the movement known as *Sturm und Drang* that was a forerunner, a precursor of what was to grow at the turn of the century into a fully-fledged Romantic Movement – Rebellion – Revolution, whatever its various historians have called it. This movement was destined to change all the arts in Europe, perhaps the last major shift in European sensibility, a change that still dominates our own attitudes and perceptions, so much so that Western culture's dominant ideology remains irredeemably romantic. Most of the main themes of Romanticism can be found alive and kicking in *Sturm und Drang*: the emphasis on the individual and individual freedom, a political idealism, the crucial importance of creative imagination, a subjective, Rousseau-esque response to Nature, the new attention paid to feeling and sensibility, the use of symbolic imagery, the championing of Shakespearean freedom in dramatic writing, as opposed to the dramatic unities, and scurrying back down the corridors of time to find themes for plays in distant epochs and other cultures.

This involved the first serious attempt at some kind of historical realism in stage settings and costumes. *Sturm und Drang* took its name from the title role of a play by Klinger. Its leading spirit was Goethe from 1771-78 who greatly influenced the younger disciples around him – J M R Lenz, H L Wagner, F Muller and F M Klinger. The young Schiller's work from 1780-85 was a later flowering from the same stem.

Schiller had good reason to be almost obsessively occupied with concepts of freedom. The fashion for looking at the early life of an artist to find the motives, often subconscious, for the main themes of his later creations, has happily waned in recent times, but Schiller was so maimed by his early experiences, it is difficult to understand the man without first grasping what terrible things they did to him.

To talk of Germany, even in 1805, is misleading. The Holy Roman Empire, which was as Talleyrand neatly noted, neither holy, nor Roman, nor an empire, consisted of a patchwork quilt of little independent states, kingdoms, dukedoms, fiefdoms, each supporting a Court and local aristocracy, depending as it had since feudal times on a labouring peasant class. Yet the increasing efficiency of the educational system was producing a talented middle class for which there were very few jobs, very little chance of status and position. This created a growing social tension which was only gradually resolved as industrialisation and increasing prosperity in the later nineteenth century absorbed and greatly increased the new middle class. In the 1790s it looked as though there was nowhere for this upstart middle class to go. They depended pathetically on the patronage of the aristocrats, particularly on the local ruler.

It is difficult to fit back into the mindset of what was, after all, a mere two centuries ago, but attitudes to the ruler seem to the modern mind not only indefensible, but incomprehensible. It must be remembered that since the Dark Ages church and state had strenuously supported each other. The ruler was not only appointed by God, he had divine authority. It was the good Christian's duty to submit. Schiller's father, of a Lutheran Swabian family, was a typical member of the emerging middle class, still dependent on aristocratic patronage.

Schiller's father spent most of his career in armies as a field surgeon, a soldier, and later as an officer. At 25, riding his own horse, with a fair sum of money carefully put by, he married the daughter of the landlord of The Lion at Marbach.

Sadly, the money was unwisely used, the family fell into difficulties and Schiller *père* once again joined the army of his sovereign, Duke Karl-Eugen, of Württenberg, gaining a lieutenant's commission. In 1763 he became a recruiting officer, charged with recruiting soldiers for his Duke's army from the imperial city of Schwäbisch-Gmund. Karl-Eugen needed to send recruiting officers outside his own borders because, in order to gain French subsidies, he not only fought with the French against Frederick the Great in the Seven Years War, but as a result of an agreement made in 1758, he sold his male subjects of sword-bearing age as mercenaries to the French army.

This tyrannical bartering of his subjects was very much a theme of Schiller's third play, *Passion and Politics*, yet in the notes Schiller *père* made for an autobiography the matter is never even mentioned. A ruler had the right to do as he pleased with his subjects. When Schiller *père* was transferred to Ludwigsburg, he planted a tree nursery behind his house, and the Duke, hearing of this, put him in charge of tree planting of the ducal country estate. Tens of thousands of trees, grown in a stony soil, were used for roads and parks. He established an economic system of fruit tree growing, and his nursery became a horticultural Mecca for gardeners from all over the world. Yet he was still entirely dependent on ducal patronage. The Duke kept a firm grip on his Duchy and scrutinised the results of the school examinations to see who was doing well. The young Friedrich Schiller showed promise. The Duke had established his own school, Karlsschule, essentially to provide the right administrative staff for his Duchy. The Schiller family had planned, with Friedrich's willing assent and intention, that he should study for the priesthood. The Duke thought otherwise. Control over his subjects' children was part of his all-embracing right. The thirteen-year-old Friedrich was handed over, until his 21st year, as a guinea pig for the Duke's teaching experiment, since the Duke personally controlled the school. The young boy agreed, although "tormented in spirit", largely out of consideration for his parents.

He found himself in a prison, not only of the body, but almost of the mind too. For the Duke had just lost a constitutional battle with his subjects, who had appealed to the Emperor, and in the satiric words of the poet, Schubart, whom we will soon come across again:

> Als Dionys von Syrakus
> Aufhören musst', Tyrann zu sein
> Da ward er ein Schulmeisterlein

> (When Dionysus of Syracuse had to stop being a
> tyrant, he became a little schoolmaster.)

There were no holidays or leave of any kind to visit home. When a pupil's request to see his dying father was refused, the Duke admonished the weeping boy "Be quiet: I will be your father." The pupils' correspondence was carefully scrutinised and censored. On the Duke's birthdays, or those of his wife, the pupils had to compose flattering speeches in prose and verse. One of Schiller's survives:

> I see before me the father of my parents, whose gifts
> I cannot recompense. I see him, and he takes my breath
> away. This Prince, through whom my parents can do me
> good, this Prince, through whom God can work his plan
> for me, the father who seeks to make me happy, is more
> praiseworthy than my parents, who totally depend on
> him. Could I but come before him with the thanks that
> such excites in me.

What is the twentieth century to make of this sycophantic grovelling?

The pupils rose at six o'clock (five in summer), had porridge for breakfast and worked from seven to eleven. Then they put on military costume, sword, top boots, blue coats with silver buttons, white waistcoats and white trouser, a three-cornered hat with silver braid and cockade, and paraded for the Duke's inspection. Lunch was followed by a precious hour in the garden, then more lessons until seven p.m. Parents had to petition the Duke for a chance to visit their children and a superintendent had to be present throughout the interview. At night there were no lights in the pupils' rooms. Schiller often reported sick just to be allowed to write by the sick room candle. If anyone of authority or the Duke himself came by, all evidence of writing had to be hastily hidden. "Any tendency towards writing poetry broke the rules of the academy, and was in direct opposition to the plan of its founder", as Schiller himself wrote bitterly four years later. There were the usual savage punishments. In 1775 a medical department was added to the academy, and Schiller transferred from studying law to studying medicine.

There were compensations for this frighteningly Spartan regime. He had good teachers. One of them, confiscating Shakespeare from the young pupil because this was not on the authorised list of books, returned it and encouraged Schiller, who went on to be greatly influenced by the poet, Friedrich Gottleib Klopstock (1724-1803), whose ambition to provide the German tongue with an equivalent for Milton's *Paradise Lost* resulted in *Der Messias*, a hexameter epic in twenty cantos, making him the leading poet of his day and spearheading a renaissance of German poetry. In attempting to imitate Klopstock's poetry, the adolescent Schiller discovered his vocation as a poet. Sadly, because his final medical thesis, at the age of 20, showed signs of independent thought, the Duke condemned him to another year at school – with the crushing discipline and all-demanding routines.

When he finally left school at 21, he had with him the secret, much hidden and cherished manuscript of a play, *The Robbers*, understandably a rebellious tirade against tyranny. He emerged into the outside world after a sentence of eight years' hard labour. No time off, no home visits, ultimately at the beck and nod of a capricious tyrant. And one who did not approve of poetry.

Just how capricious and cruel a tyrant Karl-Eugen could be was demonstrated by his treatment of another older poet Christian Friedrich Daniel Schubart (1739-1791), who left the Duke's domains and edited a paper in Ulm that gave offence to the Duke. He was enticed back over the border at the Duke's instigation and then thrown into a dark, vaulted jail, in solitary confinement for a year, with no means of reading or writing. His regime was then slightly improved, but he was kept in jail for a further nine years with no trial, no charge and no sentence. When finally released, on the direct intervention of the Prussian King the poet's spirit had been finally broken. His arrest took place when Schiller was 17, already writing poetry, an activity strictly against the school rules. When Schiller was 19, he started writing *The Robbers*, a play based on a story by Schubart. Play writing was also forbidden at the school. In 1781 the young Schiller, a year after leaving the school, bravely visited Schubart in prison. We do not know what they talked about, but we may be sure the Duke was told of the visit. Perhaps he smiled grimly and hoped the example of Schubart, the literary butterfly crushed in the grinding wheels of the state, might teach the ambitious young Schiller a lesson.

If so, he was wrong. Schiller had graduated from the Karlsschule fully qualified as a doctor, and hoped to start up in civilian practice, but the Duke, all powerful when it came to deciding the lives of his subjects, decreed that he should be a regimental surgeon in a unit consisting largely of disabled soldiers. He still required a General's permission to leave Stuttgart, even to visit his family in the countryside. The change must nevertheless have been exhilarating. At 21, although still required to live and work in the all-male atmosphere of the army, he was able for the first time to meet and talk with women as part of social intercourse, to see his mother and sisters, to respond to the challenge, the stimulus, and the physical appeal and temptation of the opposite sex. He was an impressionable, imaginative, sensitive poet. New vistas opened out before him. He wrote love poems. He paid for sex. He fell for his landlady. He behaved as absurdly as so many young men when fresh out of boarding school.

He was also ambitious as a writer. When publishers refused to consider his play, he raised a loan (the origin of much financial worry in the future) and published at his own expense. The reviews were favourable. The then popular novelist, Timme, began: "If ever we have hopes of a German Shakespeare, this is he!" In Mannheim, the bookseller, Schwan, went to Baron von Dalberg, the director of the state theatre, the most important in Germany after Hamburg, and persuaded him the play must be performed.

For the first night Schiller travelled from Stuttgart in secret and without permission. The play was a sensation. "Rolling eyes, clenched fists, strangers falling sobbing into one another's arms...everything dissolved as in the chaos from whose night a new world breaks forth." Schiller discovered a world he could conquer – the world of the theatre. He must have been almost as dazzled as the audience by the effect of the play, watching his own creation brought so successfully to life. He was lucky to have a great actor, Iffland, then only 23, taking the leading part of Franz Moor, and establishing his own reputation as much as Schiller's. The dramatist learned a good deal about stagecraft from watching his play in performance. He reassured Dalberg that his next play would be much better.

The Robbers is very much a young man's play, full of the passion and longing of frustrated youth. Perhaps not surprisingly, it is also bookish. The characters are drawn by a young writer who has read widely, is sensitive, intelligent and imaginative, but who has little knowledge and experience of real people and real life. Germany's great man of letters, Goethe, who was to become Schiller's mentor and close friend, detested *The Robbers*. The mature Schiller agreed with him. In later life he wished that it would never be performed. As Schiller himself wrote:

> Any disposition to poetry did violence to the laws of the institution where I was educated, and contradicted the plan of its founder. For eight years my enthusiasm struggled with military discipline; but the passion for poetry is vehement and fiery as a first love. What discipline was meant to extinguish, it blew into a flame. To escape from arrangements that torture me, my heart sought refuge in the world of ideas, when as yet I was unacquainted with men; for the four hundred that live with me were but repetitions of the same creature, true casts of one single mould, and of that very mould which plastic nature solemnly disclaimed.

Thus circumstanced, as a stranger to human characters and human fortunes, to hit the medium line between angels and devils was an enterprise in which I necessarily failed. In attempting it, my pencil necessarily brought out a monster, for which by my good fortune the world had no original, and which I would not wish to be immortal, except to perpetuate an example of the offspring which Genius in its unnatural union with Thraldom may give to the world. I allude to *The Robbers*.

Yet something about this "monster" of a play has kept it very much alive. It was wildly successful when first performed in Mannheim in 1782.

Although Schiller was already establishing a growing reputation as a poet, his first play was written in prose, powerful prose. As Carlyle put it:

> It is the production of a strong untutored spirit, consumed by an activity for which there is no outlet, indignant at the barriers which restrain it, and grappling darkly with the phantoms to which its own energy thus painfully imprisoned gives being. A rude simplicity, combined with a gloomy and overpowering force, are its chief characteristics; they remind us of the defective cultivation, as well as of the fervid and harassed feelings of its author. Above all, the latter quality is visible; the tragic interest of *The Robbers* is deep throughout, so deep that frequently it borders upon horror. A grim inexpiable Fate is made the ruling principle: it envelops and overshadows the whole; and under its louring influence, the fiercest efforts of human will appear but like flashes that illuminate the wild scene with a brief and terrible splendour, and are lost forever in the darkness.

The unsearchable abysses of Man's destiny are laid open before us, black and profound and appalling, as they seem to the young mind when it first attempts to explore them: the obstacles that thwart our faculties and wishes, the deceitfulness of hope, the nothingness of existence, are sketched in the sable colours so natural to the enthusiast when he first ventures upon life, and compares the world that is without him to the anticipations that are within.

The play itself is easy to make fun of. It is written in a high impassioned prose style. In German, the word *pathos* can imply a stagey almost melodramatic passion dangerously akin to bombast, and the use of the word *pathos* has often been levelled in a pejorative sense at Schiller by later German critics.

The story, too, is an unlikely one. It has two main characters, two brothers, Karl, the hero, and Franz, the villain. The brothers never meet throughout the play. Franz persuades the Count, their father, to disinherit Karl, who is away studying in Leipzig. Karl, appalled at the injustice of the world, agrees to become the leader of a band of robbers. Back home, Karl's sweetheart Amalia rejects Franz' overtures and remains true to Karl. The Count, hearing false news of Karl's death, is overcome with grief. Karl is almost equally appalled at the atrocities committed by his gang. He visits home in disguise and discovers the evil-doings of Franz, which include immuring the Count, their father, naked and starving in a dungeon. Karl sends men to seize Franz, who commits suicide. Karl is not to be allowed a happy life with Amalia, he has pledged himself to his gang of robbers. He realises he has only one choice, and surrenders to the law, recognising that social justice cannot be achieved by the revengeful action of a wronged individual.

In a sense the play cheats, both having its cake and eating it. Karl, who in fine revolutionary style is taking his revenge on a corrupt and decadent society, ends up surrendering to the law, affirming in fact that social justice depends on the very social system the play starts out attacking with such bombastic fervour.

Worse still, the characters, in any naturalistic sense, are not really believable. Has Karl really not the slightest inkling that his own brother is trying to turn his father against him? Would Karl really have reacted to the news of his disinheritance by deciding to lead a band of robbers? And what about Amalia? If ever there was a cardboard cut-out, it is she, her author displaying almost no knowledge of how women think and feel. But then how could he, immured as he was for every week of eight long years in the all-male establishment of the Karlsschule, depending for any knowledge of the opposite sex on what plays, poems and stories he could manage to read.

What Schiller does have is a fine sense of what works as drama in the theatre. He presents us with a series of exciting scenes, paced with action and emotion, that generate an undeniable dramatic energy. When Karl ties his hand to the oak tree and orders his companions to heed the monk's words and make him their prisoner, the author is certainly being melodramatic, but the scene carries its audience away with the sheer daring and unexpectedness of the action. As Carlyle wrote, "It is in vain that we rebel against the crudities and inconsistencies of the work: its faults are redeemed by the living energy that pervades it."

Most of the themes of the plot, and indeed individual incidents, can be traced elsewhere. This is not a criticism of the author, it is a reminder that the original audience were probably more prepared to swallow improbabilities, because those improbabilities were already almost conventions of narrative. Henry Fielding in *Tom Jones* used the theme of the good and evil brother as an essential part of the plot, equally improbable but apparently quite acceptable for his eighteenth-century readers. Shakespeare himself based *Othello* on an equally unlikely villain and even less likely circumstances. It is Othello's weakness, not the improbabilities of the plot, that matter, and in *The Robbers*, some of the themes that the more mature Schiller was to use even more effectively were already discernible.

Both brothers are rebelling, and both have to live not only with their grand gestures of defiance and rebellion, but with the effects of what they have done. Karl equates his own misfortune with wrongs done to suffering humanity and sets out to seek redress. He finishes by becoming as much of a villain as his brother. Franz is rebelling, too. He opposes all the usual ties of brotherly love, filial duty, the very existence of the idea of the sacredness of the family. Not only that, but as Schiller himself noted, Franz is not just a dyed-in-the-wool villain, he is consciously experimenting almost philosophically with the idea of being a villain. People to him are "as flies to wanton boys". He kills them for the sport of it.

Why was it such a sensation when it first appeared? Like *Look Back in Anger* in 1956, it had the good luck to say the right thing at the right time. In England Jimmy Porter's denunciations of the establishment struck a responsive chord with the post-Suez generation. In Germany, the young Schiller's hero combined fervour, enthusiasm and political idealism with a whole range of youthfully rebellious attitudes that caught the mood of the times. Unlike Osborne, Schiller went on to become a major poet and playwright. When the play appeared, the French Revolution was only seven years in the future. "Bliss was it in that dawn to be alive, but to be young was very heaven."

Bliss was to give way to disillusionment. The French Revolution in 1789 led to the Terror, which led to a dictator, an emperor far more powerful than any Bourbon, absolutist monarch. Schiller and Goethe retreated from the heady world of *Sturm und Drang*. The mature Schiller in repudiating *The Robbers* was really renouncing some of the adolescent attitudes of his youth. Yet it is those very attitudes, rebellion not so much directed at particular instances, but rebellion per se, that permeate *The Robbers* and keep it exhilaratingly alive. Being so grandly against so much can still strike a chord with the adolescent that lurks in most of us – still alienated and resentful, still longing to make grand if ultimately futile gestures and hurl defiance at the world.

The Duke was very angry indeed at the success of *The Robbers*. He summoned Schiller, sentenced him to fourteen days detention, and "I order you to write no more plays, or to face instant dismissal. Write no more literary work and do not communicate with foreigners!" When Schiller wrote to him requesting a relaxation of this ban, his General was instructed that if Schiller again asked for permission to submit a letter to the Duke, he was to be arrested immediately.

It is not surprising that this ambitious young poet and dramatist fled from Stuttgart. He was lucky that the Duke depended on and favoured his father, so took no reprisals against Schiller's family, nor made efforts to have him brought back. But it was a terrible risk. From 1782 Schiller was free of the Duke, free of Stuttgart. The step was momentous. Until 21, he had never had to take any decision about food, clothing, lodging, everything had been planned for him. Even in the army, having to manage on low pay, he had security and accommodation. Suddenly, he faced the wide, intimidating world on his own. He had prospects, yes, but almost no money, and was already saddled with debt. Dalberg proved unwilling to give him any kind of position in Mannheim, although he accepted two more plays, *Fiesko* and *Passion and Politics*, and contracted for a third, *Don Carlos*.

Passion and Politics is also a young man's play. It is full of idealism, prepared to sacrifice everything for the then very new concept of romantic love, and very much on the attack too. Essentially it disdains snobbery and the corruption of a ruling class which took its privileges to the manner born and by divine right.

Schlegel sneered at it: "the play is not likely to move us by its tone of over-strained sensibility, but may well annoy us by the painful impression it leaves on our mind." Carlyle felt that where *The Robbers* depended for much of its effect on "enormity of incident and strangeness of situation, *Passion and Politics* is destitute of these advantages. It is a tragedy of domestic life; its means of interesting are comprised within itself and rest on very simple feelings dignified by no very singular actions."

Yet it has considerable virtues, it still holds the stage, it still works in the theatre. Not least of its merits is its surprising difference from the young Schiller's two earlier plays, *The Robbers* and *Fiesko*. Here we see a restless creative mind trying out its considerable dramatic talent for size. The last thing the young Schiller wanted to do was repeat himself. One almost feels the "been there, done that" as he pushes his two past successes aside. The play was written in the winter of 1783-4 and performed to great success in April 1784. Schiller was staying alone in a small cottage in Bauerbach. Accustomed all his life to the hurly-burly of institutional living, solitude must have been a new experience, although food, service, linen, heating and indeed the cottage were all generously provided by a patroness, Frau von Wolzogen. The play works better as drama than *The Robbers*. Its plot is simpler and the drama comes as much from what people do as what they say. In keeping the dramatic excitement going, Schiller clearly profited from G E Lessing's *Emilia Galotti* (1772), another domestic tragedy with tension, vivid dialogue and believable characters which deeply influenced the *Sturm und Drang* writers. A copy of *Emilia Galotti* lay open on the desk in Goethe's *Werther* when his character took his own life. Lessing's Emilia, preferring death to dishonour in fine romantic style persuaded her father to kill her.

Schiller's play ends in much the same style with a double poisoning. Louise Miller, the heroine, is a mere musician's daughter but in love with Ferdinand, whose father wants him to marry Lady Milford. The older generation set intrigues going to break up the couple to such effect that at the end Ferdinand is led to believe Louise has been unfaithful to him. Hence the poison which Ferdinand administers to both of them. Only after taking the poison does Ferdinand discover that Louise has really been faithful to him all along, and dies denouncing his father. There is more of a dramatic ambivalence here than in that prototype of lovers' tragedies *Romeo and Juliet*, where the lovers die for a pure love. Ferdinand dies for an impure love, or at least he thinks that's what he is doing until the final *dénouement*. The love has been tainted by a corrupt, scheming, unscrupulous world that has lost touch with what matters. Alienation from such a world, belief in the power of romantic love, an obsession with death particularly when contrasted with dishonour, all these were to become staples of the new romanticism. The young Schiller made a taut drama out of them. We are not yet into the poetic language of *Don Carlos,* but the prose of this play is perhaps a shade too heightened for its own good. The minor characters tend to share too much of Schiller's own poetic imagination:

> Forgive me, my Lady, I was only thinking how sorry I feel for that wonderful Ruby being unable to know that its possessor is so hard on vanity.

Where Schiller's dramatic gifts came from remains a mystery of the creative imagination. He had read widely, from Greek drama, through Shakespeare, to French classical drama. But he was, himself, an appalling actor. At the Karlsschule he had ruined a performance of Goethe's *Clavigo* in 1780, reducing his audience to hysterical laughter by his hopeless attempts to act the main part. Strecher, his companion in Mannheim, has related at length how, when the Mannheim actors were invited to hear Schiller's first reading of his new play *Fiesko*, they left appalled, thinking the play a disaster. It was only when later reading the play they realised that Schiller himself had ruined it for them by his sheer inability to read it in anything but a monotonous, high-pitched gabble. Yet this man was a poet, alive to the musicality and rhythm of words, a dramatist with a born sense of theatre.

This same young man was on the verge of forming the friendships, relationships and acquaintances that would make him such a force in a movement that was to spearhead a major shift in the cultural sensibility of Europe. Where had his mental baggage, his attitudes and assumptions, the dominant ideology of a group of bright, committed intellectuals, the new *Weltanschauung*, come from? What in fact were the origins of the Romantic movement?

As we have seen in earlier chapters, the previous major shift in European sensibility had been the Renaissance. This broke the mould of medieval thought, primitive, backward, superstitious and ignorant, underpinned by a tenacious theology, and to question any theological tenets was to commit blasphemy, as Galileo and so many others discovered. The Renaissance was, as the French world implies, a rebirth of interest in the classical world of Greece and Rome, and for 200 years (1500-1700) classical writers established a growing authority that came to be seen as the Age of Reason, with perhaps its finest flowering in the golden age of French artistic achievement in the seventeenth century, particularly the work of Molière and Racine.

Everything stemmed from a firm belief in the power of reason, an engaging paradox in itself since there is nothing very rational about belief. Descartes in his *"Cogito ergo sum"* deduced man's very existence from his ability to reason. Christian Wolff, the German philosopher considered God *"reiner Verstand"* – pure reason, Alexander Pope in his *Essay on Man* maintained "that reason alone countervails all other faculties." Just as Newton had discovered laws which were universally applicable in physics, so reason would ultimately establish similar laws in the Arts as well as the Sciences. All this projected a comfortably stable view of the world.

> Nature and Nature's laws lay hid in night.
> God said 'Let Newton be!' and all was light.

The same *lumière* shone over the Arts as over the Sciences. God was in his Heaven and all was right with the world.

Unfortunately, this rational view of the arts left too much out of account. Art was seen as a skilful imitation of reality, the artist as a manipulator of the necessary skills, and the purpose of the enterprise was an intellectual, artistic medicine, as it were, with moral lessons that did those at the receiving end good, while pleasure was seen as a necessary coating of the moral pill. La Bruyère even went so far as to draw an analogy between making a book and making a clock.

The creative process is much more than this. The creative process is as irrational as it is rational. The imagination does not operate according to the rules of a textbook, and yet the Age of Reason saw it largely in those terms. When Gray was asked by a hopeful young poet how to turn prose into poetry, he answered airily, "Twirl it a little into an apophthegm, stick a flower in it, gild it with a costly expression." Here the creative process is seen merely as applying a little decoration to what is already there. Imagination is a bit like the paint kept in a paint store somewhere at the back of the premises, which if lavishly applied, can make everything seem fresh and new. There is little room in this view for the creative individual imagination.

When the seventeenth-century certainties were increasingly questioned in the eighteenth century, a great deal was at stake. Certainty is comfortable to live with. The arts functioned in a frame of reference that made for a stable, secure world. To question the system was to change security for insecurity, certainty for uncertainty, a sure sense of the order of the universe for doubts as to what the hell was going on. To exchange in fact the eighteenth century for the twentieth. When the eighteenth-century viewers eyed the starry heavens, they felt assurance and security. In the twentieth century we feel only insecurity and doubt. To put it another way, that old objective view of the world has given way to a more subjective view.

The process by which this new view was arrived at was fortunately a slow one. The Age of Enlightenment, as the eighteenth century is called, shedding new light – *Aufklärung* – on old problems, nevertheless, while still ascribing much to the power of reason, gradually came to emphasise new concepts, genius, beauty, sensibility and freedom.

The process was slowest in France, where the glories of the seventeenth century dominated art and aesthetics. In 1799 La Harpe in his *Cours de Littérature Ancienne et Moderne* remained wonderfully unaware and impervious to almost the whole of eighteenth-century thought and achievement. Voltaire, while accepting "enthusiasm" in his *Dictionnaire Philosophique,* considered it must always be *"raisonnable",* that enthusiasm must always be controlled by reason. It is clear from the study of Diderot by P N Furbank (1992) that this lively mind was well ahead of his contemporaries, but in this area his actual influence was much slighter than it should have been. It was not until the 1830s that the Romantic movement really took hold in France.

In England matters were otherwise. At the beginning of the eighteenth century, Dryden, deeply influenced by French thought, was faced with the incomparable achievement of Shakespeare. He did his best. He revised him, he rewrote him, and he tried hard to make him more "correct"; but we find Dryden finally admitting, early on in the century, that rules can be stretched or even broken rather than sacrifice any great beauty. This is a surprisingly early appearance of an admission that a work of art is to be judged on its aesthetic merits, not judged by how well it obeys the rules, nor by what moral values it propagates.

> But Shakespeare's magic could not copied be;
> Within that circle, none durst walk but he.

Yet the eighteenth century is essentially in England perhaps the age of Dr Johnson, whose influence was considerable, and who, like Voltaire, would undoubtedly have put reason first. Yet all around Johnson, the ground was shifting.

Germany had no tradition, neither Shakespeare and the Elizabethans, nor France's golden age of Molière, Corneille and Racine. Its very artistic poverty of background made it more open to innovation. Domer and Breitinger in 1739 in their *Kritische Dichtkunst*, while restating many of the seventeenth-century assumptions, were already claiming that poetry derived not from the intellect, but from the spirit and the imagination. Bodmer lauded the imagination as greater than *"Alle Zauberer der Welt"* – all the magicians in the world. Most striking of all, greatly influential, translated into both English and French, was Gotthold Ephraim Lessing's *Laokoon*, where, with the utmost reasonableness and with a brilliance that resonates even today, he effectively demolished seventeenth-century aesthetics.

A subjectively creative imagination, beauty as the standard and fantasy as their embodiment, were thus initially in place for the young Schiller to grind his artistic teeth on. From then on the unruly beauties of an unruly imagination became admissible. Not only had the world changed, but the young Schiller knew it.

Yet there was far more to this than mere demolition. "Sensibility" was a new and much admired quality in eighteenth-century art. The "unbounded feeling of a tender heart" came to be valued more highly than reason, scorning the cool judgement of a detached mind. Plays in England by Cibber and Steele, with their long rhetorical speeches aimed firmly at the emotion, illustrated changing taste. In France, the *comédies larmoyantes* (tearful comedies) of La Chaussée wrenched the heartstrings, and the lugubrious poetry of Klopstock in Germany made this clear too. In England, however, the theatre, labouring under a new censorship, was already losing ground to the novel as a potent medium of communication, both reflecting and assisting in the changing value system. English novels, positively wallowing in the new "sensibility", conquered Europe.

Richardson's *Pamela* (1740), *Clarissa Harlowe* (1747), *Sir Charles Grandison* (1754), Goldsmith's *Vicar of Wakefield* (1766), Sterne's *Sentimental Journey* (1768), Henry Mackenzie's *Man of Feeling* (1771) and Henry Brooke's *Juliet Grenville*, or the *History of the Human Heart* (1774) represent the more attractive peak in a positive Himalayan range of such outpourings. Alongside them the Continent could muster only Prévost's *Manon Lescaut* (1735), Rousseau's *La Nouvelle Héloïse* and Goethe's *Die Leiden des jungen Werther* (*The Sorrows of Werther* – 1774).

Almost all of them recount at thrilling length the trials and tribulations of a virtuous but unfortunate individual. The reader is moved by their misfortunes, and so instructed in the value of virtue. But although this is the ostensible aim, a rational aim of which Dr Johnson undoubtedly approved, these novels were in fact doing something else. They were wallowing in a display of emotion, of feeling, of sensibility, which is the real purpose of the exercise. Tears, emotion for its own sake, the eighteenth-century equivalent of the Hollywood "weepie" – very far indeed from seventeenth-century rationality – were edging centre stage. Richardson's novels were admired by Rousseau, Diderot and by the *Sturm und Drang* movement in Germany, particularly Goethe, Herder and in due course Schiller. In his use of the letter form – his stories are progressed by means of letters between the protagonists – Richardson was also emphasising not an objective approach to fiction, but the new subjective response of the individual.

It was a significant break with earlier formal techniques. No wonder the ground on which Dr Johnson took his firmly rationalist stance was positively shifting around him.

The vogue for "gothick" architecture echoed this same sensibility – but sentiment gradually merged into sentimentality, with thrills and horrors for their own sake. Ghosts and the supernatural invaded melodrama in the theatre and in the novel.

Sensibility and subjectivity – as the sensitive mind turned in upon itself – led to that other precursor of romanticism, the reverse coin, as it were, of sensibility, melancholy. This also was generally presented in "gothick" trappings, hauntingly caught in Gray's *Elegy written in a Country Churchyard* (1742-51) and at much greater length in Young's *Night Thoughts* (1742) and Harvey's *Meditations among the Tombs* (1784). Rousseau in his *Rêveries du Promeneur Solitaire* (Musings of a Solitary Stroller) (1782) echoed exactly the new mood of his time where the subjective creative imagination, the emphasis on feeling, the response to melancholy, seem a very long way from seventeenth-century French classicism.

This emphasis was not only on the natural and the spontaneous in terms of the individual and his feelings. It led to a new view of nature – as opposed to the city where more artists actually lived – a nature whose moods, sunny, full of the promise of spring or dark, thunderous and frightening as midnight chimed, reflected and embodied the moods of the artist and could become a symbol for them. A surprising number of Schiller's poems do exactly that, as in the last two verses of *Der Pilgrim* :

> Hin zu einem grossen Meere
> Trieb mich seiner Wellen Spiel,
> Vor mir liegts in weiter Leere,
> Näher bin ich nicht dem Ziel.
>
> Ach kein Steg will dahin führen
> Ach der Himmel über mir
> Will die Erde nie berühren,
> Und das Dort ist niemals hier!
>
> [Onwards to a mighty Ocean
> Bearing me its billows role;
> Vast and drear it lies before me
> But no nearer is the goal.
>
> Ah! no bridge will lead me thither
> Ne'er alas will Heaven's sphere
> Meet this nether earth-ball's surface
> And the There is never Here.]

Here the symbolism is almost too heavy for the poor ocean to keep it afloat.

Nature did more than symbolise the changing moods of the subjective artist. In Rousseau's hands it became almost a concept of value in itself. The seventeenth century, from Descartes onwards, had seen the world as a mere mechanism, whose laws Newton deduced, and which had originally been set going as it were by God. Rousseau, and Diderot too, began to see Nature as an organic whole, a growing, living entity, of which the noble savage had once been an integral part. Where the French seventeenth century had reordered their parks in rational rows and patterns, the English, in recreating a "picturesque" Nature, were embodying this new view. Instead of seeing it as one of the many tools with which man created his own world, painters and poets started treating Nature with reverence and respect, actually describing and responding to what they found. Rousseau in his famous *Discours sur l'Origine de l'Inégalité parmi les Hommes* (*Discourse on the Origins of the Inequality among Men* – 1755) not only equated decadence with civilisation, but advocated a "return to nature" as it might have been before the ownership of property, a return to living in a community where all had equal shares.

"Innocent, primitive, natural, and good" became almost inter-changeable as adjectives and there was not only a torrent in fiction extolling the natural." – Bernadin de Saint-Pierre's *La Chaumière Indienne* (*The Indian Hut* – 1790) and *Paul et Virginie* (1788), Chateaubriand's *Atala* (1801), and *René* (1805), but works which took this a stage further and posited a "natural" justice, as opposed to the man-made justice of a decadent civilisation, Goethe's *Götz von Berlichingen* and Schiller's *Die Räuber* (*The Robbers*), that first play he furtively brought out in his baggage when he finally left school.

So we have finally come full circle. It was not only the play, but a whole intellectual baggage, a framework of reference, a dominant ideology which that widely read and frighteningly intelligent young poet took with him as he faced the outside world for the first time. Clearly the Duke and Schiller had little common ground. Schiller had an all too real and humiliating experience of absolute tyranny at first hand. He also had a set of beliefs which regarded that tyranny as hopelessly outdated and morally indefensible. He was an idealist, who believed the natural goodness of the noble savage had been corrupted by a decadent civilisation, based on an unfair division of property. "Man is born free and is everywhere in chains", as Rousseau had so thrillingly declaimed. Freedom of thought was the noble savage's birthright.

Before we make any attempt to assess or analyse Schiller's contributions to European drama, we must recognise that we stare back at him across an historical divide. He was born in 1759, and was a young man as the forces that were creating the French Revolution in 1789 gathered impetus. We now know about the French Revolution, we know about its aftermath, and even more importantly, we know about that whole shift in European attitudes and assumptions that we attempt to describe with the label Romanticism. We are the end-result of this process, Schiller flourished at its beginning. If we are to grasp Schiller's importance, we should be aware of what the Romantic movement involved to create such a separation.

Western culture's dominant ideology remains firmly bound up with that same Romantic movement, we are still enmeshed within the same cultural change, so it is extraordinarily difficult for us even to attempt any kind of analysis. The patient still on the operating table is in no state to arrive at a dispassionate assessment of his condition, much less attempt an impartial prognosis. Yet somehow if we are to make any sense of what has happened to our values and attitudes in the last two centuries, that is what we must attempt to do.

If we talk of a particular generation, imbued with a vague but powerful sense of political purpose, a sense that somehow "the system" had failed them and had to be rejected and largely dismantled so that it could be built afresh, a generation that wore its hair long, and clothes that scandalised its elders, a generation consciously welcoming a laxer lifestyle, a different set of values, a generation that experimented with drugs, questioned sexual taboos, dropped out, most readers will think of the 1960s. But every single one of these attributes applied just as forcibly to the 1840s. Almost every European capital except London experienced violent political upheaval and revolution in 1848. The student revolts of the 1960s were very small beer in comparison.

When we attempt to deal with major shifts in European ideology, such as the impact of Christianity on the pagan world, or the Renaissance which was in a strange reversal, the impact of a long dead pagan world on Christianity, and then the next major change that is Romanticism, it is dangerously easy to generalise. Yet Romanticism changed the way we perceived the world, ourselves, our relations with each other, society and all the arts. Value systems altered and are still changing.

A few examples make the difference clear. There is a passage in one of Jane Austen's letters where she refers to the Peninsula campaign being conducted by the British army under the man who would in due course be the Duke of Wellington. She did not consider the Napoleonic war to be of sufficient importance to refer to it in any of her novels. In her letter she notes the heavy casualties suffered by British troops. Our troops. Her troops. "What a blessing", she says cheerfully, "that one does not care a jot for any of them!" This is the authentic voice of pre-Romanticism, sane, rational, assured. It shocks us. Even if we do not actually care a jot for victims in the latest air crash or train disaster, we feel we ought to. We would not dream of admitting that we did not. We belong to the Romantic movement.

Or take attitudes to Nature. The very fact we have to spell it with a capital is revealing. If I could take readers and drop them down on the top of Cader Idris, that much admired mountain in North Wales, on a glorious sunny day, I could be fairly sure of everybody's reaction in the 2000s. Deep lungfuls of pure air, a sense of exhilaration at the view, increased spiritual well-being in communing with unspoilt scenic wonders. Nothing in the view around has changed since people were there in the fourteenth, fifteenth or sixteenth centuries. But their reactions, as far as we can tell, would have been quite different. Surrounded by a "horrid waste", they would have been anxious to get back to civilisation. Or let me put it another way. Faced with a particular valley, a soldier looks at it with the eye of a professional, defence is possible here, troops will be vulnerable there, positions can be dug there and so on. A farmer has a different, but equally professional eye. This land can be drained, that is only good for pasture, this could make arable. A typical twentieth-century individual, faced with the same valley, is more likely to experience undifferentiated emotion. "How pretty! How unspoilt!" We have not gone soft in the head. We have gone Romantic. Even Shakespeare looked at Nature with the expert, understanding eye of the true countryman. It is just that expertise we have lost.

Is *Sturm und Drang* in any sense to blame for any of this? Not really, or only partly. There were at least two Romantic movements, and because we are at the end of a process which has incorporated both, these differences no longer seem important. To return to the analogy of the patient on the operating table, he does not care very much whether his cancer came from smoking or from chemical additives. All he cares about is the cancer. Perhaps it is not a very good analogy because I do not want to suggest that society has acquired a terminal disease. But whatever it is we have, *Sturm und Drang* helped to give us. It started us smoking, let us say. It took the Industrial Revolution to provide the chemical additives. And now the analogy is making more sense because Romanticism was spawned as much by the industrial revolution as by anything.

Let us take the *Sturm und Drang* Romantic movement first. This was a healthy development of the rationalism of the eighteenth century. As we have seen, towards the end of the seventeenth century, instead of being overshadowed by the past achievements of the Greeks and Romans, and the whole Renaissance had been devoted to picking up where the Greeks and Romans had left off, thinkers and artists began to imagine they were not only as good as, but possibly better than their illustrious predecessors. Newton had demonstrably taken science further than Aristotle. Dryden could only defend Shakespeare by setting aside classical dramatic rules about the unities of time, place and action. The eighteenth century embarked on that most dangerous of paradoxes, a blind faith in the power of human reason. It would only take so long before the scientists and the thinkers would find the necessary solutions to all the outstanding problems. Given time, we would lay bare the secrets of the universe, remodel nature in man's image, reconstruct reality, etc., etc. Wonderfully heady stuff. Rousseau in the 1760s and 70s shifted the emphasis to the "*moi*", edging the individual and his own response to his own predicament into the centre of the new world reason was itching to create. His *Social Contract*, wildly unhistorical but enormously influential, indicted the "system" for failing to honour the supposed contract by which free individuals supposedly bargained themselves into a society. "Man is born free and is everywhere in chains." Even more heady stuff. A little over a decade ago, we celebrated the bicentenary of the end result of this blind faith in the power of reason, the French Revolution.

Studying the interminable debates among the so-called experts in 1789 who set about that epoch-making event in European political and cultural history, their conceit, their naivety, their assurance in their own ability to replan the world is what *Sturm und Drang*, among other influences, has to answer for.

There is a depressing little parallel among the architects of the 1930s, 40s and 50s. They too thought they knew best and could cheerfully destroy in order to replan. "Bliss was it in that dawn to be alive" for architects among the municipal corruption and shoddy building of the booming 1960s. Middle-aged architects now have a hunted expression. After 1789 French politicians were lucky to make middle age at all. One of their many supposed solutions to social problems was the guillotine, and seldom have so many theorists had to endure so quickly and so rudely the end results of their own theoretical solutions. Many of us would like to condemn architects to live on the top floor of their vandalised tower blocks where the lift is semi-permanently out of order. Many of the most vehement French seekers after liberty, equality and fraternity, found neither liberty nor fraternity, but only the nastiest kind of equality as the guillotine reduced them to the final indignity of becoming a mere statistic.

Had anybody told French thinkers at the close of the seventeenth century that the coming century would prove to be a battle for supremacy between England and France, which England would win, to enjoy the fruits of victory throughout the nineteenth century, they would have found it too unlikely even to feel insulted. France was the undoubted leader of the arts, of thought and of military might. Spain was already looking back regretfully on a noble past. Venice no longer counted for much. Germany was a gaggle of independent little principalities.

What were the long-term effects of the French Revolution, succeeded as it was by Napoleonic tyranny, the attempt to conquer Europe? It certainly helped the rise of nationalism, largely as a reaction against the French. Nothing made a German, an Italian, or a Spaniard feel more nationalistic than a French army lording itself on their land and their goods. But the main change was ideological. In spite of all the Congress of Vienna could do in 1815, a new kind of political idealism and revolutionary fervour arrived which not even the most frantic efforts of the *ancien régime* could suppress. Democracy, as a principle, became part of the political fabric of Europe and after the French Revolution, replacing the feudal world that had lingered since the Middle Ages. Expediency might resist democracy, but its gains were all short term.

Ideas are ultimately defeated only by better ideas, and the idea of democracy survived its appalling failure in the French Revolution to continue to win the hearts and minds of Europe. That is the main achievement of the intellectual ferment in the second half of the eighteenth century which *Sturm und Drang* reflected and advanced. Democracy was not, of course, anything new. Even accepting that most of the ancient Greek and Roman world was based on slavery, a background against which Pericles' funeral speech rings a shade hollow to modern ears, democracy was a Greek word and a Greek idea. It was also the last gift of the Renaissance to modern Europe. And it started the Romantic movement.

The term Romantic, although based on the English word, was first used in its currently accepted sense by the German critic Friedrich Schlegel, who managed so to muddy the water over its definition that nobody has been quite sure exactly what it means ever since. The English word was, of course, already loaded with meaning, echoes and associations long before Schlegel hijacked it for art criticism. His use of *romantisch* can fluctuate in meaning even within the confines of a single work. In *Gespräche über Die Poesie* (Conversations about Poetry), having accepted that ancient and romantic represented almost opposite areas of feeling, he says: "*indessen bitte ich Sie doch, nur nicht sogleich anzunehmen, dass mir das Romantische und das Moderne völlig gleich gelte.*" (I beg of you, however, not to jump to the conclusion that the Romantic and the Modern are entirely synonymous to me.) He comes close to narrowing things down in his much quoted: "*ist eben das Romantische, was uns einen sentimentalen Stoff in einer phantastischen Form darstellt.*" (What shows emotional subject matter in an imaginative form is Romantic.) He then went on to equate Romanticism with Christianity until nobody was quite sure what he meant by the word at all. The debate and the problem of definition took some time to reach English literary criticism. As we have seen, Carlyle wrote in 1831: "we are troubled with no controversies on Romanticism and Classicism."

But while French and German thinkers were enthusing over Rousseau, something quite different was happening in England. We were about to step onto the centre of the world stage for our moment of glory. The agricultural and industrial revolutions literally changed the face of the land. The total population of England in 1720 was about five million, most of them living in villages. Throughout the eighteenth century land enclosures revolutionised peasant lifestyle. More food was grown with much less labour, driving surplus labour into the cities at the very time improved agriculture was providing more food to feed them. In the cities, jobs were becoming available for the new surplus labour as the factory system got under way. Steam engines provided power and improved communications enabled the capitalist system of a market economy, obeying the laws of supply and demand with as little government interference as possible, to spread octopus-like tentacles everywhere.

It is difficult for us to grasp the extent of the change which occurred within the span of a single lifetime. My father died at 104. Born in 1890, he had seen Britain, which in his early manhood owned a quarter of the globe in the largest empire known to mankind, shrink to a small, relatively unimportant island off the coast of Europe, anxious to strengthen its links with the rest of the European Community in order to compete with the new superpowers. He had survived two world wars. He had seen the advent of the combustion engine, the diesel ship, the aeroplane, the telephone, radio, film, television, computers, word processors, space exploration; yet the shape and pattern of the city in which he spent his life, while altered, did not really alter that much. Trains are still there. Railway stations have hardly changed. Horse-drawn buses have given way to petrol engines, but they still trundle up unaltered streets. Houses have been converted to flats, but they are still the same houses. Shops are still shops. Many of the branded goods had been on sale most of his life. Public libraries, museums, theatres, concert halls, even public houses are all unchanged. Yet take the London of Wordsworth, who could stand on Westminster Bridge as a young man and write:

> Earth has not anything to show more fair;
> Dull would he be of soul who could pass by
> A sight so touching in its majesty.
> This city now doth, like a garment, wear

The beauty of the morning; Silent, bare,
Ships, towers, domes, theatres and temples lie
Open unto the fields, and to the sky;
All bright and glittering in the smokeless air.

Wordsworth too lived to a ripe old age. Had he been taken back to Westminster Bridge in the last year of his life, the London of his youth would have almost completely disappeared. He could probably not have seen anything anyway, because the new bridge on which he was standing might well have been enveloped in a dense, man-made fog from all the factory and domestic chimneys belching smoke from the new city built all around him. There were no fields, nothing bright and glistening in the smokeless air. Historians tell us of the appalling living conditions of the early industrial workers. England paid a high price in human suffering for being the first to industrialise. A lifestyle that had suited village life did not adapt easily to the overcrowded living conditions of the factory system. Overcrowding, polluted water and minimal sanitation meant that life was nasty, brutish, short and cheap. Even London did not acquire Bazalgette's gravity sewage system until the 1860s. Before that it was a matter of carts, stench, along with cholera and other diseases. Marx and Engels working in London as it changed all around them, saw the exploitation, the poverty and the ghastly living conditions and came to conclusions about Capitalism containing the seeds of its own decay which, while they seriously underestimated the resilience of the system, were all too understandable.

It would make a neatly fitting mechanism of cause and effect, although history is anything but mechanistic, to read into these terrible changes in the environment the causes of the sense of alienation from society that is such a marked feature of Romanticism. Sadly, with examples stretching as far back as Schiller and the *Sturm und Drang*, or early versions of Goethe's *Faust*, this alienation is discernible even before industrialisation created a more hostile environment. Undoubtedly the Industrial Revolution helped, but perhaps it was the growing status and importance of the artist, who was therefore able to make much more of his neurotic sense of being different, which Freud maintains is one of the mainsprings of artistic activity anyway, that better explains the growth of alienation as Byronic artists paraded their separateness through a host of artistic creations.

We need historians to tell us about the terrible living conditions because the arts were almost unanimously silent about the epoch-shattering changes taking place in society. The arts were going Romantic. It is as if collectively the arts turned their face to the wall and tried to pretend the Industrial Revolution simply was not happening. There are noble exceptions like Dickens' *Hard Times*, but not many. The arts became preoccupied with other cultures, other periods, Nature, anything to escape from what was taking place around them. The most popular British novelist as the Romantic movement got under way was Sir Walter Scott. The bogus medievalism of such novels as *Ivanhoe* and *Quentin Durward* make him almost unreadable today, but his influence here and in the rest of Europe was incalculable. Reading Scott's poetry or prose, it would be difficult to grasp that the Industrial Revolution was changing the whole fabric of society:

> Tunstall lies dead upon the field
> His life blood stains the spotless shield.

What had shields and obscure medieval battles to do with factories, child labour, sewage pollution, the railway network, canals, the frantic search for markets, the booming economy, the poverty of the slums? Perhaps it was just because they had nothing to do with these realities that they appealed.

As the arts retreated from the real world, the status of the artist changed too. Artists had acquired prestige in the Renaissance. One of the ways rulers and lay governments showed off their power was through the arts. It became important which court finally attracted Leonardo da Vinci, but artists still needed a patron, still remained subservient. With Romanticism artists finally achieved independence. It is instructive to look at Haydn's contract. He was a senior servant in an aristocratic household, wore its livery, was responsible for a group of musicians who played at family occasions, was entitled to a seat at the upper servants table and so forth. He was also a composer with a European reputation. His pupil, Beethoven, also had contracts. They were with his publishers. In one generation Beethoven achieved the kind of independence that was impossible for Haydn. The market for the arts was changing. The Industrial Revolution was a period of intense social mobility. The middle class expanded enormously.

It is not always appreciated just what a trap this must have been for the women in the emerging middle class. A generation earlier in the peasant village economy, women were probably working harder than men and playing a pivotal role in the family economy. The lucky ones who emerged into the middle class in the subsequent Industrial Revolution found things quite otherwise. The men in the family were still working hard in factories and offices in the helter-skelter of the new industrial economy. They were able to buy fine houses for their families to live in. It was possible to drive from central London to the Crystal Palace passing almost nothing but these fine new houses for the new middle class.

But what of the women inside them? They were now fine ladies. They had hordes of servants to do the actual work. They were not allowed to seek a career or a vocation. They were anyway worn out in the endless business of procreation, producing surprising numbers of children to underpin the population explosion. Ill-educated, with no chance of a career, waited on hand and foot, they had to find ways of passing the time. Hence the growth of Mudies' circulating libraries, of the four-volume novel, of sheet music, magazines, of theatre, of a whole entertainment industry. Artists made large profits meeting this new demand from a newly emerging class of consumers. But as profits rose, standards fell. This is the key to the depressing lowering of standards in all the popular arts throughout the Victorian period. The new consumers, one or two generations away from the village economy, were largely female, with time on their hands, ready to be exploited. The first mass-market for the arts had arrived. With it came the hallmarks of Victorian art: sentimentality, hypocrisy and sensationalism. Ghosts and the supernatural generally, much as they must have done in the tales told round the evening fire in the village, popularised the "thrill of horror". Disembodied hands clutched from behind the wainscot, maidens immured in turrets, listening as grisly things slowly climbed the stone stairs towards them, young women died of love in almost every chapter and every play, and the arts became steadily more and more divorced from the actual, practical ways in which people lived and behaved. When we read of young middle-class girls toying with their food at the dining table and genteelly eating almost nothing, then tucking into a large tray in the privacy of their own room afterwards, art was clearly reshaping life with a vengeance.

Most of these aspects of Romanticism are still with us. Sentimentality, hypocrisy and sensationalism are as much the hallmark of our own time as of the Victorians. The Industrial Revolution in due course produced a more prosperous working class who in their turn became the new consumers waiting to be exploited. The tabloid press, sentimental horror films, lurid computer games, nightly violence on television are as symptomatic of our period as the first excesses of Romanticism were for the Victorians. Our journalists, scriptwriters, and film crews grow fat on the proceeds just as the first artists of the industrial era did. A Disneyland erected in the middle of a France full of real castles, wonderfully beautiful and historic, yet with crowds packing in to see gawdy imitations, is symptomatic of the same process.

We now view Schiller with perceptions that cannot help taking account of all that has happened since he wrote his plays. It may have been "very heaven" to be young at the beginning of Romanticism, but these days Romanticism has been around too long for us to show the same naivety. We view Schiller's early enthusiasms with a slightly jaundiced eye.

Schiller's views were anyway to change radically. The French Revolution in 1789 saw to that. The bliss of revolution turned sour. Revolution led to the Terror and to Napoleon. Schiller and Goethe retreated from the heady world of *Sturm und Drang*, but when *Don Carlos* was completed in 1787, that lay in the future. It was written by a young poet who kept his youthful idealism intact, but it was also the first of Schiller's plays that represent his maturity. He had come, artistically, a long way from the world of *The Robbers*.

He had also come to the end of his tether in Mannheim. Poverty, bad relations with the theatre, and the stress of insecurity prevented his fulfilling his contract and delivering *Don Carlos*. He moved to Leipzig where a fresh set of admirers were ready to support him, and he was anyway hoping to support himself by publishing a periodical, *Thalia*, a journal to cover literature, art, and the aesthetics, and to convey Schiller's views to his growing public. In it he published the first two acts of *Don Carlos* and part of the third.

The play is based on a work so unhistorical as to be more fiction than fact, a French romance by the Abbé de Saint-Réal. The Restoration dramatist Thomas Otway also wrote a popular play, *Don Carlos* (1676) based on the same source, but Schiller seems to have been unaware of that. He had begun the play in 1783, published the first half in 1785-86, but all five acts were not complete until 1787. In *Thalia*, in his *Letters Concerning Don Carlos,* he wrote about his increasing difficulties with the play. When he originally proposed it to Dalberg in Mannheim in 1784 it had been intended as a "family portrait in a princely home". By 1787 it had become a "play expressing a view of life".

> The work has played its part in the different changes that my thinking and feeling have been through… New ideas superseded earlier ones. Carlos fell from favour, perhaps simply because I was outgrowing him, so that Posa, for just the opposite reasons, began to take his place.

But there is one more general point to make about Romanticism. George Steiner in his *Death of Tragedy* maintains that tragedy and Romanticism do not mix, because Rousseau and his Romanticism, both at a conscious and subconscious level, established a new approach to the concept of guilt. If man was basically good, pure and noble, then crimes were committed by those whose education had not taught them to distinguish properly between good and evil, or those who had been corrupted by civilisation. Society, not the individual, was to blame, and if an individual is not wholly responsible, he cannot be wholly damned. Marlowe's *Doctor Faustus*, an Elizabethan tragedy where we watch a heroic individual destroyed, was replaced by Goethe's *Faust*, which has in true romantic fashion, a happy ending. In Steiner's memorable phrase: "Rousseau had closed the doors of hell." At the climax, remorse and redemption would save the day. From *The Ancient Mariner* – "The self-same moment I could pray/And from my neck so free/The Albatross fell off, and sank/Like lead into the sea." – to *Les Misérables*, all the way to *Götterdämmerung*, romantic fiction spread a view of life that was basically optimistic. The Hollywood happy ending, as the couple walk hand-in-hand into a technicolour sunset, or the lone cowboy heads heroically into the desert for the next adventure, can never be tragic.

The genuine tragic hero cannot run away from responsibility for his actions. The doors of hell are open and damnation is hellishly unavoidable. The tragedy of Lear will not be put right by setting up old people's homes. As Steiner says: "The twist of the net which brings down the hero may be an accident or hazard of circumstance, but the mesh is woven into the heart of life." Romanticism gave us a different view of life, liberal, optimistic, sentimental and suffused with slightly wishy-washy ideas of human goodness. The Romantic looks at tragedy through rose-coloured spectacles and tries to pretend it is not really there.

Schiller was not only a dramatist and a poet, but he was also a theorist, a genuine critic with impressive insight into the intellectual problems of his time, fascinated with questions of dramatic form. The critic debated with and inspired the dramatist. In a sense, *Don Carlos* represents a slightly uneasy compromise between them.

It is written in blank verse, a deliberate imitation of Shakespeare. To this day, many Germans not only feel proprietorial towards Shakespeare, but think that Shakespeare's language is easier for a German speaker to understand than for speakers of any language but English. Wieland's translation in the 1760s and the famous version of the complete Shakespeare by Schlegel and Tieck (1796-1833), arrived at the same time that German was arriving as a respectable language for literature. The Shakespearean manner conquered German from within, permeating the cadence and tonality of classical German, and German writers appropriated for themselves the rhetoric and dialectic that are so much a part of Shakespeare's dramatic language. It is also worth remembering that German audiences were seeing productions of Shakespeare which were faithful to the original text, almost a century before English audiences, who were accustomed to mangled and heavily edited versions right up to the 1900s. Schiller's choice of blank verse for *Don Carlos* was part of this process, acknowledging and itself spreading by vivid example Shakespeare's influence.

The plot of the play is unusually complicated for Schiller. It is set in 1568. Don Carlos, heir to Philip II of Spain, has had to conceal his passion for his stepmother, Queen Elizabeth, who was originally intended to be his bride, but was married instead to his father, the King. When his friend, Posa, arrives at Court, Carlos confesses his feelings and Posa manages a meeting for Carlos with the Queen, who attempts to direct his passion into politics, to take up the cause of the persecuted Spanish Netherlands, a cause which Posa also espouses. Philip refuses to put Carlos in charge in the Netherlands, and sends the repressive Alba instead. Carlos keeps an assignation thinking it to be the Queen, but it is Princess Eboli who, dissatisfied, denounces Carlos and the Queen as lovers to Alba and Philip's confessor, Domingo, who in turn arouse the King's suspicions. A high point of the play is the interview between Philip and Posa, who pleads for religious tolerance and democratic rule, but still impresses Philip, who gives him an official appointment. Posa tries to shield Carlos from suspicion, and in the end can only save Carlos by sacrificing himself. He barely has time to explain this to Carlos before he is shot on Philip's order. A despairing Carlos intends to raise the flag of revolt in the Netherlands, bids farewell to Elizabeth, but is then arrested by order of the King and handed over to the Inquisition for execution.

Schiller, representing all the romantic ideology of *Sturm und Drang*, was aware too of the clash between romantic optimism and the classical view of tragedy. In *The Robbers*, he had himself done much to spread the new romantic ideology, proclaiming the rights of passion, the true feeling of a noble heart, against conventional morality and an outmoded class system. In his love of freedom and toleration, his passion for wild and picturesque nature, his imaginative response to the colour and variety of other places and other times, and the tensions of an historical contest, he was a true romantic. With his plays, and in his poetry, the first generation of Romanticism found many of its preoccupations and much of its language, the whole gamut of romantic emotion.

His considerable prose writings all carry the same stamp. He believed man was basically good, that social justice was possible, and like a true romantic, he projected his own subjective imagination into everything he created.

And yet, and yet. The critic in him was always aware of the clash. Was tragedy possible for a romantic generation? His treatment of Greek mythology was a powerful source of the Hellenism that fascinated German culture from Winckelmann to Nietzche. Schiller translated Racine and had a greater imaginative awareness of the essence of French classicism than most of his contemporaries. His plays tend to reflect, much as a tide ebbs and flows, an "either/or", in one play opting for full-blooded romanticism, in another attempting to recreate dramatic conditions, to find a dramatic form that would still make true tragedy possible.

Don Carlos is the first play in which we are aware of these tensions. It is amazingly long. Originally 6,282 lines, he revised it in 1801, 1802 and 1805 down to a still unwieldy total of 5,370. Much of it belongs firmly to *Sturm und Drang*. There are all the romantic trappings of another time and an alien country. There is the passionate defence of liberty and toleration, the emphasis on the heroic individual, there is even to be found in the language a vivid awareness of nature, if only in metaphor:

> Their petty vices, kept in check, have served
> my turn, just as your tempests cleanse the world.
> Now I need truth – and digging for its source
> in the dark mud of error and delusion
> is not the fate of kings.

There is also that grand extension of sensibility and feeling, the concept of romantic love, with all its revelations, heroics and despairs.

Yet at the heart of the play there is something else. No doubt Posa stands for the political idealism that Schiller espoused so ardently. Perhaps in his interview with Philip II there was originally to be something of all the insults the young Schiller must have wanted to hurl at the Duke when he was imprisoned in the school and could say nothing. Yet Schiller was a great dramatist. Of the many gifts a dramatist displays, one of the most important is that gift for being not themselves, for stepping into alien shoes, for creating rounded characters that seem to owe nothing to their creator. Richard III, Falstaff, Justice Shallow live as themselves; and the twentieth century by an ironic twist of fate actually knows much more about them than it does about their creator.

Once he started to write, it is clear that Schiller's imagination got to work on Philip II. What would it be like to be an all-powerful tyrant, what effect would it have on a man of intelligence and sensibility? The final creation is chillingly frightening. We see that something has died in Philip. That moment when the Count of Lerma runs from the King's presence and announces to a horrified court that the King is shedding tears, has a fine dramatic resonance. The audience is suitably horrified too. Feelings long suppressed by a ruthless intelligence are briefly surfacing. Feelings? Eighteenth-century sensibility flares briefly even in this monster of cold reason. It works at a number of different levels, rational, emotional, symbolic. This is fine dramatic writing.

What could be melodrama, and sometimes teeters on the edge of becoming so, is saved by this believable conflict of ideas and this insight into character. We get bound up in the battle of ideas, and the mechanism of the plot and drama allow the issues to present themselves and the characters to take shape. There is not too much melodrama in *Don Carlos*; if anything, there is too much ideology. It is the debate of ideas, rather than the dramatic action, which dominates the play. Nothing can quite equal the intensity of the first encounter between Posa and Philip, where two rival ideologies ideally embodied in believable characters attempt to dominate not each other but ourselves, the spectators, as we almost cheer on each palpable hit and are convinced in turn by one and then the other. This has some of Schiller's finest dramatic writing, but there is an awful lot of drama to follow it.

Is the death of Carlos or of Posa tragic? In a classical sense? Are we filled with awe and pity as we watch an inescapable fate grind down the heroic individual as he is forced along the dusty road to destruction? At one level, the answer has to be yes. Since the characters stand for a set of ideas, if we sympathise with these ideas, as Schiller expects, then their defeat – and they are resoundingly defeated in this play – is tragic. But of course, the ideas are not defeated. The author intends the audience to rise up and leave the theatre determined to fight on, to keep these ideas alive, to struggle for their ultimate victory. This is romantic optimism, not classical tragedy. And is there not a sense in which by the end of the play the characters have almost ceased to be people we care about, because the author and the play so clearly care a great deal more about the ideas they represent?

Perhaps by the highest standards *Don Carlos* never quite resolves the problem of being romantic and of being tragic at one and the same time in the same play. But the dramatic energy of the attempt makes it exciting theatre. Unlike Goethe, Schiller has a sure sense of what will work in theatrical terms, and this more than anything else is what keeps his plays still in performance on so many stages. Thomas Mann said of Schiller that not even Shakespeare was a greater master of dramatic rhetoric.

But Shakespeare followed the high tension of murder in *Macbeth* with the low comedy of the Porter. He knew when his audience needed to unwind, and lowered the almost unbearable tension, only to raise it again with yet more horrors. Goethe said of Schiller that he was "magnificent even when cutting his fingernails", and here and there perhaps a British audience might wish he had been a shade less magnificent, a shade less serious, a shade less committed and offered just a touch of humour, what Clive Bell thought was the true mark of being civilised, the ability to laugh at things we take seriously.

It is salutary to remember that the Greeks enjoyed the mocking anti-war satire, *Lysistrata*, when they were in the middle of a desperate war for survival against Sparta. But it is a signally bad critic who decries an author for not writing what the critic would have liked written. We must respond to the strenuous intensity and seriousness of Schiller's imagination.

In the summer of 1787 Schiller moved to Weimar where he married Charlotte von Lengefield in 1790. He wrote a remarkably able history of the sixteenth-century conflict between Spain and the Netherlands, and in 1789 became a professor of history at the University of Jena. He became a close friend of Goethe, and although his health broke down from overwork in 1791, he was at last freed from financial worries late in 1791 with generous grants from two German-Danish aristocrats.

Poetry, belles-lettres, aesthetics, history and philosophy claimed him for the next ten years, as did increasingly serious ill-health. It was not until 1798 that he again wrote for the theatre when his trilogy *Wallenstein* brought him immediate success again. He then wrote *Mary Stuart*, finishing it in 1800.

There is, there has always been, a touch of irony in this serious professor of history delving into the past to discover juicy material for drama, and then proceeding to rewrite history with a wild disregard for the actual facts. Schiller was never one to allow what really happened to get in the way of exciting drama. He rearranged the past with the same eye for a good exit speech as Shakespeare himself. In this he was swimming against the spirit of his times. As the Industrial Revolution got under way artists did their best to escape the present by rushing off imaginatively to earlier periods, other cultures, anything to get away from what, in soot and smoke and noise, was actually taking place around them. Part of this new passion for the past was a growing desire for historical accuracy. Plays started being presented in the actual costumes of the period. Stage sets made a point of showing how things had actually been and how they looked. It became important to get it right. We still feel a vague sense of outrage at Schiller's casual rearrangement of events.

For the real Mary Queen of Scots there was no conspiratorial Mortimer – no Lord Leicester in love with her, no confession and absolution when she was condemned to death. In the confrontation between England's Queen Elizabeth and Mary, which never actually took place, Mary would not have been 25 but 45, and Elizabeth would not have been 30, but 54. The play grates on an English audience, because some of the popularity of Good Queen Bess still lingers on and makes it difficult for us to accept the cold-hearted Machiavellian schemer that Schiller creates. Even the Scot, Thomas Carlyle, was fairly dismissive. The play gets little more than a single page in his *Life of Schiller*. "This tragedy" he tells us,

> will not detain us long…to exhibit the repentance of a lovely but erring woman, to show us how her soul may be restored to its primitive nobleness by suffering, devotion and death is the object of *Mary Stuart*. It is a tragedy of sombre and mournful feelings, with an air of melancholy and obstruction pervading it; a looking backward on objects of remorse, around on imprisonment, and forward on the grave.

Sombre indeed. The play is rather better than this. Schiller's sure sense of what will work in the theatre has not deserted him. He is no longer however depicting a youthful mind intent on overthrowing the existing order. Schiller is no longer the radical avid for action. We are a long way from 1789 when the promise and excitement of the French Revolution seemed to usher in a new age. The mature Schiller, appalled at the excesses of the Terror in France, sickened by the violence and sheer brutality that had been let loose, had turned away from revolution, yet he too, like so many of his creative contemporaries, took refuge in an escape from the present. He set about showing us the tragic dilemmas of individuals in their historical context, enabling us to see the problems and share the anxieties. He was recreating the past as it affected the lives of particular individuals; romantic individuals. And just as in *Don Carlos* a high point was the confrontation between Posa and Philip of Spain, so in *Mary Stuart* it is the confrontation between the two queens that somehow encapsulates, in a poetic truth that is remarkably intuitive, the real dilemmas that faced both of them. This is Aristotle's catharsis, the working out for an audience of tensions through the pity and fear that the dilemmas of others in whom we believe imaginatively, can excite.

This is even more true of *Joan of Arc* (*Die Jungfrau von Orleans*, 1801). As with *Mary Stuart* an English audience cannot be entirely impartial. Some of our historical sympathies are inevitably involved in a depressingly chauvinistic way. The English burnt Joan of Arc as a witch. The French still worship her as a saint. Does a flavour of these ancient antipathies still linger?

Nothing could better emphasise the extraordinary difference that Romanticism effected in our culture than Schiller's choice of subject matter for this play. Voltaire, that embodiment of *"raison et lumière"* had demolished Joan of Arc in a long and scabrously amusing *La Pucelle.* As a result the saintly Joan of Arc was and had been for some time, entirely exploded, a mere figure of fun. It is difficult for us to realise how boldly Schiller set about rehabilitating her. We are almost edging into the lurid territory of Victor Hugo's *The Hunchback of Notre-Dame.* Religion, sentimentality, the oddly bizarre and the romantic past all jumbled up to tear at our heart strings.

Once again Schiller reorganised the facts with scant regard for accuracy. In his play, Joan of Arc is not burnt at all, but perishes in fine style on the battlefield. Far from being the modest creation of Bernard Shaw or Max Mell's *Jeanne d'Arc*, Schiller's Joan has high-flown rhetoric in abundance. Even more interesting is the way she see-saws between having a powerful sense of destiny, and losing her authority from a sense of guilt. Indeed in Schiller's play she verges on the manic-depressive, bouts of exultation followed by despair.

In *Mary Stuart*, Mary knew she was innocent of the Babington plot, but felt guilty about her part in her young husband's murder years before. She only regained her confidence when faced with the death sentence. Guilt gnawed at her sense of justice and authority. How could Right be on her side when she herself had done such wrongs?

This theme of guilt was continued in *Joan of Arc*. Joan, when faced by an English knight, Lionel, fights him in single combat and defeats him, but touched by love and pity, spares his life. This leaves her with a strong sense of guilt, of having failed in her divine mission and surrendered to earthly passion. When her father denounced her publicly as a witch in the play, she was too conscious of this feeling of guilt to rebut the charges, did not defend herself and was banished. Wandering in the forest (how many romantic heroines have not wandered in the forest?) she was of course captured by Lionel's guard and then resisted his physical advances. Having rejected him she then see-saws up to a state of exaltation again which allows her to escape, rescue the King, win the battle and die gloriously draped with banners on the battlefield.

Why does guilt play such a part in these later plays? Did Schiller himself equate a sense of guilt with the loss of power, of authority, of creativity? Did he himself harbour feelings of guilt? Few dramatists of his power and authority have written nothing for the theatre for a decade, almost a half of his adult life.

As we have seen, Romanticism and guilt were almost irreconcilable concepts. Romanticism, based on a wishy-washy belief that everybody is basically good, cannot cope with guilt. Redemption was always just around the corner, a happy ending part of the territory. So Schiller was flirting with the unacceptable. He was a sick man by the time he came to write *Joan of Arc*, but two further successful plays lay ahead, *The Bride of Messina* and *William Tell*. On May 9th 1805, little more than a year after *Tell*, he died. He was in his 46th year. Germany has never forgotten him, and his plays still hold the stage there. Elsewhere the world keeps rediscovering him. He was one of the first grand Romantics, so it was perhaps fitting that in his own day romantic writers repudiated him for his so-called retreat from what Romanticism stood for. Alienation, being misunderstood and reviled were all part of the Romantic mystique. But his plays, his writings and his poetry survive to confound lesser critics. "*Si monumentum requiris – circumspice*" (if you need a monument, look around you) they wrote on Sir Christopher Wren's tomb in St Paul's. Schiller too has his monument. It exists on paper, and in the minds and hearts of living audiences as his ideas and his incandescent language still set the stage alight.

7

Lenz – Three Plays:
The Soldiers, The New Menoza and The Tutor

What is surprising about Lenz is how little impact he has made on English letters and English drama. Most of us would class him with Sir Walter Scott as largely unreadable and certainly unread. By 1978 he had still not made it to the *Oxford Companion to the Theatre*. This makes it difficult for us even to begin to grasp his importance, not just for German, but for European drama. Jakob Michael Reinhard Lenz was found on 24th May, 1792, at the age of 41, lying dead in a Moscow street. His death is a mystery. His family had no idea what country he was in, or whether he was even alive. He was staying with a freemason, at a time when the Russian secret police were inquiring into freemasons as a threat to state security. Lenz was an unpredictable, at times almost crazy personality, liable to say anything anywhere. It is not beyond the bounds of possibility that he was murdered by his own circle as a security risk. At his death, whatever literary career he had achieved lay in ruins. He was unremarkable and unremarked. He died in poverty without position or financial prospects. The only certainty remains those sightless eyes staring unseeing at a Moscow sky.

Yet he had originally been hailed by some of the finest minds of his generation as "the second German Shakespeare after Goethe." He formed an intense friendship with the young Goethe and shared a room with him. He was among the leading dramatists of that strange movement known as *Sturm und Drang*, taking its name from a play by Klinger, a movement that anticipated the political idealism of the Romantic

Movement, espousing the rights of the individual, a Rousseau-esque return to nature, the championing of Shakespeare's freedom in dramatic writing, as opposed to the dramatic unities, and scurrying back down the corridors of time to find themes for plays in other countries and even more importantly, in distant epochs. This involved the first attempt at some kind of historical realism in stage settings and costumes. Almost every theme that was to launch Romanticism as a major shift in European sensibilities was to be found in *Sturm und Drang*.

Even in this group Lenz stood out as being different. For the modern reader his plays seem addressed to an audience several generations after they were actually written. For his contemporaries they must have been baffling indeed. He was constantly being rediscovered throughout the nineteenth and twentieth centuries. Georg Büchner wrote a novella on Lenz's descent into near madness, a sort of middle class Woyzeck, and Lenz's impressive theoretical work *Anmerkungen übers Theater* (*Observations on the Theatre*, 1774) might be seen almost as a blueprint for Büchner's dramatic approach in *Danton's Death* (1835), and *Woyzeck* (1836). Playwrights like Hebbel, Bleibtreu and Halbe acknowledged his influence on them. The German Naturalists in the 1880s claimed him as a kindred spirit. From 1910 Arthur Kutscher, director and critic, gradually kindled public enthusiasm for Lenz with exciting stagings of his plays, and since then they have been regularly performed as a small part of the standard repertory of German theatre. Bertolt Brecht adapted Lenz's *The Tutor* for the Berliner Ensemble in 1950. Yet if anything flashed before Lenz's eyes in his last moments on that Moscow street, it was more failure than success. His radically different play, *The Tutor*, had two performances in Hamburg, one in Berlin and over a decade a mere eleven in Mannheim. After that it was not performed for over a century.

What we can see with hindsight is that much of what Lenz stood for was disregarded or discarded as the Romantic movement gathered impetus. Indeed in a sense, by playing a part in the *Sturm und Drang* movment, he was presiding at his own literary funeral. He set out to write a new and radically different form of ironic drama at the very moment when Romanticism was about to rush off in almost every direction but the one he wanted to take. No wonder his plays met with a poor response at the time and were steadily neglected for a century after they were written. His friend Goethe was a sufficiently major artist both to encompass early Romanticism, be an influence within it, and still maintain many neo-classic attitudes and interests that were light years away from what Romanticism stood for. Lenz sank almost without trace. Happily he still spoke to a select few, and increasingly this century we have come to realise that he is remarkably well worth listening to.

Lenz can still surprise us. He was almost as much of a pioneer in the theatre as William Blake was in painting and poetry. Lenz's contribution was threefold. He set about creating what amounted to a new theatrical form. He was among the first writers anywhere, long before Marx, to perceive the importance of social class in human relationships. He seems to have been among the very first creators of fiction attempting both to depict and analyse the emotional tensions, unspoken but shatteringly powerful, that exist in various disguises within the domestic family circle, particularly between parent and child, sister and brother. These gifts did not come to him piecemeal. They are all apparent in his very first play, *The Tutor.*

This was partly the result of his own personal experience. Germany in the eighteenth century was in a state of growing social crisis. It is of course impossible to talk of Germany in the eighteenth century. The Holy Roman Empire consisted of a patchwork-quilt of little independent states, kingdoms, dukedoms, fiefdoms, ruled by all-powerful little despots, each supporting a court and a local aristocracy, depending as it had since feudal times on a labouring peasant class. Yet the increasing efficiency of the educational system was producing a middle class for which there were very few jobs, very little chance of status and position. This created a growing social tension which was only gradually resolved as industrialisation and increasing prosperity in the nineteenth century absorbed and greatly increased the new middle classes. In the 1770s it looked as though there was nowhere for the tiny, upstart middle class to go.

Lenz was very much a victim of this social process. Gifted, intelligent, educated, he spent his first year in Strasbourg as a "lackey-cum-companion" to the von Kleist brothers, sons of a local aristocrat, and a humiliating year it must have been. It was during this year, 1771, that he wrote *The Tutor*. At the same time he was gradually coming into closer contact with Goethe, Jung-Stebbing, Klinger, Wagner, Herder and Salzmann, the group which later became labelled as *Sturm und Drang*. They did not behave as later artistic groups were to do, the pre-Raphaelites in England or *Das Junge Deutschland* or the Naturalists in Germany and issue a *pronunciamento*, form a society, publish a periodical, or agree a basic set of principles. Rather it seems as though meeting with each other sharpened and intensified that vital emphasis of Romanticism, the awareness of the self as an individual, subjectively relishing and exploiting the uniqueness of a single imaginative vision. Perhaps nowhere else in Europe was the middle class so frustrated, so aware of its emasculated state as the aristocrats comfortably controlled the levers of power and authority. Even so it was a major achievement for the young Lenz to grasp objectively the role of the aristocracy as a social class and present it in a dramatic form that made the concept so apparent to his audience.

Läuffer, the tutor of the play, is humiliated by the aristocrats he works for. When he expresses an opinion about a ballet dancer, contrary to the Count's, he is publicly rebuked and sent to his room. His salary is arbitrarily reduced without consultation. He is never given the use of a horse as promised. Yet perhaps the key point is the blundering reply of the major when his brother, von Berg, asks why he has a tutor for his children. The major clearly has a tutor because he feels his social position calls for it, a matter of class vanity, rather than because he knows or understands the purpose of education, much less cares about what is actually being taught to his children, nor does his wife. Läuffer's father, although prosperous will not pay for him to achieve a university post. Von Berg will not consider him for a teaching post at the local school. The major is unwilling to use his influence to get Läuffer a post in the civil service. Läuffer is at their mercy, humiliated and helpless. The moment when Läuffer's bitter mood is transformed to servility as he sees the von Berg brothers come down the street, and they in turn fail to notice him at all (as aristocrats they only see other aristocrats), is exactly paralleled, is indeed made the central point of Gogol's novella *The Overcoat*. Yet Gogol was published in 1842. Lenz is making the same point, and getting his audience to think objectively about it in the early 1770s.

In the same way his insight into family relationships would seem to stem from his own experience. Büchner, although medically qualified, was only 23 when he wrote his novella, *Lenz,* giving an account of Lenz's descent into near madness. This account was closely based on the notes of Pastor Oberlin with whom Lenz was staying at the time in 1778. For a post-R D Laing generation it is clear from this detailed account that Lenz was schizophrenic. It has even been suggested that much of Laing's insight into this condition stemmed from his own mental struggles. Büchner, although trying imaginatively to be sympathetic and certainly telling the story from Lenz's point of view, was writing in 1835 and could not begin to grasp the emotional and mental complexities with which he was dealing. A closer study of Lenz's plays might have helped him. Lenz shows the kinds of insight into family behaviour that Laing's psychiatric studies in *The Self and Others* and *The Divided Self,* have now made more familiar territory. Laing was writing in the 1960s, Lenz in the early 1770s.

What are we to make of the major's wife's clear need to control and humiliate the tutor before she can feel at peace with herself? Von Berg, while shown as an upholder of new and liberal ideas about education, is quite unable to take the pastor's point about young middle-class men being victims of the system because that would have meant confronting the aristocracy's refusal to relinquish any of its powers. And how quickly von Berg reverts to type when he discovers his son, Fritz, and his niece, Gustchen, are in love. Lenz sees the members of a family as being in conflict with each other, a conflict they can neither understand nor control, particularly those differences between the parents' view of their role and the emotional needs of their children. Von Berg sees the affair which has flourished in secret as a threat to his authority as a father, which he immediately sets about re-establishing. Having made the lovers feel small by making fun of them he then imposes impossible conditions. They are not to meet in private and he is to read their letters when Fritz is away at university. Punishment at disobedience will be severe. Fritz will join the army, Gustchen will go to a convent. At one level he appears to be controlling their love in their best interests, but he is in effect destroying it in such a way as to make it seem that the collapse of the affair will be their own fault.

As Edward McInnes has pursuasively pointed out in a perceptive paper on *The Tutor,* what a contrast this represents between the man who has extolled the power of choice to educational growth and the father setting out to destroy any possibility of choice for these two lovers. He never attempts to see things from their point of view. It is his sense of how things should properly be arranged that is outraged. Father and son are locked in conflict for the rest of the play, although they do not see this consciously, because the victims of family conflict in Lenz never seem able to communicate their feelings of fear and emotional distress, much less analyse the process by which those they are supposed to love oppose their deepest wishes. This is familiar Laing territory, but in 1771? The major's family relationships read even more like a Laing case study. A conservative and proud officer, he cannot cope with a sexually dominant wife and as a result bullies his son, thus demonstrating his authority to her which she increasingly undermines. This creates an ever widening spiral of emotional tension. He compensates by expecting too much for his daughter and fantasising about her future so that she is made to feel inadequate. Where else in the 1770s can we find these kinds of perceptive understanding?

Surely what we are dealing with here is the stuff of tragedy. It is perhaps in his awareness of the need for a new dramatic form through which to present his insights that Lenz is at his most revolutionary. And he had few models. No member of the *Sturm und Drang* had published a play when Lenz wrote *The Tutor*. Goethe had started *Götz von Berlichingen* and had probably discussed it with Lenz. And that year saw the first mention of *Faust* as a project. Only in 1776 did Leisewitz's *Julius von Tarant*, Klinger's *Die Zwillinge* and *Sturm und Drang*, and Wagner's *Die Kindermörderin* or Lenz's own *Die Soldaten*, begin to give the group some dramatic credentials. Lenz was a pioneer.

In 1774 Lenz published his major theoretical work *Anmerkungen übers Theater*, a paean of praise for Shakespeare, seen not only as the best dramatist of the modern age, but as genius and prophet of all that was best in Christian culture. Above all, Shakespeare was praised for his creation of the outstanding individual, heroic before an awesome destiny, embodying individual will and representing mankind's endless striving towards the spiritual. Lenz was nothing, if not committed. Gerstenberg in his *Literaturbriefe* (1766), and Goethe in *Shakespeare-Rede* (1771), had praised Shakespeare's ability to create believable individuals in believable situations. Lenz sees the development of the individual hero interacting with events and other characters as the essence of Shakespeare's drama. The hero as individual is the play's very stuff and justification. The old Aristotelian unities should be replaced by a new, single unity, the unity of character. And a central figure alone could be the unifying force that held a drama together. This for Lenz was the essence of tragedy.

Lenz did not grasp the secret of the effectiveness of Renaissance tragedy. The old sense of social order and religious certainty was breaking up, but was still powerful. The new sense of individualism, of a testing of the limits of the possible, an exploration of new experiences and a demand for new meanings as the old retreated, created a fascinating tension between old and new that was at the heart of Elizabethan tragedy. By the eighteenth century, the age of rationalism, the old medieval certainties had lost too much of their hold. The tension was gone. Where in Elizabethan plays, rank implies a social hierarchy, a view of order and justice, by the eighteenth century at best this had narrowed down to sympathy and pity between private persons. Pope was simply out of date when he praised Addison's *Cato* as:

> A brave man struggling in the storms of fate
> And greatly falling with a falling State.

Addison's tragedy was a hollow façade based on earlier models. The greatness, the sense of social order and religious certainty the State used to mean, had crumbled away. Cotes was nearer the mark:

> What pen but yours could draw the doubtful strife
> Of honour struggling with the love of life?

Raymond Williams, who contrasts both these quotations in his *Modern Tragedy*, goes on to talk of bourgois tragedy as not being social enough:

> For with its private ethic of pity and sympathy it could not negotiate the real contradictions of its own time between human desire and the new social limits set on it… We hear the first weak accents of man the victim: the old far-reaching heroism has gone.

Williams suggest that it is not enough to look at the isolated martyr, but rather we should look at the social process of his martyrdom:

> And at this point we reach the profoundly ambiguous question, is it not a sin against life to allow oneself to be destroyed by cruelty and indifference and greed?

Writing on Brecht he says:

> In most modern drama, the best conclusion is: yes, this is how it was. Only an occasional play goes further, with the specific excitement of recognition: yes, this is how it is. Brecht at his best reaches out and touches the necessary next stage: yes, this is how it is, for these reasons, but the action is continually being replayed and it could be otherwise. The trap at this last moment is the wrong kind of emphasis on the undoubted fact that it could indeed be otherwise. To make it clearly otherwise by selecting the facts…is to go over to propaganda or to advertising.

What was so prescient about Lenz was his recognition in 1771 that Renaissance tragedy no longer worked, and a new theatrical form was required. The theatre needed a new kind of play, not hopefully the bourgeois tragedy that involved the "first weak accents of the victim", but a look at the "social process." He called his first play a tragedy, but by the time of publication after much heart searching and playing with alternatives he opted for the word comedy. This and his later plays are certainly concerned with the human condition, but it is a social condition. In a series of short scenes he invites his audience to consider the social forces that produce a given set of characters. And yet he is almost Shakespearian in his skill at bringing his characters to life as believable individuals in believable situations. And there is an unspoken corollary. If the social conditions were to change, "it could be otherwise."

When he wrote *The Tutor* he was dealing with a given audience accustomed to a given kind of theatre. The idea of a comedy on education must have reassured them, particularly with its subtitle, *The Tutor* or *The Advantages of Private Education* suggesting a mildly satiric view of a particular profession along such well-worn lines as Lessing's *Der junge Gelehrte* (1747), Krüger's *Die Candidaten* (1748), or *Die Geistlichen auf dem Lande* (1743), and Mylius's *Arzte* (1745). Specific plays on education like Molière's *Ecole des Femmes* or Gottsched's *Die Hausfranzösin* had already paved the way. Yet once Läuffer begins to reveal his true feelings the effect on the modern reader is surprisingly similar to Jimmy Porter's effect on British audiences in Osborne's *Look Back in Anger* in 1956; in spite of its shortcomings, it is still a saying of things that needed to be said, a breaking of a conventional tabu of silence, a facing up to changing circumstances. Porter was castigating a middle-class establishment, Läuffer was taking a hard look at the aristocrats. *The Tutor*'s actual performances were few and unsuccessful, unlike Osborne's play, but it was, nevertheless, published, read and discussed.

The plot soon gathers impetus. As we realise that Läuffer and Gustchen are caught in the same kind of trap, both longing for what they cannot have, both alienated by their very longings from the actual pressures that surround them, they have a sexual encounter. Nothing could be further from the grandeur of Romantic passion. Neither grasps the reality of the partner as another person, they clutch at each other as a brief escape from the real world which imprisons them. Neither shows much comitment or loyalty to the other. As soon as their guilty secret is discovered they flee in different directions, Läuffer to Wenzeslaus, a village schoolmaster, Gustchen to a blind beggar woman in the forest. The action of the play is now divided. Parents are separated from children, children from each other. The major searches for Gustchen. Gustchen, unable to carry the burden of her guilt at having a child, throws herself into a lake. Läuffer comes across the supposedly orphaned child and, overwhelmed by guilt, castrates himself. Fritz, learning that Gustchen is dead and was seduced by the tutor, is overwhelmed with guilt just as Läuffer was. The audience knows that Gustchen is not dead at all, which adds a fresh touch of absurdity to the whole proceedings. The readiness of everybody to shoulder guilt for what has not even happened, when the play is showing us just the opposite, that the characters, far from imposing themselves on events and taking responsibility for their actions, are themselves the uncomprehending victims of a social system they have no hope of controlling adds yet another layer of absurdity. Nobody is in control, nobody is a free agent. Lenz then adds a final icing to the layer cake. Against all the odds everything turns out happily. Patus, Fritz's friend, wins heavily in a lottery and can pay both their debts and bring them home. The major arrives at the lake precisely as Gustchen throws herself in. And from nowhere a beautiful girl dedicates herself to a spiritual love and life with Läuffer.

We know about Lenz's theory of comedy because he wrote about it, not only in his *Anmerkungen übers Theater*, but in his article, *Recension des Neuen Menoza*, which appeared in the *Frankfurter geleherte Anzeiger* in 1775. Lenz sees characters in comedy as being at the mercy of the plot, structured around a crisis which Lenz calls a *Sache*, and swept along as the complications develop. He also claims that comedy can be a form dramatists can use to present both grim and upsetting facts to an audience intent only on enjoying themselves. Whether the characters are controlled by the twists of the plot, or by a social system that imprisons them in a given set of class responses, the point is that in comedy they have little or no chance to assert themselves as individuals, much less impose themselves on events. Lenz sees this as the crucial difference from tragedy. In a tragedy the hero grows before our eyes, acquires new insights, changes and matures as a person, controls, or at least attempts to control the course of events. In a comedy the characters achieve no insight, cannot change. Von Berg remains the same father at the end of *The Tutor* as at the beginning. He accepts his son's apology. He never sees that he himself has precipitated disaster. Nothing is resolved except the plot – and the more arbitrarily that is managed, the more effectively Lenz is making his point. It is of course a humourous ironic point. German critics are notorious for having difficulties with humour, particularly irony. They have struggled with Lenz' ending to the *The Tutor* and, in general, dismally failed to understand it. In England Sheridan in *The Critic* does much the same as Lenz, at much the same time, in the conclusion to his glorious subplot, when true identities are revealed. "This is your father, this your mother, these your uncles, these your aunts, these your cousins." English critics happily responded to an equally improbable parody of theatrical form and, incidentaly, a gorgeous send-up of the critic's role. German audiences, readers, critics have been less responsive to Lenz. Even Brecht, in his adaptation of *The Tutor*, irons out much of the irony. Lenz deserved better of his countrymen.

The Soldiers, published in 1776, the very year a middle-class America was doing rather well against an aristocratic Britain, is an easier play. It is the most accessible of all Lenz's plays and because parts of it seem old-fashioned and dated, audiences can comfortably patronise it and find it charming without being too upset by it. Eighteenth-century views of women, views of chastity, views of pre-marital sex, views of the married state, now sound archaic. The *Weltanschauung*, the mind set, of a society entering the twenty-first century has moved on and left most of this unnecessary baggage behind.

Yet just as in the ballet *Giselle*, created in 1841 and loaded with Romantic flummery, but still holding its place in the ballet repertory, there comes a moment of recognition as the aristocrat, Albrecht, deceives the peasant girl, Giselle, and one can almost hear the women in the audience thinking "yes, that is what men are really like, they'll lie and cheat and deceive, they're all after the same thing!" So *The Soldiers* has its moments of recognition.

The soldiers are aristocrats, officers. They amuse themselves with seducing pretty tradesmen's daughters, ruining the girls' reputations in the process, but tempting them with dazzling prospect of marriage into the aristocracy. And the girls pursue the bubble reputation even in the cannon's mouth. Lenz is consciously inviting his audience, not only to see the officers as representatives of an aristocratic class, but much more importantly to think about the role of that aristocratic class in society as a whole. Chaucer shows us bad priests. He never expects us to question the role of priests. Lenz was pushing his audience into asking far more searching questions about the social responsibilities of the aristocracy. The French revolution was still thirteen years in the future, and Lenz's play was in many ways a revolutionary tract. Yet his characters are not cyphers. Once again he has a gift for sharp observation, for creating believable characters in believable situations, so that Marie, the daughter of a fancy goods dealer in Lille, is all too believable as an ambitious flirt, dazzled by the material things of life, only too ready to play with fire.

Once again, Lenz deliberately overplays his ending. We can perhaps still take the melodrama as her original lover poisons the man who has done her wrong. But when the father, faced with a woman whom he suspects to be a prostitute, begins fearfully to apprehend he may be talking to his own fallen daughter, "was your father a dealer in fancy goods?" is a line which deserves to rank with "out, out, into the cold snow" as one of the mightier clichés of melodrama. Once again, nobody changes, nobody grows and matures before our eyes, nobody gains fresh insights. Once again they are the creatures of chance and social conditioning. A freak combination of circumstances brings them together. By stressing the implausibility at the end, Lenz is nudging us into a recognition of the sheer absurdity of the human condition with our responses fixed by the way society has conditioned us, immersed in events we cannot hope to control. The shock of recognition here is a jolt to complacency even in the twenty-first century. In the eighteenth it must have seemed considerably more than that.

The New Menoza (1776), is a less accessible play, more difficult to read, more difficult to stage. It represents more of a challenge, because in it Lenz is looking not so much at life as at the theatrical conventions of his time. It is as though, rather than hold the mirror up to nature, he starts playing tricks with the mirrors. We must remember the predominance of theatre as a medium for fiction in Lenz's day. In England the words poet and playwright were almost interchangeable even at the end of the seventeenth century. The novel was only beginning its long rise to dominance as a literary form.

Cinema, radio, television lay far in the future. Not only writers, but audiences had almost nowhere else to go for imaginative fiction. Lenz could therefore count on the audience recognising the conventions he was making fun of.

The title is based on a Danish novel by Pontoppidan, translated into German in 1742, using the then popular formula of an oriental visitor looking at European customs as a method for objective social comment. Once again it is easy to see why the Naturalists rediscovered Lenz in the 1880s. Although they are characters in scenes which are poking fun at the different theatrical genres of the day, the characters still come vividly to life, flaring into believable existence before our eyes in a brief moment of theatrical glory. They are not really naturalistic at all, since as the same characters appear in different plots they adapt into the style of each.

The diversified plot is gorgeously complex. It is not intended to be taken seriously, yet in its own crazy way it hangs delightfully together and makes a bizarre kind of sense. Naumburg is recognisably small-town Saxony; philistine, affluent fathers misunderstand melancholy scholarly sons. Wilhelmina is beautiful, naive, unspoilt as heroines should be. Across this basic setting a variety of subplots burst like coloured streamers, each highlighting a particular kind of theatre. Prince Tandi represents the "Europe as seen through the eyes of a foreign visitor" approach. He travels to seek enlightenment. The young men Herr Zierau and Master Beza visit him to discuss philosophy, and of course we marvel at the superior wisdom he brings from exotic foreign lands. He falls for Wilhelmina, and courteously agrees to wait five years in Germany until she decides to return with him to Qumba. In mid drama we are led to believe the Prince and Wilhelmina are actually brother and sister, but a further revelation is in store. Wilhelmina is a changeling and all will therefore turn out for the best.

The Donna Diana subplot is fairly standard Spanish melodrama. Passionate and wicked, she poisons her father, steals her mother's jewels and elopes with the seducer Count Chameleon to Dresden. The Count, after failing to get his manservant Gustav to kill her, flees to Herr von Biederling, tells him he has killed a man in a duel, and is allowed to hide secretly in a house in the garden. Donna Diana tracks him down because Gustav, the manservant, is in love with her. She kills the Count and Gustav hangs himself. Donna Diana is not really a Spanish aristocrat, but a von Biederling.

The Count Chameleon subplot is again a tilt against the power of the aristocracy. The Count ruthlessly uses the von Biederlings, making Frau von Biederling fall for him because he is in love with Wilhelmina and needs her mother's help to obtain the daughter's hand in marriage. Prince Tandi challenges him to a duel, but the Count in typically villainous style will not fight. The Count throws a masked ball, ostensibly for Wilhelmina's pleasure, but really so that he can take her into a side room and rape her. Here the theatrical convention of changed identities and masks is used delightfully. Wilhelmina does not go to the party, Donna Diana takes her place, the Count finds himself raping the very woman he wants to avoid, Donna Diana stabs him, the various subplots have all interlocked in fine style and the play ends with Herr Zierau complaining at the sheer monotony of life in Naumburg.

Lenz became a sad victim of increasing mental instability. He was the son of a pastor and studied theology at Dorpat and Königsberg. He had a depressing tendency to fall in love with women associated with men around him whom he should have avoided antagonising. At Strasbourg he made advances to Friederike Brion, an affair of Goethe's, and Cleophe Fibich, a fiancée of one of the von Kleist brothers. In 1775 he convinced himself he was in love with Henriette von Waldner, an aristocrat engaged to someone else, although she was scarcely aware of Lenz at all. In 1776 he seems to have behaved so tactlessly and oddly that he had to leave Weimar and seems to have lost the respect and affection of Goethe, who wrote in *Dichtung und Warheit* of Lenz's general instability. After becoming more and more unstable, he had to return in 1778 to his family in Riga, probably not exactly a calming environment, and three years later Lenz went to Russia, first to St. Petersburg and then to Moscow where he died eleven years after leaving his Baltic homeland. He wrote other plays (the long lost manuscript of one of them was found in Hamburg in 1971) and his works were first collected and published in Germany 1828, again in 1900 and again in 1967. The letters were published there in 1918 and again in 1969. His poems were published separately there in 1968.

8

Coleridge – Remorse

Samuel Taylor Coleridge (1772-1834) has left an indelible mark on British literature and culture. We would be slightly different people if he had never lived. And yet his actual achievements, in terms of books written and poems completed, remain depressingly slight. For a time he was a young man full of promise, then he became a slightly fraudulent man full of promises, then a self acknowledged drug addict, and finally, and perhaps most preposterously of all, a grand old man of English letters.

He retained, all his life, an amazing capacity to impress those around him with his intelligence and erudition. He could say striking things, be passionate about ideas, and was undoubtedly challenging and rewarding company for many of his contemporaries, although there remains a sneaking doubt about the calibre of those he charmed. There is Max Beerbohm's celebrated cartoon of Coleridge obviously boring the rest of the company as he goes relentlessly on and on, and Madame de Stael's famous verdict, "*Avec M. Coleridge, c'est tout a fait un monologue.*"

With hindsight it is possible to see that he played with ideas like a wayward child, planning to do the most exciting projects, only to toss them carelessly aside and take up some new enthusiasm, until playing with ideas became almost a substitute for life. He did not experience the actual events of living so much as have fanciful, poetic and intelligent ideas about them. He had a wife, but he did not live with her, nor did he face up to the real problems of supporting her. He had children, but he was not involved in the actual business of bringing them up. He had relationships, made deep friendships, but they did not last. He moved on as it were to fresh circles, new acquaintances ready to come round and play with him the latest games with the newest ideas before and after tea-time. Perhaps his very eloquence was his own undoing. It clearly became much more fun to talk about doing something than to do it.

In that world it would be difficult to find anything he was not. Poet, playwright, philosopher, critic, theologian, moralist, lecturer, he still cannot fail to impress.

He had a tough schoolboy upbringing at Christ's Hospital where savage beatings enforced rigid rules. On hearing in later life of the death of one of his schoolmasters, Coleridge remarked, "Poor JB! – may all his faults be forgiven; and may he be wafted to bliss by little cherub boys, all head and wings, with no bottoms to reproach his sublunary infirmities!"

Even at school he impressed his contemporaries. Charles Lamb has written of him there, "Come back into memory, like as thou wert in the dayspring of thy fancies, with hope like a fiery column before thee – the dark pillar not yet turned – Samuel Taylor Coleridge – Logician-Metaphysician-Bard! How have I seen the casual passer-through the cloisters stand still, entranced with admiration to hear thee unfold, in thy sweet and deep intonations, the mysteries of Iamblichus, or Plotinus (for even in those years thou waxedst not pale at such philosophic draughts), or reciting Homer in his Greek, or Pindar while the walls re-echoed to the accents of the inspired charity boy." It will be noticed that Lamb refers to the "dark pillar" ahead. In later years the young Hazlitt also was to fall under the spell of Coleridge, only to fall out with him, as disenchanted with the performance as he had been enchanted by the original promise.

At Cambridge, Coleridge made a terrible mess of things. Enrolling in 1791, intended for the Church, he was by 1793 so overloaded with debt and blighted love that he fled from the university and in a wildly unlikely gesture, took the King's shilling in a regiment of light dragoons. In the first of many such manoeuvres, friends rallied, arranged his release, and his return to the university, where, in 1794, he began the friendship with Southey that was to colour so much of his early life.

Romanticism, that powerful impulse that was to change western culture so effectively, was already well under way. Coleridge was not only to reflect its values, but himself be one of the many influences that shaped its early days. Southey as an undergraduate was a fiery revolutionary. The French Revolution, with all its promise of a brave new world of Fratenity, Equality and above all Freedom, had started auspiciously in 1789, even if it was on the edge of the Terror in 1793. Responding to the dominant Southey, Coleridge became a revolutionary too. Along with Robert Lovell they planned a "Pantisocracy", a new utopian society on the banks of the Susquehanna. Like so many programmes associated with Coleridge, it came to nothing, but as part of the plan, Coleridge was allocated one of three Fricker sisters, Southey and Lovell each taking one of the two remaining. History has judged that Coleridge did not find himself with the best of the three, but however much of a paragon either of the others proved, would that have helped? Coleridge was a disaster area. The marriage to Sara Fricker in 1795 was probably never destined to be a success. What it meant however was that the strong feelings Coleridge was later to inspire in Dorothy Wordsworth had to remain unacknowledged and repressed until her finely-tuned and imaginative sensibilities finally collapsed under the strain. Coleridge seems to have been only half aware of the impact his charm, his gift for mildly flirting with the opposite sex, was then having on Dorothy. At that time, although he was married, his inclinations were firmly centred on yet another girl within the charmed circle of their extraordinarily sensitive group.

It almost goes without saying that Coleridge left Cambridge without taking a degree, thus dashing any chances of a comfortable life in the Church. What matters is the six years of his deep friendship, 1797-1803, with Wordsworth. It is worth remembering that neither wrote anything of any distinction until each had a considerable effect upon the other. Coleridge was also having a considerable effect upon Dorothy, who in a close and loving relationship with her brother, was also having a considerable influence on Wordsworth himself. Wordsworth was to prove a major poet, one of the precious few. It is no exaggeration to suggest that Coleridge was in effect the equivalent for Wordsworth of a challenging six years at a remarkably stimulating university. Coleridge was just what he needed at that particular stage of his development. But the traffic was far from being one way. Wordsworth had been in touch with real life. He had participated in the French revolution, had had a French mistress and indeed an illegitimate child. He had attempted to become a French citizen, had even possibly been involved with spying on developments in France as a British agent (much as Marlowe had been before him?). He must have done much to drag Coleridge back into the real world.

They finally agreed to function in different spheres of poetic creation. Wordsworth would attempt to display the value of real life, often in its humblest forms, while Coleridge, inevitably, would plump for the fanciful, the romantic, the supernatural. They produced together *Lyrical ballads* in 1798, a second edition with a second volume appearing in 1800. Each had sparked some of his best work from the other.

It is possible, indeed it has been proved possible, to trace almost all of Coleridge's most famous poem, *The Ancient Mariner*, as source material in his wide reading, particularly in travel books of the period. Fascinating as this exercise is, it is of course, the use he made of his material that distinguishes him as a creative poet. Yet it must also be said that this in some ways distinguishes him from other poets. Much of his source material was what he had read, not what he had observed. He was excited by words, by descriptions, by ideas, rather than by people, events, places, the look of actual things, how nature and the creatures within it actually worked. No reader is going to care a jot about this when faced with a masterpiece like *The Ancient Mariner*, *Christabel*, or the fragment *Kubla Khan*. Yet is it pushing the analogy too far to suggest that Coleridge was like a painter more excited by other painters than by the world around him, or to bring the analogy nearer home, what if I were writing these words not having read either Wordsworth or Coleridge, but only what other people had already written about them?

It cannot be emphasised too much that what matters is the final product, not how the writer gets there, but sadly in Coleridge's case, we increasingly do not get the final product. His poetic oeuvre is surprisingly small. Worse still, in much that he wrote or reputedly said in his lectures, there hangs an uneasy suspicion of downright plagiarism. Too much of the philosophy in *Biographia Literaria* (1817) seems to have been cribbed unacknowledged from Schelling, and many of his ideas in his literary lectures came from Schlegel. Yet it is impossible to dismiss *Biographia Literaria*, that long, rambling prose work mixing philosophy, politics and literary criticism.

Most literary critics cut their teeth on it and it is full of flashes of brilliance and dazzling insights, and did much to form our true understanding of Wordsworth's stature as a poet. Coleridge was writing at a time when literary criticism was becoming almost an art form in itself, and yet he still towers above contemporaries like Leigh Hunt, Hazlitt or Lamb.

Increasingly at the mercy of his opium habit, Coleridge seems to have in effect run away from all his domestic problems, touring the Mediterranean, and acting as secretary to the Governor of Malta during the years 1804-6. On his return, never again to resume quite the same intimacy with either Southey or the Wordsworth circle, he became increasingly part of London's literary scene, finally casting a questioning eye on the possibilities of having a play he had written in a flush of youthful enthusiasm actually performed on the London stage.

And how healthy was this London stage? Just as Turkey in the nineteenth century was to prove the "sick man of Europe", so drama in eighteenth and nineteenth-century London was to prove the "sick man of the arts".

Partly the blame must rest with Henry Fielding for being too good a playwright! But the causes lay deeper. The beastly Puritans had killed theatre dead. During the so-called Commonwealth – the republic set up in this country after the execution of Charles I – public theatre was forbidden. The popular tradition of theatre established by Shakespeare and his contemporaries was destroyed. When Charles II was restored to the throne in 1660, only two theatres, known as the Patent Theatres, were allowed to perform spoken drama, one patent going to Thomas Killigrew at Drury Lane and the other to Sir William Davenant (supposedly the illegitimate son of Shakespeare, which if true would have provided a bastard kind of continuity) at Lincoln's Inn Fields, which moved in 1732, after a spell in Dorset Gardens, to Covent Garden. There were however many other theatres, all of which had to pay lip service to the law by pretending not to be moving their lips! As a result all sorts of spectacles, musicals, operas, operettas, ballets, pantomimes and dumb show productions became popular. Words were allowed provided they were not the main element of the performance, and inevitably this led to more and more playing fast and loose with the presumed rules. Nobody seems to have noticed that this very process was changing popular tastes. Words were taking second place to spectacle, music and dance to such good effect, that gradually the popular taste they created forced changes in the patent theatres themselves.

This process was reinforced by the very success of Henry Fielding. In a small theatre at the Haymarket, "The little theatre at the Hay", after the dancing master Samuel Johnson had put on a burlesque called *Harlothumbro* to thunderous applause for thirty nights, Fielding had an equal success with *Tomb Thumb*, a delicious satire on heroic drama. (In our own time the adventurous theatre impresario Michael Codron had a similar success putting on the same play as an undergraduate at Oxford.) The play had a subtext of quite vicious attack on the government of the day, and the following year in *The Welsh Opera* Fielding not only overtly pilloried the government but cheerfully caricatured the King, the Queen and the Prince of Wales as well. After a further hit with *Don Quixote in England*, a stinging attack on electoral corruption, Fielding took over the management of the theatre and produced his *Pasquin* in 1736 and worse still, *The Historical Register for the Year 1736*. The much satirised government could take it no longer and in 1737 passed the Licensing Act, not only reinforcing the position of the two patent theatres, but imposing a fierce censorship on the drama, all new plays having in future to be submitted for approval to the Lord Chamberlain's office. This was not abolished until 1968.

By reinforcing the privileges of the two patent theatres, the government was in effect giving a powerful boost to other forms of theatre – spectacle, dancing, singing, musicals, pantomimes – and by making them even more popular, ensured that the taste for them would inevitably infiltrate even the two patent theatres. Sadly it was doing even more. Creative artists do not like censorship. Henry Fielding is a good example. His theatre was forced to close and became temporarily derelict, Fielding transferred his writing talents to the uncensored world of the novel, and became one of our finest novelists. The novel's gain was the theatre's loss. Writers who might have previously turned to the theatre as a vehicle for their talents, found a much greater freedom in writing novels. The nineteenth century is the age of the novel. It is definitely not the age of the theatre.

At the beginning of the nineteenth century, Coleridge was not alone in wanting to write for the theatre. Alongside Wordsworth and Southey, he represented one generation, the next up and coming set of poets Byron, Keats and Shelley also experimented with dramatic forms, and their failure is perhaps the saddest indictment of the drama's condition in their time. The poets were there, ready and willing to ply their trade, but the drama of their day had been "dumbed down" to such an extent that writing for it was probably as impossible and unlikely as asking T S Eliot to write for Disney (although his poems were used in *Cats*).

Yet in 1813 Coleridge's *Remorse* was put on at Drury Lane Theatre and proved a smash hit, making him more money than anything else he ever wrote. It was widely and favourably reviewed, was put on in provincial theatres, and was still being occasionally revived decades after its first production.

Popular taste was changing and at an accelerating rate. Coleridge had originally submitted his play, then entitled *Osorio* to Richard Brinsley Sheridan, the manager at Drury Lane Theatre, in 1797. Sheridan was well read, particularly in drama, and probably noticed the similarities between the youthful Coleridge's piece and *Die Rauber* (The Robbers) written by the 22-year-old Schiller and first performed fifteen years earlier in Germany in 1782. Schiller's play had taken Europe by storm, been widely translated, and was also about two brothers, one good, one bad, both also in love with the same woman, also set in the past, the sixteenth century, and also about revenge and remorse. At that time Sheridan had rejected it out of hand, but that had been nearly nineteen years ago.

These days we are accustomed to changes in popular attitudes. Little more than a decade ago, New Zealand was seriously proposing legislation that would herd homosexuals onto an offshore island where their supposed moral corruption would taint nobody but themselves. Now, even in Auckland, not even the capital of New Zealand, there is an annual gay pride carnival. Even in the Catholic Republic of Ireland attitudes to abortion have undergone a similar sea change in much the same period of time.

Coleridge in *Osorio* was anticipating many of the attitudes that were to become part and parcel of romanticism, attitudes which *Lyrical Ballads* both reflected and itself reinforced, as had Schiller's *Die Rauber*. By 1816 the London world was a very different place from 1797.

Drury Lane Theatre was different too. On 20th September 1808 the theatre burned spectacularly to the ground. The whole length of the facade from Drury Lane to Bridges St was alight. James Boaden wrote, "Never before did I behold so immense a body of flame; and the occasional explosions that took place were awful beyond description." Sheridan was ruined. He lost almost everything, but kept his brilliance at repartee. He sat with friends watching the disaster in the Piazza Coffee House, and to someone amazed at his calm he replied insouciantly, "A man may surely be allowed to take a glass of wine at his own fireside." Samuel Whitbread, a fellow sharer with Sheridan in the patent, saved the day by raising £400,000 to build a new theatre designed by Wyatt, which opened in 1812, essentially the theatre still in use today, then controlled by a committee, with Samuel Arnold as the theatre manager. Sheridan's reign was over. It was this committee, led by Samuel Whitbread, which decided to put on Coleridge's play, now entitled *Remorse*. Fortunately for Coleridge, they had probably never heard of Schiller's *Die Rauber*, much less read it.

Even so, what made them choose *Remorse*? Where Byron, Shelley and Keats were all to fail, what qualities did Coleridge's play possess that both made that committee opt for it, and proved them right in their decision? It should be remembered that it was in this very theatre as late as the 1870s that its despairing manager, F B Chatterton laid it down that "Shakespeare spells ruin and Byron bankruptcy." Yet Coleridge's *Remorse* kept the box office cheerful with the reassuring sound of a stream of money clinking over the counter.

Melodrama has been defined as, "Outrageously unlikely characters, in impossible situations, behaving in preposterously unbelievable ways." Yet it was melodrama that held the stage of both patent theatres as the most popular dramatic form in 1813. Audiences wanted the sensational, the gory, the nasty, and especially the spectacular. Yet Whitbread and his fellow committee members wanted above all to be what was increasingly to become the dominant theme of the nineteenth century, they wanted to be "respectable". Coleridge was increasingly seen as a distinguished poet, and as the play was accepted, was embarking on a lecture series on the arts at the Surrey Institution in Blackfriars Road that was not only the height of respectability, but was to add to his reputation as one of the foremost minds of his time. Coleridge had been giving occasional series of public lectures since 1808. He seems to have been a born lecturer, establishing an excellent rapport with his audience, and impressing them, as he did everybody who knew him, with his wide-ranging discursive flow of ideas.

He was also very much alive to the possibilities of theatre, even the rather limited possibilities of the drama of his own time. Shakespeare was a huge disadvantage for would-be playwrights in the nineteenth century. Like an Old Man of the Sea, he weighed heavily on the shoulders of later generations. Eighteenth and nineteenth-century theatre was an age of actors not of playwrights, and outstanding actors kept Shakespeare very much alive even in heavily edited and truncated productions, because they wanted to play the mammoth parts that Shakespeare had created. Inevitably Coleridge was heavily influenced by Shakespeare's achievements, particularly by the subtle and revealing way Shakespeare shows the development of character, not only by the soliloquies which allow an audience to enter into a character's innermost thoughts, but by the dramatic action which moulds character and displays a personality changing and growing as a response to the pressure of events.

Yet the fashion of the day was for caricatures rather than real characters, for sensational events rather than subtleties, for simple set pieces rather than complexities. Somehow, if he was to be successful, and yet not altogether lose sight of his more ambitious aims to analyse real people, Coleridge had to strike a balance between these two almost opposing forces, between melodrama and spectacle on the one hand, and poetry and complexity of personality and believable situations on the other. *Remorse* represents an uneasy compromise between the two. Yet it would be idle to pretend this dilemma belongs only to 1813 and to Coleridge. Modern viewers of cinema and television often face much the same dilemma. Theatre spectacle has been replaced by fast paced cinematic action, but in a Schwarzenegger, a Stallone, a Mel Gibson, can we honestly maintain that melodrama is out of fashion? Or that complexity of character development has not been replaced by simple caricature, "unlikely characters in impossible situations, behaving in preposterously unbelievable ways"?

Coleridge was also mixing with a poetic hand, a potent theatrical brew which threw in together other major elements in romanticism. Alongside love of the sensational and melodramatic, romanticism also brought a new sense of alienation from society; a desire for radical political change; escapism, from one culture into another, from the present into the past; and above all, the new emphasis on the concept of romantic love. They are all to be found in *Remorse*. Above all, Coleridge was a poet, and some of his finest writing is to be found in *Remorse*. Leigh Hunt thought it "the only tragedy touched with real poetry for the last fifty years". Indeed small extracts had already appeared in *Lyrical Ballads*. The wonder is, not so much that *Remorse* was such a success in its own day, but rather why it has been almost totally ignored and forgotten in our own.

Surrounded by the early excesses of the industrial revolution, the arts did their best to pretend it was not happening. Escapism, fleeing anywhere but the actual present of the industrial city, was a typical feature of romantic art. *Remorse* was duly set well into the distant past, in the days of the Spanish Inquisition, but in Grenada. It was a fortunate choice of location. The Duke of Wellington's brilliant series of military successes in the Peninsular campaigns had made all things Spanish particularly popular and fashionable, and by bringing in the Moors as well, Coleridge added a suitable dash of further mystery and another exotic culture.

There is a fashionable hint too of radical political change, suitably diluted for popular consumption, when Isidore, the Moresco chieftain, disguised as a Christian, fights for the independence of a persecuted minority. His wife Alhadra, sparked up by his death, addresses his fellow Moors:

> That point
> In misery, which makes the oppressed man
> Regardless of his own life, makes him too
> Lord of the oppressor's. Knew I a hundred men
> Despairing, but not palsied with despair,
> This arm should shake the kingdoms of the world;
> The deep foundations of iniquity
> Should sink away, earth groaning from beneath them;
> The strongholds of the cruel men should fall,
> Their temples and their mountainous towers should
> fall;

This is the clarion call of the revolutionary. But it is anodynely set a long time ago, in a foreign country, and anyway, the wench is dead.

The symbol of alienation in fiction is often the long exile, and in the first lines of the play, Don Alvar speaks of his "long exile" from his homeland. But even more deeply embedded in the assumptions of the play is the power of romantic love. Dona Teresa the play's heroine, has remained faithful, as all romantic heroines must, to her true love and to her lover. It is around this concept that the complex and melodramatic plot revolves.

Don Alvar, the hero, on his return from a long exile, is shipwrecked before he can reach his beloved Dona Teresa, patiently waiting for him. His wicked brother, Ordonio, who also lusts after Dona Teresa, sends a Moor, Isidore, to kill him and to tell him that Teresa has abandoned true love. Ordonio then sets about seducing Teresa, believing Alvar to be dead. Alvar, far from being dead, has won the loyalty of Isidore, but not wanting to kill his brother in revenge, seeks ways to make him feel remorse and repentance for what he tried to do. It was at this point that far from setting up a revenge tragedy, Coleridge genuinely wanted to bring real people to life and show the effects of wrongdoing on a sensitive mind. As Crabb Robinson, who sat through the first night, later wrote, "His two great characters are philosophers of Coleridge's own school, the one a sentimental moralist, the other a sophisticated villain; both are dreamers." Alvar disguises himself, even playing a wizard, and gradually tricks Teresa into avowing her love, and Ordonio his guilt. Finally the lovers are re-united, Ordonio has repented, and Alhadra has inspired a Moorish rebellion against the oppressing Spaniards.

Underlying the whole plot was the romantic assumption that people are basically good. As Schiller found when trying to write tragedy, "Rousseau had closed the gates of hell". If people are basically good, it is only what a corrupt society does to them that makes them seemingly bad. Repentance and forgiveness are just around the corner. The happy ending when hero and heroine walk hand in hand into a technicolour sunset, had become *de rigueur*. Coleridge by this time was wrestling without success with an opium addiction that was ruining his chances, ruining his hopes of making the most of his undoubted talents. Was it his fault? Was he to blame? Could it have been otherwise? There must have been times for him when the gates of hell hung all too widely open in his private despair.

The brand new Drury Lane Theatre had been equipped with the very latest stage machinery, and Samuel Arnold, the manager wanted to show it off in a spectacular production. Coleridge was on hand to make alterations, to cut, edit and rewrite, and did so willingly. The play with its suggestions of the black arts, (it has a wizard), the pervading sense of threatening gloom and inner despair embodied in the romantic trappings of dungeons, caverns, rocky precipices, and the knowledge of evil committed and unatoned, cried out for spectacular stage effects, and seems to have positively wallowed in them. The plot was simplified and made more obviously sensational. At the end, the villain Ordonio, rather than being ignominiously hustled away to prison, was stabbed on stage by the Moor's wife Alhadra, apparently to great dramatic effect. But the high point of the production, and all who saw it are strangely unanimous on this, was a haunting moment in Act III.

Just as Hamlet put on a play within the play to elicit Claudius' guilt, so Alvar presented a picture of the supposed murder of himself, which his brother thinks has actually happened. A vast picture on stage was slowly lowered through a ring of fire, while a choir of monks sang in a suitable Gothic chapel and an additional chorus of boatmen sailed gradually across the stage. As if this was not enough, the Irish Michael Kelly composed music for the slowly sung recital of a spell to raise up Alvar's supposed ghost from the dead below. Happily for the play, Coleridge's words were equal to the dramatic weight of all this; holding the audience as if in a magic trance, as the last word died away.

> Hush! The cadence dies away
> On the quiet moonlit sea;
> The boatmen rest their oars and say
> Miserere Domine!

As Michael Kelly recalled, "a thrilling sensation appeared to pervade the great mass of congregated humanity, and at the conclusion the applause was long and protracted."

Samuel Arnold made such good use of his stage props, scene transformations, lighting and design, that added such a fresh dimension to the play of sheer spectacle, that nobody in the audience or even among the many enthusiastic reviews it received, seems to have noticed anything owed to Schiller. If they had, they might have noticed that in fine Shakespearian style, Coleridge had not so much borrowed as vastly improved upon Schiller's youthful play.

In his perceptive and fascinating *Coleridge:Darker Reflections*, Richard Holmes tells us that the play earned Coleridge over £400, a large sum in those days, that it was published and ran to three editions, and that it went into Drury Lane's regular repertory, earning the management profits between eight and ten thousand pounds, the equivalent these days of a quarter of a million. It was also played in most of the big theatres in the provinces, although, there being little copyright protection, Coleridge earned nothing from that.

Coleridge was on the crest of a wave in 1813. Good money was coming in, he planned a new play for Drury Lane, planned to publish some of his lectures, and to write a new book of poetry. None of this happened. Whenever Crabb Robinson called, Coleridge "was not at home (or rather not visible)". Coleridge was to live on until 1834, emerging from his opium addiction to reveal, every now and then, tantalising flashes of inspiration and rare ability, but in Shelley's horrifying words he was increasingly "A hooded eagle among blinking owls". We must be grateful that as well as the poetry, as well as the writings on politics, aesthetics, literature and philosophy, we have this distinguished play, revealing a fine poet at work and at home in the theatre in the first flush of romanticism. It is high time we saw it once again on the stage in a live theatre where it properly belongs.

9

Dumas – The Tower

Alexandre Dumas, born in 1802, had a parentage that seems almost too aptly prepared for the Romantic Movement. His father had been a general, a contemporary of Napoleon, in the French Revolutionary army, his grandfather a French aristocrat, his grandmother a black slave in San Domingo – even Lord Byron's background seems positively pallid in comparison. In the annals of French literature, the Alexandre Dumas who wrote *The Three Musketeers* and *The Tower* is known as Dumas Père, because his illegitimate son Dumas Fils, became in his turn the celebrated author of *La Dame aux Camelias.*

By the time he wrote *The Three Musketeers* in 1845, still undoubtedly his best known novel, and still very much in print, Dumas Père had become not so much an individual writer as almost an industry, and it is still debatable just how much that book owes to the efforts of others. It is based, event by event and far too closely for artistic respectability, on *The Memoirs of Monsieur d'Artagnon, Capitaine – Lieutenant of The First Company of The King's Musketeers* by Gatien de Courtilz, published in 1700. A record is kept in the Marseilles library that Dumas took the book out in 1843 and never returned it. Even so he collaborated closely with Auguste Maquet on the book. To be fair, when Dumas had previously wanted to acknowledge another such collaboration, his publisher refused. "Anything signed Alexandre Dumas is worth three francs a line – sign it Dumas and Maquet and it won't fetch thirty sous a line."

Naturally as Dumas became ever more famous, his collaborators resented their anonymity. In 1845 a pamphlet attacking him was published entitled *Manufacture Of Romantic Novels – The Firm of Alexandre Dumas and Co.*, purporting to tell all.

So it is not surprising to learn that *The Tower*, written in 1832, and Dumas' most famous play, also had similarly murky origins. It was based on a play by an aspiring writer, Frederick Gaillardet, who had given his manuscript to Harel, the manager of the Theatre de la Porte-Saint-Martin, where Dumas had already had great success with his historical melodrama, *Anthony*, in 1831. Harel first asked the critic, Janin, to attempt a re-write, but then asked Dumas to see what he could do with the play. Still on a sick bed after a cholera epidemic, Dumas duly "improved" the play, and even generously offered to take only a fee, leaving the authorship to Gaillardet alone. Harel preferred to advertise the play as by a set of asterisks and Frederick Gaillardet, and then after suitable haggling, agreed with Gaillardet to put the young man's name first, and then the asterisks. He then busily spread the real name of the second author by word of mouth. The play was a great success, and Dumas hence-forward insisted on including it in any list of his own works. Ultimately he and Gaillardet fought a duel, pistols not swords, over Gaillardet's claim that the play was really his. Neither managed to hit the other. The play continued a hit for 800 performances and was constantly revived. Years later Gaillardet asked that the name of Dumas should be coupled with his at a revival in recognition of "the large part his incomparable talent had in the success of the play." Posterity has been unkind to Gaillardet. There is no doubt we now think of the play as belonging very much to Dumas; and like the whole tribe of the other collaborators of Dumas, Gaillardet has largely sunk from sight.

Scurrilous pamphlets, duels, rival claims from disgruntled collaborators, none of these affected Dumas' growing reputation, nor his ever increasing public. Dumas learned his trade as a writer in the competitive and demanding world of the commercial theatre. He began by writing for vaudeville, but just as Hector Berlioz was so over-whelmed by the visit of an English theatre company playing Shakespeare to Paris in 1829, that they inspired his *Symphony Fantastique*, so they opened up fresh vistas for Dumas as well. (Berlioz fell even more heavily for a young actress in the company, Harriet Smithson, than he did for Shakespeare, marrying her in 1833 and emerging disillusioned from their relationship nine years later, but with his allegiance to Shakespeare undimmed.) Dumas had the artistic acumen and imagination to realise that the new romanticism and historical drama were made for each other, and his *Henri III et sa Cour* 1829, was perhaps the first triumph of Romantic theatre. This alongside other plays by Dumas busily scurrying back down the corridors of time for sensation and scandal, put him at the forefront of the Romantic movement, and brought him the friendship and admiration of Alfred de Vigny and Victor Hugo.

Recognising the creation of a new French theatrical genre – historical melodrama – Dumas, on a rising tide of affluence, built and financed the Theatre Historique, but like so many creative artists, his ambitions outreached his grasp of finance, and continually in debt in spite of his huge earnings, he saw his creation fail in 1850. Yet throughout his literary career he never deserted the theatre. Better known in the twentieth century for his novels, in fact he wrote almost a hundred plays, even turning many of his novels into subsequent plays. Even as a novelist he never lost sight of the theatre's immediacy, his effects are largely theatrical effects, one almost hears at the end of a chapter the audience's sudden gasp of surprise at the final twist, the last effective line before the curtain trundles down. It was not where he got his material, nor who assembled it for him, so much as what Dumas did with it that mattered. The name of Dumas was worth three francs a line because his touch was unique. "Nobody had read every Dumas book or seen every Dumas play, that would be almost as impossible as for any one person to have written every Dumas book and play – but everybody had read some Dumas." – "If a Robinson Crusoe exists in 1850 he must surely be about to read *The Three Musketeers*." – "The world, including France, learned its French history from Dumas." – "Does Dumas make you think? Hardly ever. Dream? Never. But turn page after compulsive page? Always!"

He was the great populariser of Romanticism. This new movement in art turned its back on the industrial revolution, then transforming the cities in which the artists of Romanticism actually lived, as they sought excitement in tear-jerking emotions, sentimental love at first sight, the macabre, the frightening and the supernatural, indeed almost anything that got away from the present – other cultures, other times, from medieval Scotland and oriental fantasy to historical romance.

The very industrialism that art largely ignored created a new middle-class audience, richer but far less discriminating and less demanding than the smaller more exclusively educated class an author could expect in the previous century. Dumas was writing for a mass readership, the first in history, and he gave them colourful, exciting heroics dressed up in the trappings of the past. *The Tower* is a prime example of what became for him a well tried formula.

One of the first questions today's audience will want answered is just how true to the actual historical facts as we know them, is the account given by Dumas. It is one thing for Shakespeare, in the name of dramatic licence, to massage and manipulate events and people into an order acceptable within the confines of the stage, the three to four hours of the performance, and the limits of the dramatically possible. With the understandable exception of *Richard III*, Shakespeare gave his audience a set of guidelines to enable them to understand and appreciate what had actually happened in the past. In his historical plays he was recreating a sense of national identity from a re-telling of events that were much closer to real life than to myth. Dumas was doing nothing so acceptable. He was re-writing, creating a set of bogus events, that bore almost no relation at all to the actual facts that history recorded, and his aim was to sensationalise, to startle his audience with horrific scandals and events.

It is true that the prestige of the French throne at the beginning of the fourteenth century was affected by the scandals associated with Philip the Fair's three daughters in law, Marguerite of Burgundy (married to the future Louis X), Jeanne of Poitiers (married to the future Philip V) and Blanche of the Marche (married to the future Charles IV). Jeanne's innocence was established and proclaimed by a Parlement, but Blanche and Marguerite were convicted of having had as lovers two gentlemen in waiting, Philippe and Gaultier d'Aulnay, who were duly executed. The two princesses were imprisoned in solitary confinement in the Chateau Gaillard. In due course Blanche entered a nunnery. Marguerite became an embarrassment when her husband later mounted the throne and wished to marry Clementia, daughter of the King of Hungary. Rather than face long drawn out negotiations with the papacy for a royal divorce, Louis X had his wife smothered in her cell between two mattresses. How enthusiastic his second wife was to ally herself to such a Bluebeard, history has not recorded, although Louis X was known to his people as Louis the Quarrelsome. Not the sort of husband a wife was likely to pick a quarrel with.

This incident, a royal princess committing adultery with a courtier, has been inflated by Dumas in *The Tower* into an astounding series of events. Marguerite, presented as queen, has had two children by a former lover. He reappears and blackmails her into giving him high office, but both are unaware that the two children, far from being put to death, are in fact none other than the two gentlemen in waiting, Philippe and Gaultier d'Aulnay, who both die in suitably lurid circumstances with a great deal of the nineteenth-century equivalent of tomato ketchup liberally bedaubing everything and everyone in sight.

As with farce, to which it is closely allied, melodrama is a theatrical genre which develops its own conventions. Characters are simplified and exaggerated, the good are absurdly good, and in just as much caricature, the bad are unbelievably bad. To be effective the genre requires a swift moving plot, full of unexpected twists and turns. It may be almost impossible to believe moments such as:

> *Enter GAULTIER covered in blood.*

GAULTIER: Marguerite… I give you back the key to the Tower…

MARGUERITE: Gaultier, I am your mother.

GAULTIER: My mother? My mother?

(*Horror – his hand and arm out to curse her.*) Then be dammed!

GAULTIER dies.

But the swift moving narrative, dealing out fresh surprises in spades, obviously carried its nineteenth-century audience inexorably onwards and away into a never-never land of thrills and fantasy.

For a modern audience scenes like these are hard to take. Already by the 1890s Wilde could say of Dickens that "it took a heart of stone not to laugh at little Nell". Whereas Dickens still succeeds as a writer at a variety of levels, even if his sentimentality can seem mawkish, Dumas seems less rich. At the level of exciting boys' adventure stories his books and plays still work – Dumas actually took one of his plots from Fenimore Cooper – but these days an adult readership expects a more perceptive approach to characters than Dumas' broad outlines of people. Rather than developing, changing, being affected by events and maturing as they interact with one another, Dumas' characters tend to remain the same from beginning to end. They are goodies and baddies at the start and they come to their inevitable good or bad end at the finish with a certain predictability. It is, to use Coleridge's term, difficult to suspend our disbelief.

It is only with an indulgent smile at the excesses of mid-nineteenth-century melodrama, once beloved by its less demanding audience, but now impossibly dated, that we can span the gap between ourselves and the different expectations of over 160 years ago. This only applies to melodrama. We are not, as yet, cut off to the same extent from a whole range of other Victorian arts, but we have lost their taste, in that first flush of Romanticism, for melodrama. Dumas began in the theatre where melodrama then reigned supreme, and the sure knowledge of what would "go with the public", of exactly what they wanted, was once his main strength. Paradoxically, to some, it is now his weakness. Melodrama is out of fashion. Yet perhaps if we can learn to view these cardboard heroes of outdated fiction with that indulgent smile, we will realise the very solid virtues Dumas still possesses. The fun and excitement of a fast moving story, a boyish enthusiasm for heroes and bravery which never quite leaves any of us, the deft turn and turn about of a plot that is still easy to follow, the colour and romance of a nostalgic past.

Even today whenever the weather gets rough at sea, the Greek fisherman of Lemnos, hoping to calm the evil spirit of Alexander the Great's mother, thought to be blindly seeking her son in the heart of the storm, shout into the wind "Alexander still lives."

Through all the vicissitudes of changing fashion as the years have hurtled by Alexandre Dumas still lives too, books in print, plays still performed. Audience's perceptions and expectations may have changed but in Dumas' works too, at the heart of the Romantic storm, something is still very much alive.

10

Feydeau – A Flea in her Ear

English audiences and critics have always patronised Georges Feydeau. It is almost as though they liked disliking him. His plays, when occasionally performed, have invariably been a success in Britain. But British audiences, even as they laugh, even as they are captivated by the ever more ludicrous twists and turns of inexorable logic, as the mechanism of the plot drives remorselessly onwards, remind themselves this is only farce, not real drama at all. Listen to George Bernard Shaw when still only a drama critic, reviewing a Feydeau comedy in 1896:

> To produce high art in the theatre the author must create persons whose fortunes we can follow as those of a friend or enemy; to produce base laughter, it is only necessary to turn human beings on the stage as rats are turned into a pit, that they may be worried for the entertainment of the spectators. Such entertainment is much poorer fun than most playgoers respect... I class the laughter produced by conventional farcical comedy as purely galvanic, and the inferences drawn by the audience that since they are laughing they must be amused...as a delusion... For we have had it again and again under various titles. Act I John Smith's house. Act II the rowdy restaurant or casino at which John Smith, in the course of his clandestine spree meets all the members of his household including the schoolboy and the parlourmaid; Act III his house next morning with the inevitable aftermath of the complexities of the night before: who that has any theatrical experience does not know it all by

heart. And now here it is again with a fresh coat of paint on it, and as rotten as ever underneath.

Jump forward a couple of generations to Kenneth Tynan, also reviewing a Feydeau play on a visit to France in 1966. He agrees with Marcel Achard that Feydeau was the greatest master of French comedy after Molière, but thinks that throughout French theatre:

> One must not expect to find plays about poor people. Paris audiences are predominantly middle class and they prefer drama to concern itself with people who, if not actually rich, at least have sound banker's references. Second, there is virtually no chance of seeing a realistic play about contemporary French problems. The kind of theatre that subjects everyday life to critical analysis goes against the national grain, partly because the French are too patriotic to relish self criticism on the public stage, but mostly because they do not regard everyday life, realistically handled, as a worthy theme for serious drama. The tradition of humanism, which maintains that the proper study of mankind is not just exceptional or representative men, but men of all kinds, considered as individuals, has never exerted much influence on French playwrights. The clash of ideas and principles is what mainly excites them. Ordinary human behaviour, in all its irrational variety, strikes them as petty and peripheral: reality is too untidy to suit their notion of art.

What breathes through both these reviews, however separated by time, is distinctly anti-French bias. The "tradition of humanism" is apparently catered for only on this side of the Channel. Perhaps we are wiser now. What both critics are expressing is surprise at the differences between the English and French theatres. Since France represented the dominant cultural ideology in Europe during the seventeenth and eighteenth centuries, when modern theatre was busily establishing itself, perhaps it would be more modest of us to talk about the difference between theatre in continental Europe and theatre in Britain, because it is we who are culturally out of step. Shaw and Tynan are effectively complaining about the same thing. Shaw wants "persons whose fortunes we can follow as those of a friend or an enemy". Tynan wants "men of all kinds, considered as individuals".

British theatre has developed its own tradition of naturalism, presenting believable people in believable situations, so that British audiences enjoy watching fully rounded characters interacting with each other, changing and developing before our eyes in their responses to each other and the action of the plot. Continental audiences have a different emphasis. As Tynan says "the clash of ideas and principles is what mainly excites them". A British audience watching *Hamlet* may well ask "Why does Hamlet take so long to make up his mind?" A Spanish audience, watching a play by Lope de Vega, Shakespeare's exact contemporary, would be asking "What is the moral of the play, what does it mean, what message is it trying to get across?" It is an important difference. Church drama, the main form of drama throughout Europe before the Renaissance, used drama as religious propaganda, emphasing the moral. The message was the purpose of the exercise. In the York mystery play Everyman the characters represent not people at all, but aspects of the personality, Beauty, Health, Intelligence and so on. Here can clearly be seen the origins of the later plays about ideas and principles. In Elizabethan and Stuart theatre the plays of Ben Jonson, with characters representing "humours" faithfully reflected the same developments that were taking place elsewhere on the Continent. Yet we see this as a weakness in Jonson. His characters are only types we say, as if that was not enough. The towering genius of Shakespeare pushed our theatre in a different direction. Shakespeare's plays are packed with individuals. The second sentry may only have a line of two, but Shakespeare brings him sharply into focus as a real person in a believable situation. The host of other dramatists around Shakespeare tended to follow his lead; and it is Shakespeare, not Jonson, who has been continually performed ever since, apart from the brief hiatus of the Puritan commonwealth when all theatre was banned. British audiences may therefore be bringing the wrong set of expectations to a Feydeau play, and although he succeeds as all great artists must, at a sufficient number of different levels to ensure his success and their satisfaction, the less blinkered their approach, the more they are likely to appreciate. For Feydeau is wonderfully, gloriously French. He too was part of a long and illustrious tradition. His most immediate influence, as on all French nineteenth-century drama, was Scribe. A B Walkley, the British drama critic wrote in 1925 that:

> Everything of value in the modern theatre, its intellectual dialectic, its emotional sincerity, its fundamental verisimilitude, has been a revolt against that shallow theatricality we call Scribism.

How revealing in the British critic is that emphasis on "sincerity" and "verisimilitude". Walkley put Scribe's success down to: "a natural instinct for the business, skill in meeting popular demand, and a certain mediocrity of mind". Scribe, born in 1791, his first play produced in 1815, wrote over 300 plays, not one of which is now performed. Yet in his day he dominated French theatre. He insisted on and theorised about the well made play, the *pièce bien faite.* Not well made in a classical sense. Not Aristotle's protasis (exposition), epitasis (complication) and catastrophe (unravelling). For Scribe, the well made play meant using the tricks of theatre conventions so that audiences were always gripped and held by the sheer theatricality of the action, always wanting to know and unable to guess what on earth was going to happen next. Scribe's immediate and more impressive successor in terms of serious drama was Sardou, and in comedy, Labiche. Feydeau owed Scribe and Labiche much. They prepared the ground, as it were, created an audience with a given set of expectations about comedy, and in their work we can already see the main elements and approaches that Feydeau was to perfect. We know, too, that he deliberately modelled his dialogue on Meilhac, admiring Meilhac and Halévy's comedies and operettas. And that he also set out to emulate the technique and craftsmanship in plot construction of Alfred Hennequin, a deft devotee of Scribe whose string of comedies were well received in their day, although by 1891 Henry Fouquier was already attacking "Hennequin's theatre of a hundred doors", a phrase pillorying with apt economy the stage play where stock characters are rushing on and off, opening and slamming doors in a crescendo of farcical activity.

Georges Feydeau was born in 1862. His father was a novelist and respected member of the salons, the theatregoing, art loving upper hierarchy of Parisian *haut-bourgeois.* Feydeau, encouraged and indulged by his father, was already writing plays as a child and generally adoring the theatre. His first performed works were monologues to be delivered in the salons of the day. A favourite form of entertainment, recited even by such theatrical luminaries as Cocquelin Cadet. This led to sketches and one-act plays, also performed in salons by both professionals and amateurs, including Feydeau himself, until finally his first play, *Tailleur pour Dames* was produced on the professional stage on 17th December, 1886. It was an immediate triumph. From then on it was not, of course, roses all the way. Like all creative artists Feydeau had periods of self-doubt, fallow years, agonies of anxiety. He collaborated with Maurice Desvallières, he tried other forms, attempting in plays such as *La Main Passe* to move away from the stock types of farce to a more philosphical, in-depth approach to his characters. He even in 1898 wrote the libretto for a ballet, *La Bulle d'Amour* with music by François Thomé. Yet his main achievement, on which his fame securely depends, remains over sixty farces for the theatre. In spite of a stream of theatrical successes, and few dramatists have been so consistently popular with their public, he had money troubles. He dabbled on the stock exchange unwisely, was almost always in debt, and in 1901 had to put up his art collection, over a hundred works, for sale. In 1911 he left his wife and family to live in a Paris hotel and stayed there until mental illness finally forced him to take refuge in 1919 in a sanatorium at Reuil, where he died in 1921. His last play was *Hortense a Dit 'Je m'en fous'* produced in 1916.

What was the secret of his appeal, his mesmeric hold on Paris audiences for over three decades of a richly creative life? He belonged to what the French called the Boulevard theatre, the vaudeville. America has adopted the word vaudeville and given it a different meaning, but for the French it meant a light-hearted form of comedy, cleverly constructed, depending on farce for its effects. Farce is an ancient tradition in European theatre, certainly going back to classical Greece. The scurrilous mime drama that existed throughout the

Middle Ages as a commercial, alternative theatre in fairgrounds and market places, and which for hundreds of years the Church tried so ineffectively to banish, continued classical traditions that were pre-Christian. This mime drama had yet another flowering in the Renaissance with the *commedia dell' arte*, a major influence on French theatre in the seventeenth century. It used stock characters which the audience knew, recognised and felt comfortably at home with. Harlequin, the clever agile hero: Columbine, the pretty heroine, much desired by all and sundry: the cuckolded husband, the older man who wants to marry the heroine and is fair game for trickery: the doctor, more quack than expert and so on. Words never counted for much in the *commedia dell' arte*. The Italian Comedians had their own theatre in Paris. It was the dexterity of their clowning, the speed and pace of their quick fire theatrical situations amid the sheer verve of their solutions, unexpected, physical, brilliant, that audiences flocked to enjoy. Mime drama survived, much loved, in the Parisian Boulevard theatre well into the nineteenth century. It went in for bold, obvious theatrical effects. Scribe and his followers annexed many of these elements from the *comedia dell'arte* into their *pièces bien faites*.

It is this tradition which Feydeau inherited; base metals which transmuted into pure gold. His plays do not attempt to depict real life, nor real characters. That is not their point. Certainly they take place in recognisably real life settings and they show characters who at first sight are remarkable only in being very ordinary. What matters is the way the plot develops. Gradually it acquires a momentum and a logic of its own. We watch the characters swept up in it, carried along by it, crushed, defeated, humiliated by it, struggling vainly against it and sometimes blissfully saved by it in the nick of time. They are as helplessly unable to control the solution as they were to prevent disasters in the first place. Allied to this is his mastery of pace. The build-up to each climax, the sheer unexpectedness of each new development, which as soon as it happens seems so logical as to have been inevitable, has something of the perfection of a geometric equation. It is in the logic of his plots that Feydeau shows his dramatic supremacy. Unlike almost any other dramatist it is well nigh impossible to cut anything in a Feydeau play, not even to alter his detailed stage directions. Everything depends on everything else. Anything left out will vitally affect some piece of business, or something crucial elsewhere. As the plot begins to take hold, an audience responds delightedly to each twist and turn of its crazy logic with that burst of collective laughter which can make the theatre such a special place. It is this laughter which Shaw describes as "base".

Now a sense of humour would appear to be one of the very few things we do not share with the rest of the animal kingdom to which the human species belongs. A sense of humour is a specifically human attribute. Yet all our attributes have a biological function, so what is the function of humour? It acts, we are told by psychoanalysts, as a release from tension, we laugh about things that matter very much to us. A French audience laughing at a Feydeau play is not only laughing at the cruelty of life and at their own lack of ability to control the inexplicable destiny which orders human affairs, they are laughing at the very logic they have been brought up so to admire. The French pride themselves on being logical. Their whole culture spends much of its time congratulating itself on just how logical it has managed to become. In a Feydeau play a French audience shrieks with laughter at a logic gone mad. The very idea of madness, things thrust down into the subconscious taking over and subverting the conscious mind, reminds us how illogical so much human behaviour actually is. The more logical they claim to be, the more the French are glossing over the illogic of the actual human condition. Feydeau is aiming unerringly at a specific area of weakness in French culture. As a playwright, he is therefore not only universal, but also specifically French. Ancient Greek theatre's concept of tragedy was that of an overproud man, blinded by his own hubris, ground down by an exterior set of events that he cannot control. The springs of both comedy and tragedy lie dangerously close to each other. Laughter or tears can act as a release from the same overwhelming tension. Shaw is sadly unaware of just how powerful are the elements with which Feydeau creates his comic effects. There is nothing galvanic, nothing knee-jerk about the audience's response to a Feydeau play.

A strong element in much humour is the selecting of a scapegoat to laugh at. We reassure ourselves as we laugh, that we belong to the solid majority, and as social animals we need to belong, even as we laugh at the unfortunate, the outcast, the scapegoat. Deep down in our insecurities we know as we watch these outcasts struggling in vain, that there, but for a kind destiny, we too might be equally defenceless against a fate we cannot control. Our laughter is a glorious release from fear.

Feydeau is not easy to translate. That fugitive quality, a writer's style, shimmering and evanescent, is the first casualty in any translation. Most attempts at translating Feydeau transpose him into approximations, claiming to remain true to the spirit of the original, but importing English colloquialisms, inventing whole sentences and, in effect, erecting a barrier between an English audience and Feydeau's original intentions.

La Puce à L'Oreille, (A Flea in her Ear) was first performned on 2nd March, 1907, and is a fine example of Feydeau at his typical best. Accused of being influenced by Feydeau, although he claimed to have neither read nor seen Feydeau's plays, Eugène Ionesco, foremost protagonist of the Theatre of the Absurd in the 1960s, found when he read *A Flea in her Ear* he was: "surprised at the similarities between Feydeau and myself, not so much in subject matter, more in the rhythms, and the way the play is built". But whereas Ionesco has to import a rhinoceros or a bald soprano to achieve his effects, it is surely one of Feydeau's many strengths that he can create absurdities with banal objects like Camille Chandebise's false palate, or Poche's porter's uniform.

The play is predicated upon three delightful propositions. The first is Camille's false palate and his general incomprehensibility without it. The second is the existence at the Cuddly Kitten Hotel of a porter who is Victor-Emmanuel Chandebise's double, and looks just like him. The third is the depressing inability of Victor-Emmanuel to achieve an erection when trying to make love to his wife. (We can notice here that Millamant's "country matters", more suitable to the farmyard than to Victorian middle-class houses or theatre audiences, were always treated so lightly and delicately by Feydeau that he "somehow" always managed to mention the unmentionable without giving the slightest offence.) We willingly accept all three propositions, partly because they are cleverly presented to us in a manner most likely to make them believable, partly because we know Feydeau is going to use them to run rings around our suspension of disbelief, and create gorgeous mayhem on stage in the process. And so he does. What a superb ending it is when, finally, Poche is comfortably blamed for everything, and the whirlpool of the plot leaves us happily stranded on the shore so that we can hastily tuck away all our secret fears and comfortably face the world outside the theatre as one of its reassured majority. "Alas regardless of their fate, the little victims play." And what a play it has been.

11

Ackland – Two Plays:
After October and The Dark River

When in 1990 I wrote an introduction to Rodney Ackland's *Absolute Hell* for Oberon Books, I was very much aware that the author was, as it were, peering critically over my shoulder. Then 82 years old, he was touchy, difficult, quick to take offence and depressingly bitter about the way the world had treated him. He was living in a council flat, bemoaning his poverty, and seemingly restricted to the bare essentials of life. He also had irresistible charm, an amusing and often salacious fund of all too believable stories about the great and the not so good in theatre and films from the 1920s onwards; to say nothing of a thirst for vodka that could look unquenchable until it led to sudden and total collapse. I was absurdly pleased when he told me he approved, enjoyed and was flattered by what I had written.

To a certain extent he managed to create his own mythology, which has survived him. The talented playwright, in advance of his time, neglected by the commercial theatre, savaged by a worthless tribe of critics, "obscene ravens clamourous o'er the dead, vultures to the conqueror's banner true, who feed where desolation first has fed and whose wings rain contagion". He was fond of quoting Shelley on critics and felt strongly that his own treatment was equally horrendous.

Sadly he died on the 6th December 1991. No more will he be able to bark acerbic wit down the telephone, pen the crushing note with despatch or rush to his lawyer. He was indeed so litigious that Terence Rattigan once suggested Ackland's fond farewell should be rephrased as "Sue you later!"

Perhaps now that he is no longer so very much with us, jumping furiously up and down to make sure the scales incline in his favour, we are better able to face the many paradoxes, like an endless series of Chinese boxes, one within the other, that made up his engaging personality. Wonderfully organised in his writing, with an impressive grasp of detail and a fine sense of structure and balance, he was hopelessly disorganised in his own life. He ran up debts, could be hugely extravagant, shamelessly lied and attempted to cheat over his income tax, and generally spent his life in financial chaos. This meant that he never settled in one place but in a series of moonlight flits, was always trying to keep one jump ahead of his creditors and the Inland Revenue. Sometimes his residence could be very grand indeed. He once even lived in the Albany, but nothing lasted and ignominy was always just around the next corner.

Sexually he was almost equally protean. He moved from men to women and back again with a rapturous abandon that seemed happily unaware of sexual boundaries or social conventions. He had an affair with Emlyn Williams' wife behind his friend's back; Williams' too was bi-sexual but remained unaware that Ackland was cheating him. One of the major loves of Ackland's life was a man, Arthur Boys, but the affair was over by the end of the 1940s. Perhaps the deepest of all his relationships was with Mab Poole, the second daughter of Frederick Lonsdale the playwright. She had started adult life as a married woman with a son, but left that to come to London in war time to work for Alexander Korda in London Films, where she had an unacknowledged but important role in a wide variety of film scripts. She had an affair with the distinguished American war correspondent H R Knickerbocker, who was about to leave his wife and children for her, she claimed, when he was killed in an air crash. Ackland and she met in 1950, married two years later, and for twenty-two years until her death from throat cancer in 1972, they were inseparable and marvellously satisfied with each other. Paradoxically soon after her death, Ackland would seem again to have found sexual satisfaction with men rather than women.

Then there is the paradox of the unappreciated writer. By any standards but his own, Ackland was a very successful writer, particularly in film. If anything he was arguably more enthusiastic about film rather than the theatre and had a distinguished film career. As well as lesser known pictures, he wrote the scripts for two of the major British films of the 1940s, Emeric Pressburger's *Forty-Ninth Parallel*, with a star cast which included Laurence Olivier, and *The Queen Of Spades* with Edith Evans and Anton Walbrook. Irritated by the way his scripts were altered and reshaped in the process of making films, he managed to persuade his studio to let him both write and direct and the result was *Thursday's Child*, 1943, with Sally-Ann Howes and Stewart Granger. In films his range was surprising. Those connoisseurs who remember with relish the skill and effective dialogue of *Thursday's Child*, will be as surprised to find the name of Rodney Ackland as one of the script writers for Cecily Courtneidge and Jack Hulbert's 1938 film farce *Keep It Under Your Hat*. Ackland even wrote a book with Elspeth Grant, *The Celluloid Mistress* published in 1954, giving a deliciously amusing account of the trials and tribulations of his cinematic career. Writers for film earned more than from any other form of writing except the most astronomic best sellers. Ackland earned good money. With unremitting insouciance that out-

Micawbered Micawber, he proceeded to spend more than he earned, long before trying to explain anything to the Inland Revenue.

Even more of a paradox is the unappreciated writer for the theatre. It is difficult to gauge the exact yardstick by which a playwright is to be considered successful or unsuccessful, but Ackland had a pretty good run for the money he was over-spending. His first play *Improper People* was produced at the Arts Theatre when he was 21. Not many would-be playwrights would complain about that, even if one critic did consider "it was nearly as boring as Chekhov." His next two plays were both given productions. His fourth play *Strange Orchestra*, after a first run at the Embassy Swiss Cottage was produced in the West End by John Gielgud in 1932. The director, Frith Banbury who was to play such an important part in Ackland's life as admirer of his works and financial benefactor, was enormously impressed by it. "From then on I made a point of seeing, generally more than once, every Ackland play that was produced". It is worth pointing out that Ackland's plays were produced, acted and presented on stage. Banbury had a chance to see them, generally more than once. So here was a playwright busily writing plays that were produced in the theatre, seen by an appreciative audience.

After October (1936) and *The Dark River* (1937) had no difficulty in getting on stage. Ackland himself acted in *After October*, which had a respectable run and made a profit. Although Peggy Ashcroft was generally praised as Catherine Lisle in the final production of *The Dark River*, which Ackland directed, it did not prove a commercial success. Admittedly most of Ackland's plays started in club or fringe theatres, and if and when they did transfer to the West End, not many of them had long runs, but at least his work was produced, acted by impressive casts and given a fair chance.

Even more irritatingly for him, his theatrical adaptations generally made more money and were much more frequently revived, than his original plays. These included in 1933 *Ballerina* from the novel by Lady Eleanor Smith in which Anton Dolin had both a speaking role and danced in the ballet in the last act. Dolin says of it:

> This lovely play, so closely associated with the ballet came before its time. Today, with the tremendous public that has grown up, understanding and knowing so much more of the history and inner workings of the ballet, it would have been an entirely different matter.

Among his other adaptations were *The Old Ladies* (1935) from the novella by Hugh Walpole, directed by Gielgud for Edith Evans, Mary Jerrold and Jean Cadell, revived in 1968 with Flora Robson, *The White Guard from Bulgakov* (1938), *Crime and Punishment* (1945) with Gielgud, Edith Evans and Peter Ustinov. *Before The Party* from a Somerset Maugham story and his version of Ostrovsky's *Too Clever By Half* both in 1949 were major West End hits. The latter was very successfully revived at the Old Vic in 1988.

This is not a picture of an "unappreciated writer". On the contrary, in the world of the theatre, Ackland was appreciated, admired and encouraged. Directors of the calibre of Frith Banbury, one of theatre's finest, thought highly of him. Many of his adaptations and translations of other people's works were commercial successes and made good money. Until the end of the 1950s Ackland was thought of as one of our most gifted writers for the theatre. In the Plays of the Year series chosen by J C Trewin, Ackland was twice published, in 1949 with *Before The Party* and in 1957 with *A Dead Secret*.

Yet there is a reverse side to all this. Ackland, with a paranoia that was real and painful for him, expressed himself forcibly about it to his friends. His case is excellently put by Charles Duff in his book *The Lost Summer*, a perceptive account of the heyday of the West End theatre from the 1930s onwards, which devotes a whole chapter to Ackland. It is essentially the case I put for *Absolute Hell*. Ackland was in advance of his time. In the 1930s and 40s the middle-class audience for theatre wanted to be amused, titillated and entertained, but preferred to leave the grander subjects, the great issues, the deeper feelings, outside the theatre much as they discarded their muddy boots at the door before entering the drawing room. This was the heyday of drawing room comedy, with its stereotype of the comfortably prosperous interior set with large French windows giving onto well-kept lawns, through which scantily clad and lissome characters appeared, inquiring "Anyone for tennis?"

Ackland did not belong to this milieu and nor did the characters in his plays who, urban, seedy, threatened and "not quite nice" would never have been invited to grace the drawing room of a typical West End play of the period. If ever there was anyone not for tennis it was Ackland's fully believable characters, desperately trying to ignore an all too menacing reality. Ackland brushed aside the role models, the fashionable playwrights of his day. Frederick Lonsdale, Ben Travers, Vernon Sylvaine, Noël Coward. It was the plays of Chekhov in Komisarjevsky's brilliant season at Barnes in the mid 1920s that first opened up for him the drama's potential for tackling the social, sexual, political and intellectual challenge of the time. It is precisely because Ackland opened up these issues, that he still speaks effectively to a modern audience, where his illustrious contemporaries now seem almost pathetically frivolous.

We respond to his deft originality in the writer's craft, the skill with which he creates believable characters in the round, his ear for the rhythms of spoken language, his rare ability to present deep emotion on stage without trivialising or sentimentalising it. Leavening the whole, there is the wit scattered in glory across his scenes without any heavily laboured "funny moments". Perhaps best of all, and much more usual to playgoers at the end of the twentieth century, there is the absence of what in the 1930s was a *sine qua non* of the well made West End play, an immediately accessible and understandable plot. As in Chekhov there tend in Ackland's plays to be almost as many plots as there are characters, and it is the skill with which these intertwine and interact on each other that create his dramatic tension. The dialogue may seem inconsequential, disjointed, not getting anywhere, but in fact, not only does its humour delight and its content hold our interest but gradually through it the characters reveal themselves to us so that we begin to accept and understand them as real people.

Ackland was fascinated, and persuades his audience to be fascinated too, by themes that continually recur in his work and are very apparent both in *The Dark River* and *After October*. The haphazard way people affect the lives of others, often unaware of the havoc they create around them. Worse still, the persistent way so many people cling to hopes without having the energy and determination to bring them to reality, so there is only in the end self-deception. Ackland's characters often desperately seek any company but their own, because they cannot bear to face the truth about themselves in the dark loneliness of the soul. The alcohol, the drugs, the sex, the false bonhomie of the groups that really have so little in common, are all clearly delineated in Ackland's plays as so many defences against self-recognition.

Many people consider *The Dark River* (1937 but presented on stage in 1943), as his best play. Hilary Spurling claims it is "perhaps the one indisputable great play of the present half century in English". These are very grand words. Perhaps to assess its importance we need to put it a little too much in context. England in the 1930s was behaving almost as absurdly as America where isolationism ruled. Americans stuck their heads firmly in quicksand and pretended the rest of the world, including the Japanese and the Germans, simply did not exist. Pearl Harbour understandably blew the pants off them. How could it have been otherwise with their heads so firmly in the sand. They were not caught with their pants down so much as letting the Japanese blow them off!

Britain was no less ridiculous. Throughout the 1930s we did our best to pretend that World War One had never happened, the old class system was still not just intact but flourishing, the British Empire was thriving, and Nazism and Fascism at least kept the trains running on time for British tourists. It is in this context that *The Dark River*, where the characters comfortably ensconced in an old house on the Thames, a house which the audience comes to realise stands for England, makes such a radical impact. Like the French aristocracy before 1789, Ackland's characters remain happily oblivious of what is happening in the real world around them. When it was staged in 1943 the audience was all too aware of what awaited these characters. By then the war which broke out in 1939 was busily changing everybody's lives. One cannot but admire the prescience with which Ackland was trying to alert his audience when he wrote the play in 1937. Charles

Duff while recognising the play's "conflict of mood and poetry" considers it "relies too heavily on coincidence" and finds the film director Reade "unconvincing". The play was not a commercial success. Perhaps it was a little too close to the bone for most of its war-torn audience.

After October has real charm. It is perhaps the most auto-biographical of Ackland's plays. Ackland was born in 1908, Norman Ackland Bernstein, the child of a Jewish businessman and Ada Rodney a popular performer in music hall and a practised principal boy in pantomime. Before he was seven, his father was made a bankrupt and the family found themselves with nothing. His mother sold stockings from door to door to make ends meet. Ackland had hazy memories of early affluence, a large house, servants, but all too vivid memories of real poverty. This may explain some of his irresponsible attitudes to his own financial affairs.

After October, written in 1936, shows a feckless family in the grip of poverty, with a young playwright scenting the possibilities of escape – affluence and extravagance. Charm is indefinable, but this play has it, and so did Rodney Ackland. He kept his friends in spite of rages, temperaments, threats of law suits and generally impossible behaviour. In the words of a Victorian musical hall song, (did his mother ever sing it?) "What was there was good!"

Index

INDEX

INDEX

INDEX